About the authors

Jan Parker is a journalist and writer specialising in child and family issues; an accredited parenting group facilitator; and an honorary member of a Child and Adolescent Mental Health Service Family Team. She writes for many newspapers and magazines, including the *Guardian*, the *Independent* and *The Times*. She has three children.

Jan Stimpson is a leading parenting adviser and facilitator for the charity Parentline Plus. She runs courses and workshops in community centres and schools, and works privately with parent groups. She has two sons.

Jan and Jan met at ante-natal classes before their first children were born and have remained friends and colleagues ever since. Their first book, the childcare classic *Raising Happy Children*, is now a much-loved bestseller.

D0733345

Also by Jan Parker and Jan Stimpson

Raising Happy Children

Raising Happy Brothers and Sisters

Helping our children enjoy life together,
from birth onwards

Jan Parker and
Jan Stimpson

HODDER
MOBIUS

Hodder & Stoughton

First published in Great Britain in 2002 by Hodder and Stoughton
A division of Hodder Headline
This paperback edition published in 2004

A Mobius paperback

3

A CIP catalogue record for this title is available from the British Library

ISBN 0 340 83475 7

Typeset in New Baskerville by
Phoenix Typesetting, Auldgirth, Dumfriesshire

Printed and bound by
Mackays of Chatham Ltd, Chatham, Kent; Griffin Press, Netley, Australia

Hodder Headline's policy is to use papers that are natural, renewable
and recyclable products and made from wood grown in sustainable
forests. The logging and manufacturing processes are expected to
conform to the environmental regulations of the country of origin.

Hodder and Stoughton Ltd
A division of Hodder Headline
338 Euston Road
London NW1 3BH

Foreword
by Dr Dorothy Rowe

Raising siblings isn't easy, and being a sibling isn't easy. For many of us it's one of the most difficult roles we have to play.

I'm always being given suggestions about what kind of book I should write next. When someone suggests siblings, my blood runs cold. One day I might be brave enough to tackle that one, but not yet.

One comfort I get from these conversations is the knowledge that I am not alone in finding my relationship with my sister the most difficult one I have ever encountered. People who speak to me about siblings often reveal much pain and bafflement. They may have successfully resolved many of the issues they had with their parents, but the issues they have with their siblings continue to confound them.

Of course, the issues we have with our siblings are not separate from the issues we have with our parents. One man told me how, in his childhood, his parents had been unfailingly loving and kind. The misery he suffered in childhood was at the hands of an older brother who persistently bullied and assaulted him. Why, I asked, had not his parents stopped this? The man started to find excuses for his parents, and then stopped. He had suddenly realised that his parents had not been as perfect as he had wished them to be. If our siblings are particularly unpleasant, we can idolise our parents in order not to feel completely rejected and abandoned. If our parents persistently fail us, we can turn to our siblings for comfort.

Each of us is either a sibling or an only child and, whichever we are, we feel strongly about it. Miriam Cosic, an Australian writer, in her book *Only Child* said:

'I am an only child. All my life I believed this to be my single most defining characteristic and I didn't like it. Although I knew that all the great pleasures I enjoy every day arose out of my experience as an only child,

I also ascribed to it every problem I encountered. And, being of a catastrophising turn of mind, the negatives outweighed the positives whenever I contemplated my situation. As each of my friends gave birth to their first child, I started on them to have another: "Don't have just one, it isn't fair to the child".[1]

Many first-time parents, encouraged by friends and family to have another child, do so and then discover that a second child doesn't just double the issues they have to face, it triples them, because they now have to support their two children *and* the relationship between them.

Yet compared to the volume of literature about relationships between parents and children, especially relationships between mother and child, the literature on siblings is limited.

It is very brave of the authors of this book to tackle the subject, because sibling relationships concern not just how each child sees themselves and their sibling, but also how each parent sees each child, and how each child believes they are regarded and treated. And no parent can deal with each and every conflict or crisis in a way which both children see as exactly right. If ever you come upon my dear friends Milo (aged eleven) and his sister Adele (aged eight) fighting ferociously, as they often do, don't step in to protect Adele from her brother because, if you do, she will immediately turn against you for daring to criticise her beloved brother. It is impossible to completely separate sibling rivalry from sibling love.

Yet sibling conflict shouldn't go unchecked. Otherwise the rivalry, the fights, the hurts can go on for the rest of the children's lives. Family occasions, like Christmas or the reading of the parents' will, become battlefields where the fighting is even more bitter than it was in childhood. The people we hate the most are the ones we love. Such sibling love and hate can be denied and repressed, and then reappear as bitter conflicts.

When I was writing my book *Friends and Enemies*[2] I planned to include a chapter on the family which posed the question, 'Can family members be friends?' This proved to be a very long chapter because family relationships can be fraught in so many different ways, but out of it came my definition of a happy family. Friendship is a reciprocal

1. Lansdowne, Sydney, 1999.
2. HarperCollins, London, 2000.

relationship where both members see one another as an equal and who relate to one another with the very best of human virtues – affection, trust, truthfulness, loyalty, tolerance, generosity and kindness. A happy family is one where all the family members see one another as a friend.

It must be wonderful to grow up with another person and be the best of friends.

All parents who want to create an environment where their children can do this should read this book. Jan Parker and Jan Stimpson have garnered the wisdom and knowledge that parents, professionals and academics have acquired from their successes and failures in dealing with and understanding children.

As this book makes clear, it is not just what parents do which determines their children's behaviour but how their children interpret what they do. And no two children ever interpret anything in exactly the same way.

This is what makes parenting so difficult. We each have our own way of seeing things. And it is only through understanding this about ourselves, and our children, that we can find a *satisfying* way of uniting sibling rivalry with sibling love.

Contents

Raising Happy
Brothers and Sisters

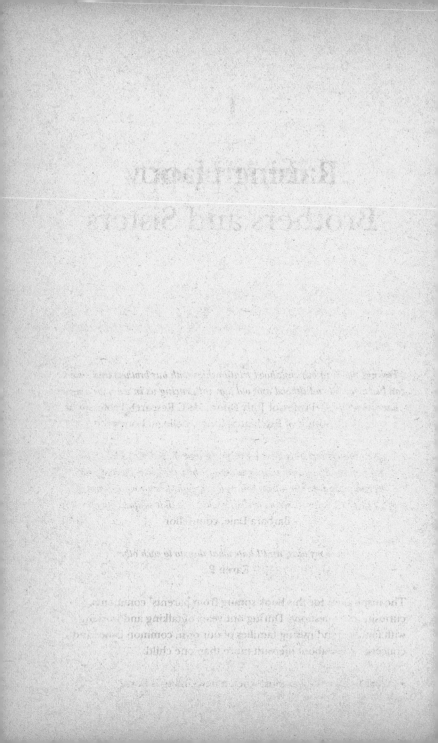

1

Life support

'Feelings rooted in our childhood relationships with our brothers and sisters can last right into adulthood and old age, influencing us in ways we'd never have imagined.' – Professor Judy Dunn, MRC Research Professor at the Institute of Psychiatry, King's College, London

'My siblings certainly gave me as much and shaped me as much as my parents. Exploring sibling relationships – the good, the bad and everything in between – puts you in touch with the enormous forces of life, I think. It helps us see more clearly what it is that shapes who we are.' – Barbara Dale, counsellor

'I love my kids, and I hate what they do to each other.' – Karen P.

The inspiration for this book sprang from parents' comments, curiosity and questions. During our years of talking and working with families, and raising families of our own, common issues and concerns arose about life with more than one child:

- What helps children most when a new sibling is born?

- How can we encourage caring, sharing and considerate behaviour?
- What can we do when our children's needs clash?
- How do we help each child feel they shine when their abilities differ?
- How can we have more good times together?
- How does what we do now affect our children's relationships in childhood? Adolescence? Adulthood?
- What makes some siblings close and supportive, and others distant and hostile?

Most childcare books focus solely on the bond between parent and individual child, as if having two or more makes barely a difference to our lives or theirs.

Yet bringing up more than one child is far more varied, rich, complex and demanding. Different issues arise and different approaches help.

Raising Happy Brothers and Sisters shines welcome new light on these,

---

 Brothers and sisters

'The sibling relationship is very important, and one which tends to get overlooked. We don't pay nearly enough attention to what goes on between brothers and sisters. After all, they grow up together in extraordinarily intimate, close and generative circumstances. It is a fascinating and important subject.' – Peter Wilson, child psychotherapist and director of Young Minds

- The bond between siblings is generally the most long-lasting of all family relationships – outlasting that with parents, partners and children.
- Siblings are likely to spend far more time together in their formative early years than they spend with anyone else.
- Around eighty per cent of children grow up with siblings.[1]
- Most of us are siblings. Most of us have more than one child.

exploring the nature and development of sibling bonds and the many ways we can help our children fight less, flourish as individuals and find mutual fun and support in their relationships.

This matters. Our children's relationships with each other are often the longest of their lives. How brothers and sisters play, fight and feel about each other will help shape the nature of our family life, their childhood and the people they'll become. Their experiences of siblinghood will influence their confidence, aspirations and behaviour, and even major life decisions from career path to partner and the number of children they choose to have.

Raising Happy Brothers and Sisters brings together the collected wisdom of parents and leading professionals to offer insight into how we can help build foundations of happiness for each child, developing their respect and appreciation of themselves and each other, their tolerance of difference, their abilities to resolve disputes and problem-solve, their capacities for affection, fun and consideration, and their abilities to delight in life's highs and cope with its knocks.

Our heartfelt thanks go to all those mothers, fathers and children who have shared their experiences with us so honestly, and to all those working with families who have offered their insights and under-standings so generously. With their help, *Raising Happy Brothers and Sisters* has become a warm, accessible, thought-provoking and genuinely helpful book that is rooted very firmly in the real world, in real-life experiences and respected research into what *really* matters within our children's relationships.

This is a book for families as they are, not as some pretend they should be. It's for families with children who hurt, laugh, fight, bicker, play, talk, conspire, love, want and need.

It is a book for parents who value the bond between their children, and who want to help them have healthier, happier relationships from their earliest days together to adolescence and beyond. These are gifts for life.

Jan Parker and Jan Stimpson

2

Mum, you can send her back now:

a new baby arrives

'I was excited about having a baby brother or sister and when dad came in to school to take us to the hospital I was quite glad because it got me out of maths. But when I saw him I was a bit frightened because he looked strange. He was all screwed up and had no hair.' – Kate, aged six

'I couldn't believe we could really, truly keep her.' – Daniel, aged nine

'Amy was three. She gently tucked up her new sister in the cot blanket, snuggled up next to me in bed and whispered, "Mum, you can send her back now".' – Margaret N.

Life after birth is a time of huge transition for the whole family, and especially for our older child or children. Think of it from their point of view. Their parents may display the bizarre behaviour of the sleep-deprived, friends and relations may ignore their cutest or wildest antics in the rush to hold the baby, and life's former certainties are disappearing fast.

As parents, our lives are turned upside down but at least we've done it before and know that it will return to something like an even keel eventually. Our children may have little idea of what their future holds. Hardly surprising, then, that older siblings, and especially first children, so often display signs of distress and resentment.

It hurts us to see it – which is why it is so important to keep a sense of proportion and perspective. Of course, they'll sometimes view their new sibling as an unwelcome intrusion, but their new sister or brother is also a potential source of support, understanding and great fun in their lives.

If we can encourage our child's affectionate interest in the baby, while also understanding their upset, we will lay the foundations of more positive, affectionate and fulfilling relationships between our children. And we can begin even before the baby is born.

'It is pretty clear that how the firstborn feels about and relates to the laterborn has more influence on the sibling relationship than the other way round, how the laterborn feels about their big brother or sister. So in the early years at least, being sensitive to what that first child is experiencing or feels about the new baby is worth special attention for everyone's sake.'
– Professor Judy Dunn, developmental psychologist

Preparing the way

'My son was anti a girl for months. If we had to have another child at all, he said he wanted a brother. If it was a girl he said he was going to drown it. Later in the pregnancy he listened to the baby's heartbeat. He was completely and utterly mesmerised because he realised this was a live human being. That was the turning point.' – Adrienne Katz, founder and executive director of the youth charity, Young Voice

'We took her with us for the ultrasound, and she seemed fascinated by the fuzzy picture of the unborn baby on the screen. But next day I heard her telling her friend it was spooky and the baby looked like ET.' – Clare M.

Preparation for the arrival of a new baby won't eradicate an older child's feelings of jealousy and hurt once the baby arrives. As adults, we know in advance that moving house is stressful, but that knowledge doesn't make the processes stress-free. Advance warning does not remove all anxiety.

Yet we can help our children feel less threatened and more relaxed about expressing hopes and concerns. We can reduce their fear of the unknown by letting them know how their lives may change and what will stay the same. And by recognising and respecting their needs and feelings – even the negative ones – we can show them that we understand and that we care (see Exploring emotions, page 125).

Timing

'Obviously much depends on the age of the first child but, if possible, I would wait at least until the mother is changing shape before talking about it. Nine months is a very long time to make a baby, and little children can't grasp that kind of time scale.' – Carol Ann Hally, health visitor and community practice teacher

When we tell our child about having a new brother or sister will depend on many factors – their age and understanding of what others may discuss in their hearing, what else may be going on in their life at the time, whether they have already sensed something important is happening. Whatever we decide, it helps to remember that young children don't have an adult's understanding of time. When told they are going to have a new brother or sister, they often expect the baby to arrive tomorrow, or at least next week. Quite understandably, their enthusiasm and excitement may have worn off a little after months of waiting. Explaining that the baby won't be coming until after the summer holiday, after Christmas or any other family celebration, may give them a better grasp of the time scale involved.

'I've noticed time and time again that as soon as the mother is pregnant, it seems to have some impact on the behaviour of the child, even though the child supposedly still does not know. In sleep clinics, I've often seen toddlers whose sleep is disrupted when mum is pregnant. It is almost that they are unconsciously aware. When this happens, the sooner children know about and can be involved in discussions, the better, I think,' – Christine Bidmead, RGN RHV, Training Facilitator, Centre for Parent and Child Support

Togetherness

When the enormity of what is about to happen begins to dawn, children are full of thoughts, feelings and questions. Sharing relaxed times with them will help them feel valued, and gives them the chance to put feelings into words, for questions and concerns to unfold gently, or for them simply to enjoy much-needed cuddles.

Playing, enjoying shared activities or snuggling up together with a book may encourage more communication than setting aside time for 'meaningful' conversations (see Message received? page 187). Stories, especially, can be a gentle, indirect way of helping children explore their feelings, and may prompt questions and communicate difficult concepts, such as the mixed emotions they may feel when the new baby arrives. Even young ones can enjoy looking at picture books or listening to us read aloud. Some of the best books about siblings are extremely funny, and nothing is quite so threatening if you can laugh about it.

Talking about the baby

Some children view new babies as alien invaders – uninvited, threatening and not 'one of us'. Helping them understand that their new brother or sister is a little person – with vulnerabilities, needs and the capacity for pleasure – seems key to encouraging friendly, affectionate relationships between them (see Encouraging affection, page 15).

Even before the birth, we can talk about how the baby may feel and how he or she may respond to their big brother or sister, emphasising the potential relationship between them: 'I wonder if the baby will like you to blow on her toes?' 'I wonder if the baby will suck her thumb like you did? Maybe it's sucking it right now.' 'The baby will be able to hear you singing even though it's still in my tummy. That must be nice.'

Some children are curious and full of questions about the new baby, while others become anxious if it is a constant topic of conversation. So it helps to be alert to signs that a child is interested and wants to know more – and when they've maybe had enough.

The same goes for including children in preparations – choosing equipment, discussing names, getting the cot ready. Many delight in such involvement, but others may find it boring or threatening. Putting pressure on children to show interest or enthusiasm will only fuel resentment.

> *'I think I went over the top. I did the books, the video, the reassurance and didn't stop to think if he'd had enough until we went to the library and he shouted, "NO MORE BOOKS ON BABIES! I'M SICK OF BABIES!"'* – Lisa G.

> *'Some toddlers are very interested in what's going to happen. Pre-schoolers and older often ask questions. But it is not worth making a very big deal about it if the child isn't particularly interested. Whatever you choose to tell them, keep it simple, short and truthful.'* – Professor Judy Dunn, developmental psychologist

> *'My friend was telling me how well her young son was adjusting to the idea of a new brother or sister, and that buying him a baby doll to play with had helped. Just as she was saying it, he started bashing the doll and throwing it around the room.'* – Julie M.

Talking about love

This is crucial. Many adults worry whether there'll be enough love to go round after the birth of a new baby, so it's hardly surprising that children do, too. We need to tell our children that we will love them forever, that our love grows every day and nothing can take that away.

> *'However much we know we can love as many children as we have, for the children it's as hard as it would be for us if our partner got another girlfriend and said, "Don't worry. I'll still love you just as much".'* – Sarah Darton, health visitor

Talking about the older child as a baby

Talking to our older children about what they were like as babies is a great way to introduce a positive view of newborns without being too heavy-handed. It may also reassure older children that they were once 'babied', too. It's a simple point, but an important one as most children won't have any conscious memory of their infancy and may consider our necessary attention to the new family member as grossly unfair and unequal treatment.

Before the new baby is born, we can reminisce with our older children about the moments they made us laugh or melted our hearts. They may enjoy watching family videos of their younger days, or making a book of photographs, mementos and memories of their infancy. This may become compulsive 'reading' in the months ahead.

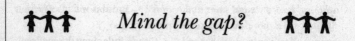

Mind the gap?

'I think the gap must make a difference. I've got a brother who's two and half years older than I am and a sister who's twelve years younger and there is quite a different intensity in our relationships. Completely different. And I'm not even sure intensity means the same thing as closeness. Siblings close in age experience intense rivalrous feelings, too. You can't have the same rivalry with someone who's twelve years younger than you, you just can't.' – Pat Elliot, psychotherapist and parenting trainer, tutor at the Psychosynthesis and Education Trust

'Every gap has its plusses and minuses.' – Professor Judy Dunn, developmental psychologist

Some studies have indicated that an age gap of two to four years may be optimal for 'greater mental stimulation from one another while minimising conflict'.[1] But 'optimal' is the language of the lab, not the family home. There is no perfect gap. Each has its advantages and disadvantages and formulaic predictions tend to ignore crucial factors, such as the temperaments of the children and what else is going on in parents' lives.

Some parents believe a larger gap makes for a less conflictual relationship; others believe that an older child responds with greater resentment after many years of being the

'It is so helpful to remind them of the things you used to do together when they were little and to talk about special times you had with them when they were babies. Let them know just how special that was because they won't remember and may not believe they were ever like that. Also, talk about all the things that are special about them now – how lovely it is when they give you a hug, or how much you like to talk and play with them. These sorts of things do help them feel appreciated for the baby they were and the child they have become.'
– Sarah Darton, health visitor

sole focus of parental attention. Siblings born more than six years apart tend to play less together and a gap of two years may be great for children who get on well, but less so for children who don't. Either way, a small gap may exhaust working parents coping with an infant and a toddler, and this will affect family relations.

Clearly, little about the children's future relationships can be predicted from age gap alone. There are trends, but simple conclusions and reductionist predictions have little relevance to real life.

'Many parents think that when the older child is about two is a good time to have another. I'm not terribly sure that's a perfect age. That's a personal feeling rather than a professional opinion. The two-year-old has so much going on for him developmentally. I certainly wasn't prepared for the impact of a second child. It's easy to forget how time-consuming a baby is and how difficult it is to share your time also with an attention-seeking toddler. It can be an enormous strain.'
– Christine Bidmead, Centre for Parent and Child Support

'I think your experiences will depend on the age gaps. I have three children, a two-and-a-half-year gap and a four-and-a-half-year gap. With the shorter gap it is really about masterminding the care of two babies and being in twenty-five different places at once. With the larger gap, it can be difficult to keep both children happy at the same time because they have such different needs and interests.'
– Belinda Phipps, National Childbirth Trust

A dash of realism

> *'One of the best times was watching the video of* Rugrats the Movie. *We both sat on the sofa, laughing at these anarchic cartoon babies with their smelly nappies. It was a welcome antidote to all those cutesy baby images that older kids find so off-putting.'* – Melanie P.

> *'Joe doesn't play or anything like that. He doesn't do anything really.'* – Jemma, aged four, sister of Joe, aged three weeks

> *'Attempting to prepare a child with stories of someone to play soccer with and so on can be a bit of a crushing blow when actually what they have is a wailing baby rather than a ready-made playmate.'* – Professor Judy Dunn, developmental psychologist

Our society has a tendency to airbrush images of infancy, and this can leave adults as well as children feeling guilty and confused when the reality doesn't match the fantasy. Preparing well for the birth of new brother or sister involves talking about what real life may be like after the baby is born. Little babies do take up a lot of time, cry a lot, wake up at anti-social hours and turn everybody's world upside down.

It helps to be honest about what babies can and can't do, or children expecting an instant friend may feel bitterly disappointed. Contact with real young babies, especially wrinkly newborns, helps children have a better idea of what to expect.

Keeping changes to a minimum

Not surprisingly, children who have major disruptions to their usual routines around the time of the birth tend to experience more difficulties coping with the baby's arrival. As far as possible, it makes sense to keep routines fairly predictable and to avoid too many other life changes.

Talking about care arrangements

Chatting about arrangements for our children's care when we're having the baby may help allay worries.

Ideally, the chosen carer should know the child well, have cared for them before and be aware of all they need to help them feel at ease – their usual routine, comforters, likes, dislikes and favourite treats. A little indulgence may go a long way right now, but an understanding of what behaviour we allow and what we don't will reduce the risk of the carer unsettling our child further through well-meaning over-indulgence or unnecessary restriction.

Thinking of our child's world

Children often attach great importance to significant objects, so are they aware, for example, that their teddy will always be theirs and won't have to be shared? Or that we can put special toys out of baby's reach to keep them safe? If their cot, blankets and baby toys are to be used when the new baby arrives, do they know? Have they had time to get used to the idea?

Thinking of our child's world from their perspective helps us recognise issues that concern them but which we may have overlooked. What matters to each child will vary, but you will know what your child cares about most.

Once the baby is born

'I liked giving him baths. I didn't like it that he cried and I felt a bit annoyed that he'd taken my cot without anybody asking me whether it was OK. But now I love him. He's very funny' – Eddie, aged seven, brother of Miles, aged two.

'He was enthralled and delighted with his little sister. And absolutely devastated.' – Christine F.

'Parents say having more than one child is hard work but also that it's more fun.' – Belinda Phipps, National Childbirth Trust

When a new baby is born, our older children have to watch someone else hold our affectionate attention and hog the family limelight. While friends and relations seem delighted, the child may be experiencing the primal fear of loss of love and abandonment. No wonder our children sometimes seem resentful, hurt and downright furious.

How we respond and help our children manage these emotions can have an enormous impact on how they negotiate the months ahead. How we talk to them about their new brother or sister will help shape the relationship between them. And how we look after ourselves when there are so many demands on our love and attention will affect how we feel and cope.

No two family experiences can be the same as there are so many variables, from birth experience to children's temperaments, from family size to social circumstance. So, as ever, you are the best judge of which of the following suggestions from professionals and parents will best help you, your family and the developing bond between your children.

🏃🏃 *The first meeting* 🏃🏃

'Holly came in and stood by the crib, then ever so gently stroked his head and said, "Hello you".' – Sally S.

'I was in hospital for five weeks before the baby was born. My son came every day but it was hard, with all these emotions crammed into short visits and everyone trying to be jolly. When the baby finally came and they met for the first time, Tom refused to even look at him and spent the whole visit hiding under my bed.' – Jane P.

We can hope, we can plan and prepare, but we can't write the script. Some first meetings with a new brother or sister go blissfully well, others less so. Some firstborns show awe, some anger, some anxiety, some disinterest. And it doesn't really matter overmuch.

Great store is set by the first introduction, but research shows children's initial reaction has little bearing on the siblings' long-term relationship. Their bonding and relationship-building does begin within the first few days and weeks, but does not seem greatly influenced by the first meeting itself.[2] That said, parents report that some approaches do seem to help:

• Giving the firstborn a present, either from you or 'from the baby'.

Encouraging affection

'Mothers who encourage concern between children are helping to foster a loving relationship – Professor Judy Dunn, developmental psychologist

'Their self-esteem must take a terrible blow when they have a sibling, but it's not the end of the world. There are resilient parts of children and we should look to those and help them cope.' – Brenda Meldrum, Head of Training at The Place to Be, a charity offering emotional support to children in mainstream primary schools

A groundbreaking study by British developmental psychologist Professor Judy Dunn and colleagues[3] has shown that where families

- Trying to avoid cuddling or feeding the baby when the child first arrives, so you can cuddle the child without having to ask them to be careful not to squash their new brother or sister.
- Asking visitors in advance to greet the child before the baby.
- Ensuring that the same trusted person brings the eldest child to the hospital and takes him home again, so the child 'doesn't feel passed around like a piece of lost property'.
- Bringing something for older children to play with so they don't get bored. They may not want to spend much time 'adoring' the new arrival.

'I had my three children at home and each new sibling was greeted with delight by the others, who couldn't wait to help me dress the new baby and have their photo taken holding their sister. Since then, of course, they've fallen in and out with each other, but certainly their first meeting seemed a very positive experience for them .'
– Belinda Phipps, National Childbirth Trust.

'I certainly remember the day I brought my second baby home from overnight stay in hospital. My first child was twenty-one months and everybody had said this first child won't notice, she's too young. Absolute rubbish! She looked in the cot then burst into tears. She knew things would never be the same again.' – Mary MacLeod, chief executive, National Family and Parenting Institute

talk to the older child about the new baby's needs and feelings in the first few months, the older child tends to develop an affectionate interest in the infant and both children show more friendliness towards each other over time. This is one of the most significant findings of recent research into the roots of happy sibling relationships, and it can begin in their first days and weeks together, with our help.

It is also a powerful illustration of some of the main themes of this book – the value of understanding and respecting children's feelings, the potency of family interaction, and the importance of playing to children's strengths rather than focusing most attention on negative behaviour.

So how does drawing attention to the baby's feelings help affection grow?

Once our older child begins to understand the baby's likes, dislikes and moods, and how they can influence these, they can begin to develop interest and concern for their new brother or sister. This will help them respond sensitively to the baby.

Once the baby experiences big brother or sister responding sensitively to their needs, they will respond more positively in return – smiling at the child, showing pleasure when they enter the room, etc. This will prompt even more sensitive, friendly attention from the older child. Which prompts yet more positive responses from the baby . . .

This is the beginning of a loving relationship, and we can encourage it by:

- **Emphasising the baby's interest in the older child:** 'I think he's watching you, can you see?' 'He likes it when you make that funny face!'

- **Showing our older child how to elicit smiles from the baby:** with gentle strokes, rattles, etc. 'Let's see if he likes this. I think he does. What do you think?' 'Look, he's smiling at you! You've cheered him up.'

- **Encouraging joint play**, such as peeping games or mimicking the baby's noises and expressions. Pointing out how the baby 'joins in': 'She's watching you.' 'Can you see how she sticks her tongue out when you do? She's copying you!' (See Let the fun begin, page 44.)

- **Discussing what the baby may need or feel:** 'Do you think he needs a new nappy?' 'He sounds upset. Do you think he needs a feed or is he just tired?'

- **Giving opportunities for older children to join in the care of the baby** without overloading them with inappropriate responsibility. 'Do you think he'd enjoy a bath now? Can you run the water?'
- **Pointing out when the baby begins to treat the child as an object of love** by recognising, reaching out and smiling at big brother or sister.
- **Talking about feelings** generally within the family (see Exploring Emotions, page 125, and Feelings in the family, page 18).

It may also help to

- **Emphasise a relationship** by sometimes talking about 'your sister' or 'your brother' rather than simply referring to the baby's name.
- **Begin to establish rituals of affection**, such as bedtime rituals of kissing and saying goodnight, etc.
- **Talk about things that the child can do and the baby can't** – eating different foods, enjoying different sorts of fun, having different toys – anything that will help the child feel their life isn't so bad in comparison.

Allowing feelings

'How parents manage the older child's feelings has enormous impact on how that child is going to cope. Every evening for weeks after my second baby was born, my daughter would just slap my cheeks when I was feeding her, as if to say "How dare you!" I think it's terribly important to understand why. If you don't handle things exactly as you'd wish, it's not the end of the world. Things can be got over. But these first weeks and months are a critical period for everybody, and it can colour feelings for a long period thereafter.' – Mary MacLeod, chief executive National Family and Parenting Institute

'When an older child has a constant moan of "It's not fair" it often helps to accept that. Instead of contradicting them, we can say, "You're right. It isn't fair. Now you have to share our attention and that feels hard."'
– Brenda Meldrum, Head of Training, The Place to Be

♟♟♟ *Feelings in the family* ♟♟♟

Developmental psychologist Professor Judy Dunn's research into sibling relationships highlights the importance of encouraging children to recognise and respond sensitively to the new baby's feelings.

'In families where the first child showed marked affectionate interest in the newborn, the young child was likely to be particularly friendly to the elder child a year later,' she explains. 'Even little children, as young as two years, are interested in and can reflect on a sibling's wishes and feelings, and the baby will become more friendly because of it.

'We can help by drawing our child's attention to the baby's feelings and responses. This is important and has been borne out in other studies, at least in terms of children growing up in European or American cultures. We have to be a little wary of giving too western a view of things. It might well be that there are some cultures where talking about feelings is not such a big deal, but certainly within western society generally that sort of understanding and expression of what feelings are about, that level of family interaction, does seem to be significant.'

Talking about emotions generally, as part of everyday life, is also important, suggests Professor Dunn. 'It might be about how grandma might be feeling, or a character in a story. Some parents, reading a book with a child, will discuss why a character might be feeling as they do. It's not simply a matter of parents explaining what the baby is feeling, it is also whether discussions of feelings are a general feature of family interaction, whether they are talked about or not. That does seem significant.'

'*If you are constantly denying that part of this process may be horrible for the child, they will feel they can't speak about these things. That's when feelings can build up.*' – Eileen Hayes, parenting adviser to the NSPCC and vice-chair of the Parenting Education and Support Forum

Many children feel genuine interest, affection and care for their new baby brother or sister. Yet a new baby can throw even the most eager and well-adjusted child off balance, as what they held to be safe and stable – their own family – is transformed beyond recognition.

Our children need to know it's all right not to feel wonderful about the baby all the time and that they may sometimes feel angry, upset and jealous. Telling children off for resenting the baby or suggesting that they should be feeling otherwise will only fuel hurt and resentment. Even well-meant comments – 'You must be thrilled!' 'Don't be silly, of course you love her!' – can make a child sense they should hide their true emotions. And hidden feelings don't disappear, but tend to be 'acted out' in negative behaviour or explode with even greater force another day.

It's far better to let children know that negative feelings are not taboo and can be admitted openly: 'I guess it feels strange having a new baby around. I can understand that'; 'Does her crying drive you mad? It's so loud, isn't it.'

Allowing our children's feelings doesn't mean we have to agree with them, but does require us to accept and understand them, allow them to air anxieties and ask uncomfortable questions (see Exploring emotions, page 125).

It also helps to keep a sense of proportion. A child who says they hate their baby brother or sister may well be telling the truth at that moment, but it is not an indication of long-term sibling rejection. It is a positive sign of a healthy relationship if our child loves and trusts us enough to share their thoughts and feelings with us, even if we find them hard to hear.

'It is normal for children to feel jealousy. That is how we are as a human race. It is one of our survival techniques to make sure we get as much as everyone else, if not more.' – Dr Sarah Newton, Consultant Clinical Psychologist and head of Clinical Psychology Services, Plymouth Primary Care Trust

'Because we hate the idea of our children being jealous of each other, we have this resistance to acknowledging it for what it is – a completely understandable emotion. One of my twins went into a complete decline when his little brother was born. He'd been extrovert and sunny, then plunged into total misery. Then he seemed to get over it and his twin brother went downhill, perhaps because Joe was six months by then and beginning to mess with his things. Each child will find it hard, but they may find different aspects hardest to cope with.' – Sarah P.

Children calling . . .

The following 'snapshots' of recent calls to ChildLine indicate some of the many worries children may have about the birth of a new baby.

- One girl called because her mum is pregnant and she's the only child. She is worried she'll be rejected. At the same time, she was looking forward to helping mum with the new baby.
- An eight-year-old boy felt his 'parents are too busy, they hardly notice I'm here; they've given my bedroom to the baby'.
- Another boy said his mum had a new baby two weeks ago and does not pay attention to him now. 'If I ask for something, she just shouts at me'. He feels 'let down'.
- A girl aged fourteen called about having frequent rows with her mother. Her baby brother is now two years old. When he was born she felt 'left out' although the family are quite close. 'Now I can't imagine being without him.'
- A ten-year-old girl felt like 'running away' because she felt she received no attention at home since her parents had another baby.
- One eleven-year-old girl had been asked by her mother to be there at the birth as her dad was away at work. She had said no but now she wants to be there.

Reproduced with the kind permission of ChildLine[4]

Understanding temperament

'The temperament of the child is so important to the way relationships develop in the family, and to the level of exhaustion of the parents. For one thing, life is very different if you have a sleeper. I keep meeting people who had sleeping babies, and I still think "Why not me!"'
– Mary MacLeod, National Family and Parenting Institute

'Having a second child, you realise just how different babies can be. Temperamental differences are there from the time they are born, and that can be quite a shock.' – Sarah Darton, health visitor

How your children respond to each other will be influenced by their individual temperaments from their earliest days together. These temperamental differences, partly rooted in each child's genetic make-up, are not set in stone but do influence how children react to each other and how others in the family react to them. They will influence each child's development and the nature of their relationship.

Studies into the effects of temperamental differences on sibling relationships suggest, not surprisingly, that easygoing and highly adaptable children tend to cope much more easily with the birth of a brother or sister than less adaptable, more anxious children[5] – which means some sibling relationships are more troubled from the start, and some parents have a much tougher job on their hands. This is worth remembering when either we're racked with guilt or (God forbid) feel tempted to judge another's parenting abilities by the apparent nature of the relationship between their children.

The temperament of the new baby is, of course, another essential ingredient in the mix. A distressed, fretful baby is harder for a big brother or sister to welcome into the world, while a calmer, jollier baby is easier for a sibling to recognise as a positive addition to the family. The influence of each child's behaviour 'style' will continue to affect the other children in the family as they grow. The more sociable babies are at twelve months, for instance, the more sociable their older siblings tend to be towards them at eighteen months.[6]

That said, how we support each child and nurture their relationship will have a major impact on how they feel and behave toward each other, whatever their mix of temperaments (see But aren't kids born that way? page 171). How we respond to them will influence their relationships for life. We can help each child feel secure in our love, respect and understanding, and this will make them feel less threatened by their siblings' demands on our attention and affection.

'We can pick out the children who are going to find major change in their family life difficult to adjust to. It will show up in the way they react to the sibling birth, as it will show up in their response to other changes such as starting nursery school or moving house. Some children are simply more anxious and more easily upset than others. Parents will know if they

have one of these children, and may well find their next child isn't like that. It's an important point to make. It may help parents feel less guilty.'
– Professor Judy Dunn, developmental psychologist

Mummy's little helper?

'I hear a lot of adults telling children, "You're such a good girl, you are mummy's helper". I'm hesitant about placing children too much in the helper role because they can feel resentful. It is valuable to appreciate when they help, so if they bring you something you could say: "Wonderful, thank you so much, that's a real help to me". But that's not the same as expecting them to always be the big, sensible helpful one. That's what can set up problems.'
– Sarah Darton, health visitor

'He seemed to thrive on his new role. He welcomed the attention he received by being caring and it helped him display qualities that perhaps had been harder to see when he was an only child.' – Jenny S.

Whether and how we expect older children in the family to help with the care of the baby will vary greatly according to family culture, expectation and circumstance. It is also hard to predict how each child will respond; some are proud to assume a new role as important older brother or sister, others feel put upon and slaves to their kid sibling's whims. Yet how they feel is also influenced by what we do, so it may help to consider the following issues:

- **Allowing them to help care for the baby** with our assistance and when they want to often eases tensions.
- **Commenting on the baby's responsiveness** to the child will encourage the child to become more interested in the baby's feelings. They may then want to become more involved.
- **Babies can be a great audience**. By making helping fun, and encouraging games, a child is more likely to enjoy it.
- **Watching for mood changes** can help us judge whether a child is likely to enjoy helping or feel taken for granted. This can change from one moment to the next. Pressurising them to help will only backfire.
- **Avoiding labels** for our children: 'She's an angel'; 'He's a

nightmare'; 'She's such an easy baby'; 'He's mummy's little helper' (see Kids don't fit in pigeonholes, page 159). These generalisations can begin from our children's earliest days – and they can stick. Even positive labels delivered with good intentions may be damaging if a child feels parental love is conditional on them being the 'good girl' or responsible 'big brother'.

- **Think small and specific**. Manageable and defined tasks that a child can do without getting bored or belligerent have a much higher chance of happy completion than time-consuming chores or vague directives to 'help Mummy'.

- **Letting older children soothe and comfort the baby** may encourage the bond between them to grow, but we need to be on hand to help. Children can be frightened by the intensity of a baby's distress, and shouldn't be made to feel responsible if their attempts at soothing don't work.

- **Praising any help we receive** will make the child feel good and increase the likelihood of them helping in this way again (see Acknowledge the good times, page 70).

The baby isn't always first

'We need to show the older child very clearly that their needs are still important to us, and we need to listen to them and notice them so they feel they have our love, attention and affection just as much as the little one.'
– Sarah Darton, health visitor

Studies have proved what many children already know – that older children may experience a startling drop in parental attention and happy joint activities once the baby arrives.[7] The reasons are obvious. Babies are absolutely dependent on their carers and cry when in need. Older brothers and sisters are less dependent and, according to age and temperament, may use more subtle methods to make their needs known or express them in negative behaviour. Either way, older children are often pushed to the back of the attention queue.

There will be many times when the baby requires immediate and preferential care, but there will also be occasions when they can wait. By sometimes attending to our older child first, we can help redress the balance.

'Try to put the baby down occasionally so you can give your child some time. This is so important. If your child is miserable or tired, they'll need to take priority.' – Carol Ann Hally, health visitor

Time together without the baby

This can feel as rare as gold-dust and is often lost under the weight of other demands, but is essential if we are to support and nurture the bond between ourselves and the older child, and the fledgling relationship between our children. Time together without the baby, to read, play or just enjoy each other's company, can reduce resentments and help parent and child relax and chat. It may also make our lives easier by reducing 'testing' behaviour.

Familiar routines

Let's be realistic. Routines are often broken in the months following the baby's arrival because there's no other way to get to the end of the day. We can, though, aim to keep as many basics in place as we can – and this is important. Children whose daily routines carry on pretty much as before following the birth of a sibling tend to show fewer signs of upset than those whose daily life becomes unpredictable.

Timing of meals and bedtimes seem particularly important, as does ensuring that older children continue to see friends. As sleep problems are common around the time of a sibling's birth, it may make sense to introduce a longer calming-down time before bed.

If the older child attends nursery, playgroup or school or spends time with another carer, ask to be kept informed of what's happening in their day so you can continue to show care and interest in their activities and achievements.

The box of tricks

After the birth of the baby, the drop in our attention and our occasional inability to respond immediately to demands may push a first child into flashes of dejection or fury, especially if they are still too young to understand the concept of waiting (see Testing, testing, page 29).

So what can we do? The first is to accept that we're not superhuman – we can't meet all demands at all times (see Looking after you, page 36).

On a practical note, many mothers suggested having a 'special' bag or box close by when feeding or attending to the baby. This could contain books to read with the older child, crayons and paper, toys, treats, anything the child may need, want or enjoy. Putting it within easy reach may help us negotiate competing demands more often and help the child feel less sidelined.

'Lots of mothers feed the baby at the same time as the older child has a meal-time, so they can all sit at the table together. That's helpful. Many read a story to their child while they're feeding, or let them watch something on the box. Don't feel guilty about letting them watch a bit of TV. These are survival techniques!' – Carol Ann Hally, health visitor

Think positive

'The increase in negative comments to the older child is very understandable under the circumstances because often the child is behaving diabolically and the mother is exhausted and on the whole gets much less support and help than the first time around. The practical lesson would seem to be to get as much help and as many breaks as you can.' – Professor Judy Dunn, developmental psychologist

Studies show a dramatic increase in the number of negative, critical comments made by mothers to children after the birth of a new baby, partly in response to the older child's demanding and challenging behaviour[8] (see Understanding and managing signs of upset, page 28). Yet that challenging behaviour is likely to increase if the child feels rejected or undermined.

To break the downward spiral, we can praise our children whenever the opportunity arises, telling them exactly why we like what they are doing (see Descriptive praise, page 72). This helps them feel better about themselves, and children who feel better about themselves tend to behave better.

🚶🚶🚶   *Does birth order matter?*   🚶🚶🚶

'I think theories are interesting but would be wary of accepting them as some sort of ultimate truth.' – Desa Markovic, family therapist supervisor; assistant director at The Institute of Family Therapy, London

'A lot of the folk belief about personality and birth order in my view haven't been borne out by the careful and very large number of studies. It is one of the factors that might feed into the giant equation to explain what you are like as an adult, but it is not a major one. To be honest, the myths don't stand up to scrutiny.' – Professor Judy Dunn, developmental psychologist

'I defy anyone to tell me birth order doesn't make a difference. It made a difference to me and it makes a difference to my children.' – Sarah P.

Birth order may make some difference to our children's development – but not as much as we may think. Its impact will also vary between cultures, with their different expectations of eldest children and gender roles, and between families and individual children. The last child in one family may be laid back and easy going and in another demanding and competitive. Both families may put this down to them being the 'baby'. In families generally, very few clear patterns emerge about the impact of birth order on development and personality.[9] It does not determine the sorts of people our children will become. That's not to say there aren't clear links between birth order and behaviour.

- Firstborns tend to be more dominating in the pre-school years. Their degree of affection or hostility will influence their younger brother or sister far more than the younger child's behaviour will influence the firstborn.

If we are alert to any caring and sensitive gestures made towards the new baby, we can express our approval and appreciation: 'You've brought me her bottle. Thanks, that's really helpful'; 'You've put on your own shoes. Now we can get out before the baby cries. Thank you!'

- Parents frequently expect more sooner of their firstborn, and are often far less anxious with their later born children.
- The first child generally has greater attention and interaction with parents before the second child is born, and the birth of the second child seems a greater jolt to all family members than the birth of subsequent siblings.[10]

Yet how these factors will influence each of our children long-term will depend on the individual child, their life experiences and family expectations and relationships. Factors other than birth order have far stronger and more significant influence on our children's relationships and the sorts of people they will become, including:

- Individual parent-child relationships
- Family and social circumstances
- Children's temperamental differences
- What our children learn from and feel about each other. The affection, intimacy, warmth or conflict one child feels for another have no clear link with family position and are of far greater importance to the nature of their relationship.

Childhood is not an assembly line of pre-determined experiences but a complex interplay of varied influences and circumstances. Birth order matters far less to our children's emotional and social development than the nature of family relationships.

'In some ways I baby my youngest. I've carried him for longer because I don't have another little one to pick up. I'm more understanding and tolerant of his ways and treasure his babyness more because I know how quickly it passes. But then he has to cope with the hurly burly of family life and just get on with things in a way his older brother didn't have to. So in that way he's less indulged. It's less clear cut than perhaps we think.'
– Helen B.

If we also praise our children for being themselves and not just for their involvement with the baby, we will reassure them that the baby isn't the sole focus of our attention. 'That's a beautiful picture. I like how you've drawn the sunshine'; 'What a wonderful smile. That's cheered me up.' Our children are now actively searching for clues about our feelings for them and will pick up on conversations and remarks never intended for their ears, so it helps to keep all comments about them positive unless we are absolutely certain they are out of earshot.

Understanding behaviour changes

'My middle daughter seemed deliberately provocative, doing and saying things she knew would annoy. My eldest became excruciatingly good – tidying her room, being very quiet, displaying impeccable manners, doing her homework without protest. It took me a long while to realise these were signs that she was struggling, too.' – Helena V.

'My health visitor described it as testing behaviour, and that's exactly what it was. It was almost as if she was saying, 'I'm not sure you love me enough now you've had this new baby, so I'm really going to test it to the limit.' – Emma B.

'It takes great patience to continue to express love unremittingly in the face of some of the awful things children do. It is very hard, and no parent should expect a totally easy ride. But behaviour problems tend to improve greatly over the first few months. It's also important to remember that children who are particularly difficult and demanding are not especially likely to get on badly with their siblings over the years that follow.' – Professor Judy Dunn, developmental psychologist.

Even with our love and concerned support, children may still display problematic behaviour. This is perfectly normal and perfectly understandable. Almost all behaviours associated with the arrival of a sibling will fade with time and are not a sure sign of trouble ahead. Strikingly, children who seem most disturbed after the birth are sometimes also the most interested and affectionate towards the baby.

So our first task is to not feel guilty about behaviour swings. They are not a sign of poor parenting, ruined lives or disastrous sibling relationships. The second is to help our children come to terms with their new, bigger family. Being alert to the ways children may express their confusion and hurt will help us respond more sensitively and constructively and help the child feel valued and less threatened.

I'll show it my way

All children can feel jealousy and distress at the changes in their lives caused by the birth of a sibling but the way they react tends to differ with age and temperament.

- Firstborn children tend to be more upset when a sibling is born, for the simple reason that they have tasted life as a single child and have more to lose.
- Children under two are likely to be clingy and miserable. They may temporarily lose their ability to concentrate on play. Older toddlers will often give up newfound toilet skills or experience sleep problems.
- Two, three and four-year-olds may take their feelings out on their mothers, becoming demanding, contrary and difficult. Some may be aggressive and bossy towards other children.
- Over fives seem less likely to be upset at the birth of a sibling than under fives.[11]

Testing, testing . . .

'Firstborns often do the one thing that their mothers had expressly forbidden or which will particularly irritate them when the mother picks up the baby to feed or cuddle. I've watched lots of children at home with their mothers and new siblings, and seen firstborns rip wallpaper from the wall, deliberately tip water on the floor, repeatedly switch off the television while the mother was watching – the ingenuity of the actions was remarkable.'[12]
– Professor Judy Dunn, developmental psychologist

'Often when the baby arrives, a child is between about two and four years old – when they are already testing all the boundaries. My son put a floorcloth over his baby sister's face as well doing all sorts of other horrible things.' – Brenda Meldrum, Head of Training,
The Place To Be

'I was two when my brother was born. It was December. My mum said that when he was a few weeks old they couldn't find us. I'd taken him outside and tucked him down in the snow.' – Eileen Hayes, writer and parenting adviser to the NSPCC.

Many studies have documented children's disturbed behaviour after the birth of a sibling, and indicate increased problematic behaviour in anywhere between fifty and ninety-three per cent of children.[13] That's the bad news. The good news is that for most of them, the peak of uncooperative, disruptive behaviour will pass in the first two or three months.

Testing behaviour needs handling kindly but firmly. We can let our children know we understand their angry or upset feelings while also being firm and clear about what we regard as unacceptable: 'I know you are feeling angry and I understand why, and *you* know that you are not to throw things. It could hurt someone.'

Children who suffer a particularly marked drop in parental attention are likely to be the most upset. Cuddles, stories and shared play may give a child the extra reassurance they need and shift the focus towards more positive behaviour – but it is best to wait until tempers have calmed and there's less risk of them associating grotty behaviour with the reward of an immediate and affectionate response.

'I often see a baby at ten days, with an older child who the mother says is being marvellous, great with the baby, great with mum, eating her food. Four or five weeks down the line, suddenly this little darling starts doing all the things she hadn't done previously. Won't cooperate, won't go to nursery, won't get dressed, won't stay in her bed. There is a danger if the behaviour boundaries start to go – children won't know where they are. It helps to gently but firmly remind them of the family rules, and they do eventually come through it.' – Carol Ann Hally, health visitor

Mother bashing

'I was prepared for her to show resentment towards the baby. I wasn't prepared for her being so angry with me.' – Julie M.

'In my experience, negative feelings often come out directed at the mother rather than the baby. I've come across that a lot.' – Sarah Darton, health visitor

'Sometimes even little children realise that expressing anger towards the baby will incur them their mother's wrath, so they express it at the mother. This can be very painful.' – Christine Bidmead, Training Facilitator, Centre for Parent and Child Support

Some mothers report children hitting or kicking them, screaming, refusing to comply with the most reasonable of requests or, perhaps most painful of all, seeming to reject them. Children may cling to daddy or granny and glower at mum, refusing to allow her to dress them, read them a story, bath them. This is fairly common and very painful.

It doesn't mean your child's love for you is in any way diminished. It does mean they are feeling hurt. As ever, responding harshly is likely to be counterproductive; damaging a child's confidence and security further is a sure way of increasing their insecurity, anxiety and jealousy. Being warm, supportive and clear about behaviour we find unacceptable is much more effective: 'I think you're feeling angry with me because I've had another baby. That must be hard. You must not hit me but you can tell me how you're feeling.'

Regression

'I don't think there's any huge harm in regression. You can weather it and have faith it will pass, staying very low key and accepting. But if you feel strongly that you really don't want him to behave like this because it is going to drive you bonkers, then it's best to say so, calmly and clearly, right at the beginning.' – Sarah Darton, health visitor

'It is really important to maintain boundaries of behaviour but also to have some compassion and understanding for regressive behaviour. If your toddler wants to feed from a bottle or your three-year-old suddenly asks to wear a nappy, it's not the end of the world. It could all seem to be going pear-shaped but it will get better.' – Christine Bidmead, Training Facilitator, Centre for Parent and Child Support

In one study, more than half the children who were toilet trained around the time of their siblings' birth had setbacks.[14] Even four and five-year-olds often lapse. Other children simply want to be babied,

ᛏᛏᛏ *Heart belongs to daddy?* ᛏᛏᛏ

'Often fathers seem to get more involved when the second child arrives, at least more hands on and particularly with the older child.'
– Belinda Phipps, National Childbirth Trust

Fathers, trusted relatives or adult friends, can make a huge difference to how children feel about themselves and cope with the birth of a new baby.

Studies show that older children often feel particularly close to their fathers in the first year after the siblings' birth. This is probably due to fathers' increased efforts to give their children support and attention. When dads are closely involved in this way, conflict with the mother following the birth tends to be less marked. However, children may display more jealousy when dad plays with the new baby.

It need not be the father who supports the child. If he's not available, a grandparent or other trusted relative or friend may provide the love, attention and understanding the child needs.

'It is still important for the older child to have time alone with mum and it is important to think about how that can be negotiated. It won't help the older child if mum is always with the baby and they are always with dad when he's home.' – Christine Bidmead, Training Facilitator, Centre for Parent and Child Support

and receive attention in the same way as their little brother or sister. This can manifest itself in clingy demands to be cuddled and carried, wanting a bottle, feeding problems and sleep problems. Forcing or demanding that children 'grow up' is only likely to make the issue a battleground. And there's nothing more certain to encourage continued 'baby' demands.

Children do grow out of regressive behaviour, and often do so more quickly when supported by parental understanding and calm. If we find the behaviour hard to handle it's best to let the child know rather than simmer with resentment. Presenting it as our problem rather than the child's reduces the risks of confrontation: 'I'm finding this bottle business really hard because it makes even more washing up, so would you let me know when you can do without it?' rather than 'Why do you want a bottle? You're not a baby.'

> *'Look at regression from the child's point of view. The baby is getting such a great deal. Relatives are rushing round, admiring the baby and buying gifts. It's completely understandable that children want some of that. I'm all for letting them be a baby for a while if they want. There's a lot of pressure on parents to get them out of a cot before the baby comes, be potty trained before the baby comes, to grow up fast. All that can backfire. It would be far easier, I think, to be laid back and think okay, I'm going to have two babies for a while, no matter what age they are.'* – Eileen Hayes, writer and parenting adviser to the NSPCC

Withdrawal and sadness

Some children become withdrawn or quiet after the birth of a brother or sister. They may be undemanding and uninterested, perhaps even unable to focus on play. Such behaviour needs to be handled with great sensitivity and care, as these are often the children whose distress is most difficult to spot but in most urgent need of our support. Studies suggest that where a child becomes very withdrawn, the relationship between the siblings can become very hostile and angry.[15]

We need to make extra efforts to reassure and show these children how much they are loved. Calm and sympathetic acknowledgement of their feelings, without undue exaggeration, will help them express their emotions and anxieties (see Message received? page 187, and Exploring emotions, page 125).

We might also mention our concerns to playgroup or school staff, and grandparents. Children may be reluctant to tell their parents how they feel, but may be able to talk to someone outside the immediate family. Many parents find this hard, but it is far better that our children have someone they can talk to openly and honestly.

Irrational fears

Children may also show a dramatic increase in fears and worries after the birth of a baby brother or sister. Some of this is age-related –

♼ *What if the child hurts* ♼♼♼
the baby?

'Often children need to be shown what a gentle touch is. Toddlers especially don't always know. Sometimes you need to take their hand and stroke the baby with them, and say, "Look, the baby likes that, that's a really gentle stroke".' – Sarah Darton, health visitor

'Direct physical aggression is quite rare in the first weeks home, though the firstborn may deliberately provoke and irritate the baby by shaking the crib and so on.' – Professor Judy Dunn, developmental psychologist

Most children have ambivalent feelings towards their baby brother or sister – and protective love, resentment and jealousy are a heady mix. The deliberate harm of a newborn baby by its older sibling is rare. However some children can turn the most lovable hugs into the fiercest tweaks by the time the baby is three or four months old. There is much we can do to help our children get their feelings under control. Here's what parents and professionals have suggested may help:

- Stay calm (see Exploring emotions, page 125) and be very clear: 'It's not OK to hit.'
- Have a firm family rule that any toys used to hurt are taken away.
- Remove the baby rather than the child, so the child doesn't get

three and four-year-old children often display previously unseen anxieties – yet they do seem to peak in the first year following the arrival of a new baby, especially in the under fives.

Belittling or ridiculing children's fears, even with the very best of intentions – 'Don't be daft, there's nothing to be afraid of' – can devastate a child trying to express a real anxiety. Talking with our children, comforting them and respecting their fears, will help them feel much more safe, supported and able to cope: 'That's a scary feeling. I remember feeling scared when I was little and it wasn't

immediate attention for hurtful behaviour.

- If your child is cuddling too tight, say so and find your child something else to do: 'That hurts her and she isn't enjoying it. Let's leave her be and find the Lego.'

- Look to the root cause. If your child is bored, missing your attention or feeling less loved, try to spend more fun time together. Do this soon but not straight away, or the child may feel rewarded for negative behaviour.

- Be clear, be firm, but don't go overboard. An overly harsh response may fuel resentment and increase the risk of pinched cheeks and tweaked hair.

- Try not to label the child or his relationship with the baby (see Kids don't fit in pigeon-holes, page 159). He isn't a 'naughty boy' or a 'nasty child', he has simply done something he should not.

- If you feel the child is really trying to hurt the baby, separate them and don't leave them alone together. Put a safety gate across the door when you put the baby down to sleep.

- Let your child know you understand his feelings and that he must understand he is not to hurt. 'I know you feel angry, and you know it's not okay to hurt the baby.'

- Give your child alternative ways to express his feelings. 'When you feel that way come and tell me and we'll have a hug.' Some children like to paint; some like to run about to get rid of their aggression; some like to read books about irritating little siblings. Choose what you think suits your child's age and temperament best (see Exploring emotions, page 125).

nice. What would help you feel better?' (See Exploring emotions, page 125.)

Looking after you

'I remember trying to get up off the chair, still in quite a lot of pain, feeding the baby, trying to stop my toddler climbing on to the windowsill, and thinking, "Where the hell is everybody?" I had much more help first time round. And more flowers.' – Helen D.

'Some parents find it easier second time around. They have often adjusted to the responsibility of attempting to meet the needs of another human being and know that phases pass. There is often less panic.'
– Sarah Darton, health visitor

'Whether you have one child or two or more, parents need friends. Children are much more fun when you can share your worries and the fun with others.' – Belinda Phipps, National Childbirth Trust

Recognising and respecting our own physical and emotional needs will help us care for our families and ourselves all the better. We can start by being aware of how parents may feel after the birth of a second child – and what may help.

Rest and sleep

'Meeting the needs of more than one is tiring and exhausting. Trying to juggle the differences leaves you very little time for yourself.'
– Sarah Darton, health visitor

Tiredness is often a fact of life with a new baby, and we may have far fewer chances to catch up with sleep or even sit down now we have two children, so it is especially important to snatch what rest we can. Offers of practical help and support also tend to be fewer second time round, so we need to make the most of those we have and to ask for help if it's not forthcoming.

👫👫 *Under pressure* 👫👫

'Just think of the relatively usual situation of having another baby with a toddler. Physically you are worn out by the pregnancy and birth, mentally you are worn out by a full-on toddler whose needs if anything increase while you are pregnant and having a baby, then you have all the responsibility of keeping these children safe and as happy as possible with next to no sleep. I am often in awe at how parents cope but especially if they are on their own. I have total admiration for parents just getting through the everyday stresses that face us all.'
– Margaret Harrison, founder and life president of Home-Start

Having a second child can push women out of the workforce, according to new research. A study of 400 women tracked by psychologist Diane Houston of the University of Kent shows that seventy-five per cent of mothers go back to work after their first baby, but half of these stop work completely after they have their second child.[16] Houston says that when a woman is pregnant with her second child, having found life hard enough with just one, she often decides she has to make radical changes to her working life.

Belinda Phipps, chief executive of the National Childbirth Trust, agrees: 'Parents are often surprised that having a second child involves a further big adjustment. When a second child is born, the mother may move from part-time or full-time work to being at home because the costs of childcare can be prohibitive. This means a whole different way of living and requires a lot of rethinking and adjusting for parents. The transition seems to be so huge sometimes because of the combined needs of the children *and* the dramatic change in lifestyle for the mother.'

'So many factors go to make up the context in which a baby is born and how the parents may feel. Is this child expected, generally wanted, is the timing right for the couple, is the timing right for the child that's already there, what kind of supports are in place? How was the pregnancy, how was the birth? What is the health of the child? Are the father and mother working? Is there enough space in the house, in the relationship, in the resources, to welcome the child? All will influence each family member's experience of what this new baby means to them.'
– Mary MacLeod, National Family and Parenting Institute

🚶🚶🚶 *Support as an investment* 🚶🚶🚶

'We all need encouragement and someone to say we are doing a good job, and parents so rarely get that,' says Christine Bidmead, training facilitator at the Centre for Parent and Child Support. 'We also need someone to turn to for support and informed advice. This could be your health visitor, or other parents, friends, local community groups, helplines, support organisations. Whatever feels right for you. When should you ask for help or information? When you feel you need it. Also, if you are tearing your hair out or feel so wound up that you're worried you may snap, or if you're not sleeping. Without sleep it's very hard to cope. But the main aim should be to look after yourself so you don't reach that point, if at all possible.'

If you feel you may be depressed, it is important to consult your GP or health visitor as soon as possible so you can receive the help and support you need. This is important for you and all family members. Withdrawn behaviour is more common among firstborns whose mothers are depressed or extremely tired following the birth of their sibling, and this has been linked to hostile sibling relations in future years (see Withdrawal and sadness, page 33).

The guilt trap

'If you are still in the 'holy phase', as I put it, with the first child, when you are so delighted they are there, still hugely invested in this first child who is everything, then you can witness the advent of the second child from your first child's point of view. This can be very tricky. You can feel "What am I doing to this little child? I haven't given her enough. He or she will find it terribly difficult. How can I make it all right? However will they cope?" I remember those feelings very well'. – Mary MacLeod, National Family and Parenting Institute

Parents have a tremendous capacity for guilt, and we can turn ourselves inside out at the thought of the damage we have inflicted on our firstborn by the birth of another baby, so it helps to keep matters in perspective. There will be many occasions when we won't

Time for you

Try to do a few things just for you – even a bath in peace can feel like luxury. Spend some relaxed time with your partner. Also meet up with old friends and other parents – talking through issues with people who really understand can be an invaluable support, as can having fun times and conversations that don't revolve around the children.

'You can't go on giving and giving and giving because in the end there will be nothing else to give,' warns Christine Bidmead, training facilitator at the Centre for Parent and Child Support. 'Think of your emotional and physical energy as the water in a jug. Unless you stop and refill it, there will be nothing left to give to others.'

Christine often begins group discussions with mothers by asking them to note down the one thing they like doing for themselves. 'And they look blank. They've actually forgotten what they liked to do "BC" – before children. When the second child arrives, parents are much more in touch with the reality of what it means to have a child, but not necessarily in touch with the reality of managing two children. It can be tough.

'Society is not changing as fast as we would like to think and the mother is still the main child carer, they are the ones who take the most strain. So mothers need to take time out, just to relax. The very last thing on their list of priorities is to look after themselves, sometimes even to have a bath or go to the loo on their own. Yet it's so important, for the mother's mental health, for the couple and for relationships between all family members.'

be able to meet all demands immediately and at least one of our children will have to wait. That's life, and our children will learn from it.

As long as we redress the balance when we can and ensure each child feels loved, they'll be fine (see You may want me but your brother needs me, page 142).

'Top of the list of pressures on parents with a new baby is guilt. There is still this idea of the perfect family unit and people aren't prepared for how difficult it can be to negotiate everybody's needs. The truth is that we can never get it perfectly right. It's relatively easy to deal with one

person at a time, but that's not how life is in families.'
– Eileen Hayes, writer and parenting adviser to the NSPCC

Your past, their future

The birth of a first baby often prompts us to reflect on our childhood
and our relationships with our parents. The birth of a second child
may start this process anew, and also trigger a reappraisal of our own
sibling relationships.

The memories stirred may be warm and comforting or upsetting
and unsettling, and may colour how we perceive the potential bond
between our children. An awareness of this may help us recognise and
support the unique, developing relationship between them rather
than viewing it through the prism of our own sibling experiences (see
Exploring emotions, page 125).

*'Distinguishing between my past with my brothers and my kids' future with each
other has been incredibly helpful. It's a simple but crucial point. Just because my
relations with my brothers were hostile, doesn't mean hostility between brothers is
inevitable. Actually, my boys seem to quite like each other!'* – Gary H.

Different baby, different you

*'I was able to tune in to my second child straight away, in a way that
hadn't happened with my first. But in a very real way it strengthened
the bond between my firstborn and me. I realised the love I felt for my
baby son was something my daughter had helped develop in me,
that it was her gift.'* – Helen D.

*'Our first two children were relatively calm, easy to soothe, placid little
things. Then came Nicola. We felt like we'd been hit by a tornado. We
were totally unprepared and I think we all went into shock for a
few months.'* – Simon P.

Some parents feel a special affinity with their first child; others feel a
more immediate bond with their second or subsequent babies (see
Exploring our feelings as parents, page 146). This is only natural.

No relationship is the same, and that applies as much to parents and their children as it does to relationships between adults. As our relationships with our children grow, it may help to remember that 'different' need not mean 'less than' or 'unequal to'. What matters is that each child in the family feels noticed, valued and loved.

For strong family bonds to form our children will need time together and we will need time with them, as a family and with each child, one-to-one. There is a huge amount to do as the parent of two or more children. Yet sometimes the most important step we can take is to try to 'do' a little less. This may help us look after our own needs more – and allow developing family relationships to flourish.

A new baby arrives: key approaches

Understand upset	The birth of a baby is a time of dramatic transition for the family. Almost all children feel some distress and resentment; regressive and testing behaviour are common. Our children will sometimes need us to be firm. Most of all, they need our love and understanding.
Prepare the way	This won't eradicate jealousy and distress but may help. We can answer our child's questions sensitively and honestly; reminisce about their infancy; involve them in preparations if they wish; keep changes to a minimum, talk about love and how the new baby may respond.
Nurture the new relationship	The relationship between baby and child begins to develop in their first

	weeks together. We can help by encouraging their first 'games'; talking about the baby's needs and feelings and emphasising the baby's interest in the child; involving the child in the baby's care if they enjoy it; and expressing appreciation of any sensitive responses to their new brother or sister.
Find one-to-one time	So hard, and so important. The baby doesn't always have to come first. Ensuring time alone with our child, accepting and allowing them to express feelings or simply finding pleasure in each other's company, may help them cope better with the dramatic drop in parental attention.
Put ourselves first sometimes	Parents' physical and emotional needs tend to get pushed to the back of the queue. Yet only by caring for ourselves will we have the reserves we need to care and support our children and their developing relationship.

Key message:

Our children's worlds are changing fast. Each needs our love.

3

Caring and sharing:

building positive relationships

'With siblings, there is terrific potential to support each other and be there for each other. You can learn so much from each other, from each other's experiences, friends, differences and interests. There is a very rich social fabric there to learn from. Great if you've got it'.
– Peter Wilson, director of Young Minds

'Adults who are close to their siblings say that their shared early experiences are a key part of their affection for each other. Those who played together a lot as children were likely to be close in adulthood.' – Professor Judy Dunn, developmental psychologist

'I think seeing your kids play and laugh together has to be one of the greatest pleasures of parenthood.' – Ros N.

How we encourage caring and consideration between our children will make a difference now and for the rest of their lives. Whatever their mix of temperaments, ages and genders, we can:

- help them have more fun together through play
- encourage turn-taking and the skills they need to share

- foster concern, empathy and cooperation
- acknowledge and encourage good times through praise
- establish family rules for positive behaviour

All these approaches help build healthy and happier bonds between brothers and sisters. The benefits to them will spread far beyond their childhood and homelife. And if our children get along better, we'll have a better time, too.

Beyond rivalry

The few books that have considered sibling relationships at all have tended to focus narrowly on conflict and rivalry. These are important facets of our children's relationships, but not the whole story. Clearly, siblings may feel love, admiration, pleasure, protectiveness, concern, warmth, joy, pride and much more. Their relationships are more rich, complex and potentially positive than concentration on conflict alone suggests. And only by recognising the positives can we hope to build on them.

How our children play together has as much bearing on the people they will become as how they fight. Their mutual understanding and knowledge of each other can be a source of support as well as the fuel behind their well-aimed slights. Their warmth and love are as powerful as rivalry and conflict in shaping who our children are, how they treat each other and how this affects our family life.

Let the fun begin!

Free play is being squeezed out of many childhoods, partly due to adult-engineered 'activities', screen-based games, packed school curricula and increased traffic levels. Yet it is through play that children learn to be social beings. It's how they begin to develop a deep understanding of themselves, their world, their brothers, sisters and other important people in their lives.

We can help put free fun back into childhood, where it belongs.

Play with a new brother or sister

Encouraging fun games with the baby helps joint play become second nature – and our children can find pleasure in each other's company from their very first weeks together.

Children need to play together because they want to, not because they 'have to', so anything that smacks of heavy-handed instruction is best avoided. Instead, we can show an older child how to enjoy simple games with the baby or toddler by playing them ourselves, pointing out the baby's happy responses, and inviting them to join in. 'Look, she's smiling when I shake the rattle/tickle her toes/stick out my tongue! Here, you have a go.' (See Encouraging affection, page 15)

If the child doesn't take up the offer, it doesn't matter overmuch. Play is meant to be fun, and will backfire if they begin to feel they have disappointed or are under pressure. By watching us and seeing that play with the baby is enjoyable, they'll be learning all they need to be able to do it for themselves when they're ready, which may be when we're not looking on with such eager anticipation.

'When the older child starts having fun with the baby is when they start seeing that there's something in this for them, that maybe having a little baby sister or brother might actually be pretty good sometimes.'
– Marie M.

Play with older babies and toddlers

The same principles apply as our children grow. We can start off a game, perhaps rolling a ball to each child in turn, then back off once they've got the hang of it so they can play between themselves. We can suggest games or set out toys for toddlers and older children, involving each child in the arrangements – 'How about a game with the dinosaurs?'; 'Joe, which animal would like some water?' – then retreat once they seem to be getting into the swing.

This isn't as easy as it may sound. Some parents find it hard to prioritise play – perhaps they've forgotten how, or dismiss it as trivial or 'childish'. Some find it difficult not to take over or dominate. All of us have a million and one other things to do. Yet is is through play together that our children first learn the mutual benefits of fun, consideration and cooperation.

Occasional games that include parents as well as children helps joint play become part of the family 'style' (see Games for life, page 54). These can also help maintain links between children who, for any number of reasons, are going through a stage of playing with each other less.

> *'Children grow in and out of compatibility. Two pre-schoolers may play quite happily then, a year of two down the line, they may play less as they develop different interests. Later on, they might come back together again. If their interests start really diverging it can be quite tricky, but we can still encourage and set up cooperative activities.'*
> – Eileen Hayes, writer and parenting adviser to the NSPCC.

Games and rhymes

Turn-taking games and songs can be a source of huge pleasure between young children, while also encouraging fundamental skills of sharing and negotiation. Kids who are told they 'must share' may revolt and hang on to their toys with an iron grip. Through play, children can learn that sharing and turn-taking are safe and mutually beneficial without even noticing the 'lesson' (see Rory and Michael's new start, page 47).

Little brother, big mess

> *'When I first saw him I thought he was great. Now he's bigger, I'm not so sure.'* – Josie, aged eight

Even adored, smiley, cooing baby brothers and sisters learn to crawl, grab, bite, destroy games and take delight in knocking over older siblings' treasured constructions. Helping an older child cope is important if our children are to remain on relatively friendly terms.

♟♟♟ Rory and Michael's ♟♟♟ new start

Kate and her husband adopted two young boys two years ago, and have used play to strengthen the bond between them. The boys are now four and a half and three years old.

'Although they are full brothers, they had been cared for by different carers prior to coming to us and they had never lived together. So effectively we adopted two little boys who barely knew each other. We needed urgently to build a relationship between them,' Kate explains.

'We did that gently but purposefully. Right from the start we used lots of turn-taking play and singing games; you know, "One for Michael, one for Rory". We did lots of physical games like rolling backwards and forwards, Row the Boat, slapping and bashing bags, popping bubbles – you pop one, I pop one; Michael does one, Rory does one – every game we did we tried to introduce the turn-taking element.

'We then moved gradually towards giving them skills to negotiate with each other (see Searching for solutions, page 67). Now, if they both want to hold the car keys, I say, "I'll hold the key while you two work it out." They'll go off and have a mutter together and maybe suggest it's Rory's turn today and Michael's tomorrow. They learned quite quickly that if it's their brother's turn now it will be theirs next time, so it's no big issue. That's a huge help.

'Although adoption is part of the reason I worked so hard to develop our family identity – the glue that sticks us together – it's important for birth families, too. I feel passionately that there is so much parents can do in the early years to enable children to have positive brother and sister relationships.'

The following are suggestions that professionals and parents have found useful:

- **Understand that little brothers and sisters are a pain sometimes**. It's perfectly reasonable that our older children feel frustrated or angry at some of the things their little siblings do. They need to know we understand their feelings: 'It's annoying when something precious gets spoiled, isn't it? Let's see if we can fix it.' (See Exploring emotions, page 125.)

- **Talk about ages and stages**. Children have little understanding of how babies and toddlers develop, tending to judge a sibling by their own standards and capabilities and presuming a kid brother or sister's actions to be deliberate or indefensibly careless. This is one reason why they become so angry.

  By explaining the way babies explore the world – often knocking things down along the way, by accident or to experiment – we may help reduce our child's simmering resentment. Sharing funny stories or photographs of the older child at the sibling's age can help them realise they did much the same when they were 'little'.

  Pointing out that babies and toddlers are often trying to join in, in the best way they know how, may help a child see their sibling less as an irritant and more as a little person still learning how to play with others. By also recognising that toddlers can deliberately provoke their brothers and sisters (see Who? Little me? page 98) we may better understand our older child's frustrations.

- **Create a special space**. Is there somewhere – a tabletop, a bunk bed, a corner of a room – that can be the older child's own, relatively safe from the ravages of little brother or sister? All children benefit from a personal space where they can play quietly, uninterrupted by other children if they wish, and where their creations and games can stay undisturbed.

- **Watch for mood shifts**. We can generally spot times when an older child has had enough or when the youngest may be bent on destruction. Removing the invader and finding something else for the baby to do before the situation overheats is far easier for everyone than waiting until tempers explode.

- **Respond when they need us**. Children can be pretty brutal in their methods of sibling control. If at first they don't succeed in persuading a kid brother or sister to leave them alone, they may shout, push or worse, which isn't going to do much for harmonious family relations.

If, on the other hand, we tell our children to call on us if there's trouble they really can't sort out themselves, we reduce the risk of them hurting each other in frustration. We also have a chance to show them how to deal with situations constructively and calmly. Even if they're too young to put this into practice, our example will serve as a powerful lesson for future use.

'If your child is confident that if she needs you, you will remove or control the baby invader, you'll reduce the risk of direct action on the older child's part.' – Professor Judy Dunn, developmental psychologist

Play between older children

Leaving them to it

'It is important for us not to get too wound up or over-involved in our children's play. Of course we don't want to leave them to kill each other in the back room, and observing the way our children relate to each other and to their friends can allow us some important insight. But if taken too far it can also open the door to more anxiety, less spontaneity, less fun. Sometimes we need to relax, and free our children to find their own way together.' – Mary MacLeod, chief executive, National Family and Parenting Institute

'You don't have to be hanging over and instructing them in fantasy play. It is absolutely something children are better at than parents.' – Professor Judy Dunn, developmental psychologist

Sometimes the hardest thing for us to do is nothing. Yet allowing time for our children to play freely, without repeated adult direction or intervention, is essential if they are to reap the full benefits and fun. As with so many aspects of parenthood, the aim is to get the balance right, between being watchful of our children's needs and retreating far enough for them to learn to get on with life together.

Being nearby is important, but we can observe without being a participant. Without an adult in the frame, children usually feel much more free to experiment with different roles and indulge in fantasy play, which is key to their growing understanding of other people's

The importance of 'Let's pretend'

'Fantasy play allows siblings to explore roles, rules and emotions. This is important and there are things parents can do to encourage it. One is to not always have the telly on. Another is to suggest. Children usually light up and relax if you say something like "Why don't you pretend the teddies are having a picnic?" Also, we can choose toys that lend themselves to children playing together cooperatively. I'm thinking of things such as Lego, playhouses, play figures and so on, whereas one super remote control car is unlikely to lead to that sort of play.'
– Professor Judy Dunn, developmental psychologist

Children who frequently share 'let's pretend' or fantasy play with a brother or sister tend to be especially good at understanding other people's emotions and intentions (see Encouraging concern and cooperation, page 61). Indeed, studies suggest that children with siblings develop an understanding of other people's 'inner states' at a younger age than 'single' children.[1]

So the importance of play spreads far beyond having a good time. Once children begin to understand how others feel, they can begin to understand the consequences of their actions on others. This helps them begin to develop a moral sense of right and wrong. Their more highly developed social feelings, thoughts and actions (see The importance of 'Let's pretend', this page).

'Some people want to separate children when they are small, but sharing a room gives them a chance to talk and play together in the mornings. As they get older they may want a room of their own, but in the early years they can get a huge amount from sharing a special space.'
– Carol Ann Hally, health visitor

'The noise levels from their room sometimes! But if they're happy noises, I try to let them get on with it.' – Hannah C.

understanding can also help them negotiate new experiences, such as starting nursery or school.

Whether fantasy play leads to increased understanding, or whether increased understanding leads to a greater tendency to fantasy play isn't known for sure. 'The influence is most probably in both directions, so it is a positive cycle of reinforcement, or what political pundits call a win-win situation,' says Professor Judy Dunn. 'The better a child is at understanding emotion and mental states, the better companion they'll be, and the better they are at sharing a sibling's imaginary world. They are then more likely to be invited into games – "You be Henry and I'll be Thomas the Tank engine", and so on – which is a context that will foster further understanding.'

Not all siblings will be playmates. Temperament, age and stage can all influence how much they play together. We can't force our children to play together when they simply don't want to. But we can recognise the importance of fantasy play and encourage it by providing space, screen-free time and freedom from adult interference to allow it to unfold.

'Some of the best fun times between my kids have been when other activities have been cancelled and they have time on their hands. That's when they build great camps together or make up intricate games. A little bit of boredom seems to spark a lot of creativity!'
– Angela C.

Time apart

Most children, like most adults, don't like to be taken for granted or feel forced into situations, however pleasurable. Children who play happily with siblings when they want to may not take kindly to a kid brother or sister when instructed to play together.

By encouraging joint play rather than insisting upon it, and by respecting each child's need for privacy, separate play and time apart, we up the chances of them being nicer to and happier with each other when they play together.

When friends come to play

'Having friends round can be tricky. Sometimes my youngest will spoil the bigger boys' games; sometimes my eldest son spoils his little brother's games with friends by playing the big hero and butting in. That's when I have to say, OK, you've got half an hour to all play together then you must leave your brother and his friends alone. If you want, I'll play with you instead.' – Jenny T.

Before a friend comes to play, it may help to set simple ground rules about siblings not interfering or trashing games.

We can remind the child whose friend is coming that their sibling may feel left out, and we can chat through different ways of dealing with any interference: divert the sibling with another activity? Let them join in for a short while? Call for our help?

We can talk to the other child about having their friends round, so they have a timely reminder that keeping out of siblings' games cuts both ways. It might also help to set up games or activities to keep them occupied. These needn't be anything grand. A child who feels left out needs attention, so anything they do with us may be fun enough if they get attention and appreciation along the way.

'A study I did in Cambridge followed children from their second year to adolescence.[2] When they were adolescent we talked to them about their sibling relationships and what had happened to make them better or worse, and on top of the list was friendships. When one had a close friend the other was jealous, or when one friend came round and played too much with the sibling, that led to trouble. Supporting children's friendships is important, but they can impact on the sibling relationship. As usual, it's a complicated story.' – Professor Judy Dunn, developmental psychologist

Play outside the family

'I think playing exclusively within the family is a recipe for potential disaster.' – Professor Hugh Foot, Professor of Psychology, Strathclyde University

Just as play with siblings is linked to the early development of some social skills (see The importance of 'Let's pretend', page 50, and Encouraging concern and cooperation, page 61), so play outside the family, between children and their friends, is crucial.

The reason is simple. Children can be as horrible as they like to their sibling and the sibling will still be there next morning. Friends, on the other hand, can withdraw from the relationship, so children need to develop different skills of compromise and negotiation to keep the friendship alive. Friends also tend to be closer in age than siblings, whose age differences may provide a ready-made hierarchy. Roles and relative positions tend to be less rigid among friends, providing further opportunities to explore, experiment and develop ways of getting along.

Even the closest of siblings need opportunities to develop separate friendships and experiences if they are to develop a sense of who they are as individuals. Without this, they can become too dependent on each other for understanding and support, which can limit individual development and lead to increasing frustrations and resentment as they grow (see Twins and more, page 230).

'Children in the privacy and intimacy of their own home with their brothers and sisters can show their emotions up front and can play pretty wildly. With friends, children need to be more considerate, to be more controlled and restrained, to temper their responses and put the brakes on a bit. Playing in other environments and with other children allows children to expand their repertoire of play activities and social skills. This can have a positive impact on their relationship with siblings and others.'
– Professor Hugh Foot, Professor of Psychology,
Strathclyde University

Understanding rough and tumble

'My mum always says her boys never fought. We did. We just didn't do it in front of her. We'd go out to play, then thump each other! But many kids can't do that now. I know I tell my boys off for playfighting because they're doing it under my feet. But where do they go? Or do I put a stop to it altogether?' – Martin W.

Games for life

Learning how to win and lose well isn't easy, but is an important lesson for life. Most children recognise the desire to win and can tolerate outbursts of rage or despair from a little brother or sister who's just lost Snakes and Ladders, yet they may become irritated or lose interest if the child doesn't develop some perspective with time. The simplest way to speed up the process is to play family games.

'Board games are a good way to learn that we all win and we all lose sometimes, and it helps children to learn that early,' says Dr Elizabeth Bryan, paediatrician and founder of the Multiple Births Foundation. 'One child I know is the older brother of twins, with a five-year gap between himself and his sisters. He'd had no previous experience of losing, was such a bad loser, and any competition was really difficult for him at any level, either with his own contemporaries or with the younger ones. In other ways he was a delightful child, but to lose a game was just agony. Playing games together helps educate children for life.'

Robert Fisher, Professor of Education at Brunel University and director of the Centre for Research in Teaching Thinking, agrees: 'Board games provide opportunities for practicing cooperative behaviour, for working things out

'Rough and tumble play is very important. It is teaching the child not only what are acceptable forms of physical contact but also what hurts, what is potentially dangerous and so helps them control the excesses of their physical contact later on. It helps children learn where to draw the line. Obviously, the early lessons may be difficult ones because you may overstep the mark and hurt, and you may be chastised, but through that you learn what is excessive, you learn to play in a more restrained way.' – Professor Hugh Foot, Professor of Psychology, Strathclyde University

Our society tends to frown on rough and tumble play, mistaking it for aggression. With fewer opportunities for unsupervised physical play outside the home, and understandable parental concerns about safety of people and possessions, it may be tempting to ban it inside the home, too.

Yet boisterous play can help children understand the limits of their

for themselves, and for solving problems together. They also help them cope with losing within a supportive environment. Children can be strengthened by that experience at home. It can help them develop the resilience they need to cope with failure in other, more competitive environments.

'No child, no adult, likes to lose all the time; some children, like some adults, don't like to lose any of the time. It's then a question of combining soft with tough parental love. We can let them know we understand that losing is painful and that it happens to us all sometimes and we have to learn to cope. Children have to experience frustrations and failure to know how to deal with them, and sharing failure with them will help them in their sibling and other relationships. The way we as adults respond in the face of our own frustration and failure will help them understand how they can struggle and overcome their problems.'

We can encourage big brothers and sisters to take pride in their superior abilities by showing younger siblings how to play, and by helping them when they get stuck: 'Looks like he's confused. What would you suggest he does next?' It may also help to have a quiet word with any siblings with a tendency to gloat over victory: 'Rachel's still learning to cope when she loses, so let's help by being kind if we win and letting her know she's done well.'

bodies and tempers, help them cope with competing, winning and losing and learn how to control their aggression, all of which will help them fight less, not more.

What you choose to do about physical play will depend partly on personal and family circumstances. It is much easier to tolerate rough and tumble if you can escape to another room. Much also depends on the age gap and relationship between your children. Any signs of bullying, real aggression or distress should be a signal to call an immediate halt (see He started it! page 83). Clear ground rules can also help: 'Rough and tumble is OK as long as no one is harmed, everyone is enjoying it and nothing gets damaged.'

'I don't think there's any need to worry if children don't rough and tumble, but there's no need to worry if they do because it is a natural way for boys

especially to interact and they normally have fun. You want to keep an eye open for signs of distress on anyone's part and maybe talk to the older one about not getting too rough if they don't realise their own strength. But this is one way children learn how far they can go and still keep it playful, that if you hit too hard or take too much advantage of someone they are not going to enjoy it and it will get nasty. Most children learn that pretty fast and it is a very important lesson.' – Professor Peter Smith, Professor of Psychology at Goldsmiths College, University of London, and Head of the Unit for School and Family Studies

Property principles

'Property disputes between children are very common, but peers seem to outgrow this issue while fights over possessions and ownership continue to occur between siblings. Property remains a contentious topic and sparks serious conflict between children in many families.' – Professor Hildy Ross, Professor of Developmental Psychology, University of Waterloo, Canada; research specialist in sibling conflicts

'It happened again today. I bought them each a ball, but they still wanted the one the other one had. It drives me to distraction.'
– Mike C.

'Sometimes when there are two things to choose from, and I badly want one and Catherine wants the other, it makes me want the one Catherine wants because it might be better. If she changes her mind and wants the one I originally wanted, I go back to wanting that one.' – from *Multiple Voices*, Twins and Multiple Births Association[3]

Trying to eradicate toy wars and force sharing at all times puts parents on a fast track to failure. Sharing demands a level of social confidence and understanding way beyond the capabilities of most very young children. Demanding it can backfire, making children clutch on to their possessions more tightly, fuelling frustration, anger and more sibling arguments. For a more cooperative relationship between our children, we need a more constructive and patient approach, recognising the reach of their abilities, encouraging respect of their own and other people's belongings, and equipping them with skills to negotiate and compromise.

It's mine, all mine!

'Honestly, he throws himself on top of the toy box, arms and legs spread-eagled, and tries to stop any of the others getting a single thing. He can't play with the toys because he's so busy protecting them.'
– Jenny M.

Sharing doesn't come naturally to most kids. The trouble often starts as the youngest child becomes mobile and starts to explore their world – which includes their older brother or sister's toys (see Little brother, big mess, page 46). Squabbles may also break out when the youngest is around eighteen months and can actively compete for objects as well as parental attention, clutching toys and declaring them 'Mine!'

According to developmental psychologist Professor Judy Dunn, 'Obsession with possessions starts to wane when children reach their fourth year.'[4] This may mean a reduction in the more out-rageous displays of claim-staking and ownership, yet sibling disputes over belongings can remain an issue for life. It's up to us to reduce the risks.

Turn-taking

Turn-taking can be a more acceptable concept to competitive siblings. Sharing may imply giving something up. Turn-taking, on the other hand, suggests ensuring that they get their way as often as everyone else. This may only be a matter of spin but, for battling brothers and sisters, saving face and not appearing to have 'lost' can be as important as claiming the toy. We need to show younger children how turn-taking is done, through games and example – 'You have a go first, then it will be my turn, then you can have a go again'; 'Let's take turns, then everyone has a chance' (see Rory and Michael's new start, page 47). Eventually, they'll pick up the basics and be able to negotiate it themselves. Once turn-taking becomes familiar, it can be used to negotiate issues of choice as well as ownership.

> *'Turn-taking is often a more realistic aim than sharing, and children do seem to accept it more readily.'* – Dr Elizabeth Bryan, paediatrician and founder of the Multiple Births Foundation

- **One divides, one chooses**. A strategy for dividing food, treats, building bricks . . . One child divides, and the other chooses which of the halves to have. Simple but often effective.

- **Removing the object**. If children continue to quarrel over a toy, it may help to remove it for a while. We can then explain why we've taken it, offer alternative activities, and tell them they can have it back once they can agree how to share or take turns.

Treasured possessions

> *'Children have very special possessions they don't want to share, and it seems fair to respect that, just as we would not want to share our most treasured belongings. It's all to do with being recognised as an individual, and being treated fairly.'*
> – Pat Elliot, psychotherapist specialising in bereavement and parenting

Most adults have treasured possessions that they would not share with others, be it jewellery, their car, their children's first lock of hair. Children have treasured objects, too, and expecting them to share these seems unfair and unrealistic. Far better to accord them special status and to explain this to siblings and friends: 'That bear is her most precious thing and no one can play with it without her permission'; 'That blanket is his most treasured toy, like your fireman's hat is to you. Let's put it back where it belongs.'

Keeping these special belongings out of sight or out of reach of others is often the easiest way of avoiding disputes when children are too young to understand family rules.

One toy, two kids – what next?

Encouraging children to see the benefits of compromise and consider siblings' feelings is key to their ability to share, new research suggests.[5]

'We have studied how young siblings resolve conflict of interests. We asked siblings, aged between four and eight, to divide a small set of toys between the two of them. The ones they chose, they took home,' explains Dr Hildy Ross, Developmental Psychologist and Professor of Psychology at the University of Waterloo, Canada, and director of a research programme on young children's conflicts. 'When they liked different toys, the children generally took turns to choose which they wanted. Unsurprisingly, the arguments began when they each wanted the same ones.'

About ten per cent of the children in the test couldn't reach a resolution at all and didn't divide the toys. 'Some just gave up. These kids were hot in contention almost over a piece of paper then said, "Okay. I give up! You have it!" Professor Ross explains. 'Shortly thereafter that same toy became an issue of contention again. But other children got creative, finding a way to share a toy they both wanted, dividing it somehow or even trading it off against something valuable they had at home.

'One thing that divides these two groups, the children who can't solve this problem and the ones who do, is their willingness to accept a compromise. They have regard for one another. The children who solve it care about what they want but also care for their sibling. These solutions are a result of this dual concern. It takes them time and energy and some contention to work out a solution that's going to satisfy them both, but they can do it, and often do it beautifully, creatively.'

Two of everything?

'A friend of mine buys two of everything to avoid the fighting over toys but I think that's nonsense. The fighting's all part of learning to live together.'
– Karen C.

Toys provide children with their first experiences of negotiation. By supplying two of everything, we may deny them the chance to learn. It won't prevent toy wars, in any case, as younger children often want whatever their sibling has in their hand at the time.

Recognising ownership

Children care very much who owns which toy and parents forget this at their peril. Asking older children to always hand over their toys to younger ones can cause them to seethe with injustice, as will telling children to always give way to guests who've come to play. In disputes over possessions, when parents don't interfere, the owner of the toy in question usually wins, regardless of birth order, gender or usual family status.[6]

Underestimating the significance of ownership can make sibling conflict worse, or at least last longer. Recognising it as a factor to be acknowledged and considered by all appears to be much more effective (see One careful owner, page 61): 'I know it's your car, and it's for you to decide, but Emma's really sad. If you'd like to play with her toys sometimes, maybe you should let her have a play with yours?'

If we really want our children to share particular items, especially large ones, it may help to buy them as family gifts so joint ownership is emphasised from the outset.

- **Let them decide**. Children often show great generosity and ingenuity in sorting out disputes, if we express our confidence in their ability to do so: 'I know this is your train, but Daniel's really upset. Can you think of anything else he might like to play to cheer him up?' (See Searching for solutions, page 67, and One toy, two kids – what next? page 59.)

Recognising success

We can help children feel good about sharing and turn-taking by praising them whenever it occurs (see Acknowledge the good times, page 70): 'You were sharing really well with your sister. Thanks. You sorted it out without fighting.'

If opportunities for praise don't arise naturally, we need to create them, perhaps encouraging children to hand round biscuits or

One careful owner

'Children are often urged to share what they own with their peers, but then to hand back a toy to a friend because it belongs to that child,' says Professor Hildy Ross, a research specialist in sibling conflicts. 'It's a mixed message, that the owner should control the use of the property, and that they shouldn't. Sharing without respect of ownership is also something we expect of our children but not of other adults.

'Children, on the other hand, tend to respect ownership. It's not that they don't have disputes over property but that more times than not, the child who is the owner tends to prevail and win, particularly when parents don't intervene. A younger child can even defend property he owns against a more powerful older sibling. Ownership is a principle children understand and use to resolve their differences.

'If we respect ownership, children may feel the situation is properly understood and can then decide whether they want to share what is theirs. Parental intervention might be much more effective if it included respect for ownership and reciprocity, by saying, "That toy is yours and the choice is yours whether or not to share with him, but that choice will have implications for you down the line when you want to play with his toys." Obviously pick your words to suit the child, but it's an idea kids grasp.'

other treats to siblings, and praising when they succeed. Expressing our confidence in a positive outcome also makes one more likely: 'Lucy, will you let Holly know when you're ready to share?'; 'Andrew will share when he's ready. He understands it's your turn next'; 'I know you two can work this out fairly. Let's see you do it.'

Encouraging concern and cooperation

Siblings often develop an understanding of their brothers' or sisters' feelings from a strikingly early age. This ability to empathise – to

The brother and sister bond

'There is often a friendly bond between even very young children and their brother or sister. This can be seen in concern at their siblings' distress and their attempts to comfort them. It has been seen in children as young as fourteen months. This is strikingly sophisticated behaviour at such a young age.' – Professor Judy Dunn, developmental psychologist

'Having siblings helps you develop an understanding of others' thoughts and feelings. Children with older siblings acquire these abilities something like six months to a year earlier than those who don't have older siblings. It's quite a big factor at that age and has created much interest in why that's so; maybe it's the pretend play between siblings; maybe it's the conflict between them, which they have to think through and resolve. Whatever the cause, there's much evidence to show that it's happening.' – Professor Peter Smith, Professor of Psychology, researching children's social development

The significance of a child's 'attachment' or bond to a parent or other 'primary' carer is well known. The effects of a child's attachment to a brother or sister have tended to be overlooked or underestimated, yet the findings of recent research are impressive.

In one study, babies as young as eight months seemed devoted to their older siblings; by fourteen months many missed an absent older sibling and would attempt to comfort them in distress.[7] They seemed to view their sibling as a source of security and comfort, and would show their concern by stroking them and fetching and offering comfort objects.

It is still not clear what the

imagine how someone else may be feeling – is the foundation stone of children's moral sense, helping them grasp the consequences of their actions on others.

long-term consequences of this early understanding of others' feelings may be once children move through adolescence and beyond. But we might as well try to make the most of it. 'If we can foster good relations between siblings, it may be an extremely effective way of promoting moral development and pro-social, positive behaviour. There may well be beneficial effects for the rest of those children's lives,' explains Dr Gavin Nobes, senior lecturer in Developmental and Forensic Psychology at the School of Psychology, University of East London.

'Why do siblings develop such understanding of each other's feelings? Siblings know each other really well. They spend a great deal of time with each other, particularly for the first five years. Their closeness in age and similarities in interests, abilities and inabilities mean there is much greater equality between siblings than could possibly be the case between parents and children. It's a very simple point but absolutely fundamental – that because of this familiarity, and the fact that siblings matter so much to each other, they probably understand each other better than they understand anyone else.

'They can respond to each other's distress, they can be empathic and imagine what it is like for the other, they can anticipate each other's feelings, they have a special insight into this special person.

'All in all, it's likely that siblings first learn about morality through interaction with each other. You learn what is right and wrong, learn why it is wrong to hit somebody, to steal from somebody, to lie to somebody, by observing the effect of your behaviour on other people, so siblings offer tremendous opportunities to learn.

'Take four year olds; there is often more aggression shown at this age than at any other. But they soon notice that although it is nice to win a battle, to get your own way and have power over somebody else, there are also other effects. The sibling may cry or be in pain, and because even young children are empathic beings, the perpetrator feels bad when they make somebody else feel bad. That's an important lesson in life.'

This understanding develops naturally, largely through play (see The importance of 'Let's pretend', page 50), but we can enhance and encourage it in ways that will benefit each child, their sibling relationships and the family as a whole (see The brother and sister bond, page 62).

Talking about feelings

'Parents can educate children about emotions, by acknowledging feelings and encouraging them, for instance, to think about what another child may be feeling, in appreciating one child's efforts to soothe another. The world of the imagination is a world of developing empathy, too, so story telling, watching the TV together, watching videos, can all provide opportunities for relaxed talk about feelings and consequences of actions.'
– Pat Elliot, psychotherapist specialising in
bereavement and parenting

Helping our children understand feelings is fundamental to their ability to get on with brothers, sisters and others (see Exploring emotions, page 125).

Our own emotional expressiveness and how we discuss feelings in the family will help shape their understanding of emotions and their ability to 'read' other people's feelings and thoughts.[8] Studies show that when families talk about emotions, children as young as two, not yet able to use language confidently, tend to display greater social understanding.[9]

The simplest way to encourage this is by showing our respect for each child's feelings and talking in an everyday, relaxed way about the feelings of other family members – why they may be feeling and acting as they do, what may help – 'You seem upset. Are you okay?'; 'George seems angry today. I wonder what could be the matter?'; 'He really enjoyed that game with you'; 'Brothers and sisters sometimes get angry with each other when they're upset about other things.'

We can also create opportunities for our children to consider and cooperate with each other (see Made by me for you, page 65, and Chocolate cake is good for kids, page 69) and boost their understanding and enjoyment of their own positive behaviour through practise: 'When you stroked his arm, it made him feel a bit better. Thanks'; 'You let him join in for a while. That's kind'; 'I think you both enjoyed making that.' (See Acknowledge the good times, page 70.)

Made by me for you

'I think it helps to think ahead, and to ask ourselves "What can I do to boost this relationship?"' says Adrienne Katz, executive director of the youth charity, Young Voice.

'So many things can help. I love making little books for children, for example, and an older child can make the book with you, pasting in the pictures. They can then present the book to the toddler or baby as something beautiful they've made. This is such an easy thing for a parent and child to do together. It makes the baby happy and makes the older child feel a hero.

'Children also enjoy recording stories with sound effects, on to tape, for the younger child. They can make footstep noises by running in and out the room, thunder effects with a biscuit tin lid.

'I've known eight-year-olds stay absorbed for whole rainy afternoons with a tape recorder and a vivid imagination. Their younger siblings absolutely adore it, because it is made just for them.'

Mirror, mirror

'It is important to keep our expectations of our children age-appropriate and realistic, but we can model how we'd like them to grow to behave.'
– Kitty Hagenbach, transpersonal and child psychotherapist

'The development of altruism and considerate behaviour in children takes place more by example than by instruction. I think if parents show consideration to each other, hold doors for people, say thank you, these little acts of consideration for other people's needs are the kinds of messages children soak up and start applying themselves.'
– Professor Hugh Foot, Professor of Psychology,
Strathclyde University

How we treat other people – including each of our children – will influence how they behave with each other. A huge body of research now shows the link between positive parent-child relationships and more positive behaviour between brothers and sisters. Similarly,

🚶🚶🚶 *Kids don't need perfection* 🚶🚶🚶

'Working with adults, it's clear that some people have grown up to believe in the fairy tale that all is sweet, people are good and everyone lives happily ever after. When they find that life can be quite difficult they are often taken aback and find it hard to cope. A little bit of reality in family life, and named as such, is often quite supportive.'
– Kitty Hagenbach, child psychotherapist

Sometimes we get it wrong. We may fly off the handle, we may act too late or too soon, we may think of a much better way of dealing with our children two days after a crisis has passed. That's life. We're human, and children need to learn how to live with real human beings, with all their mistakes, limits and needs.

This has nothing to do with being harsh or punitive with our children, or accepting habits in ourselves that we know to be counter-productive. It has everything to do with being more understanding of our needs and our limits, and not beating ourselves up when we occasionally slip from our own high standards.

There will be bad days, there will be mistakes, our children will wind us up and wind up each other, and if this happens in the context of generally loving, warm relationships, they will be fine. In fact, recognising that people and life are sometimes imperfect will better equip our children to cope with life's knocks and with relationships inside and outside the family.

'If the overall relationship is secure and loving, parents who lose their temper or step beyond their own boundaries of behaviour for a moment can rescue or repair the situation very easily. In a sense, it's a good thing to happen occasionally because through it the child can learn that reparation is always possible.' – John Bristow, chartered psychologist and psychotherapist

over-controlling or harsh relationships between parents and children are often associated with aggressive and self-protective behaviour between siblings.[10] So what they see is often what we get (See He started it!, page 83 and Kids don't need perfection, this page.)

Think positive

Much of our children's time is spent being told what not to do. Negative comments are sometimes necessary: 'No hitting in this house!' and 'No!' may be the quickest way of getting an essential message across. Yet, telling children what they are capable of achieving – rather than what they're doing wrong – is generally far more effective in communicating our expectations of behaviour and encouraging care and consideration.

Some children take negative commands as a challenge. 'Don't you dare throw that at him!' may introduce a previously unthought-of but ultimately irresistible option. If, instead, we tell our children how they could approach a situation positively – and show our appreciation when they do – they're more likely to comply, feel good and repeat the behaviour in future.

> Compare:
> 'Not like that, she'll drop it.'
> With:
> 'Put both her hands around the bat, then she'll learn to hold it properly. Well done.'
>
> and:
> 'Don't run off with her spade.'
> With:
> 'Put the spade back where she can reach it. Thanks.'

Reminding children of the power they have to be considerate is often the only prompt they need: 'You know how to be thoughtful and kind. Use those talents and we'll all have a better day'; 'You know how to get what you need without hitting. Let's see you do it.'

Searching for solutions

Encouraging siblings to tackle mutual difficulties and attempt joint endeavours can also pay huge dividends:

1. **It can help strengthen bonds** between them and boost their confidence in the potential of their relationship.

2. **They are more likely to put their conclusions into practice**
   because they have thought the matter through and understood
   it more fully than if solutions were imposed by their parents.
3. **It is habit forming**. Once our children realise they can work
   through situations without our direct intervention and
   guidance, they are in a far stronger position to negotiate the
   ups and downs of their relationships and to avert major sibling
   battles.

It's best not to wait until big problems arise, but to practice on the
small stuff – encouraging them to make choices, use their initiative,
enjoy cooperative activities (see Chocolate cake is good for kids,
page 69) and practice negotiation and compromise in simple situations.

To do this, our children need:

1. **Encouragement**. Let children know we think they are capable of
   working out issues between them: 'You both want the scooter,
   and we've only got one. How could you work this out so you're
   both happy?'
2. **Time**. Children may need time to brainstorm and come up with
   solutions. We should allow this, where possible, perhaps moving
   to another room and asking them to tell us when they've some
   answers.
3. **Suggestions**. If time's running short or our children seem
   genuinely stuck, we could suggest possible options and ask them
   to pick which they prefer.

If a situation becomes heated, or a problem is recurrent or particularly disruptive, our children may need our more active help to sort
matters out (see He started it! page 83). This is fine, as long as they
still have other opportunities to work through situations calmly,
constructively and for themselves.

We don't always need to know what our children decide, or
how. Sometimes they won't find a solution or complete their joint
venture. But the very act of trying may boost mutual understanding and communication (see Choices and responsibilities,
page 70).

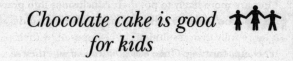

Chocolate cake is good for kids

'Parents can think up recipes for cooperative activities ahead of time, with a role for each child according to skill. You know, things that would fall apart if each one doesn't do their job, with each job appropriate to their abilities, so they all feel important,' says Adrienne Katz, executive director of the youth charity, Young Voice. 'These are great for encouraging children to work together and for proving to them what they can do when they cooperate and communicate.

'The best success in our family was the chocolate cake, with the little one doing the stirring. Each child felt their role was vital and that without them the whole thing would have failed. The most basic job could be the grease monkey who butters the baking sheet, smearing stuff all over it, but without which the cake wouldn't work. Rather than having them fight over tasks, we can separate out the tasks and praise them because without their cooperation

it couldn't have happened.'

To be effective, the joint task has to be meaningful and important to all children involved, explains Hugh Foot, Professor of Psychology at Strathclyde University. 'There is a famous social psychology experiment in which people have to cooperate and contribute in order to achieve a set goal. Cooperation was most evident when it involved a meaningful task, and when achieving the goal was important to them all.

'If kids in a family are making a birthday cake together for their dad, for example, the goal is not only making the cake but winning their father's approval. I think that's very important. It's not just them recognising that they've achieved something, it is the external recognition from an authority they both love and respect that's important too. If they didn't like their father, the idea of them making a cake together for him would lose its appeal.'

🏃🏃🏃 *Choices and responsibilities* 🏃🏃🏃

'It is important for children's motivation and self-esteem that they are allowed choices, and to know that what they feel and think are valid. This is taken away from them in the school environment because it is not viable for thirty children to make choices all the time. We can promote motivation outside school by giving them choices in what they do.' – Corinne Abisgold, educational psychologist

'If we are interested in children taking control of their lives in a responsible way, the earlier they begin the better,' says Professor Robert Fisher of Brunel University. 'When I was in Africa I saw children as young as six and seven in charge of a whole flock of animals for the day and that would represent the entire wealth of the family. That was right for them in that cultural context. Parents expected their children to be responsible and to solve problems, and children tend to become what their parents expect of them.

'We need to encourage our children to solve problems and make their own choices because ultimately we won't be there to do it for them. We can begin by letting them choose the clothes they want to wear, what they want to take to the park, how they want to approach a situation with their brother or sister. They will make better choices the more experience they have of using their judgement.

'Some choices have to be imposed, and children need to know the limiting factors on choice, such as safety and cost. But to value them as individuals we need to encourage choices within those limits and allow them to make choices that are both different from their siblings and different from the choices we would make.

Acknowledge the good times

'It is so important to keep a weather eye out for opportunities to appropriately praise, and to praise not just success or achievement, but helpfulness, friendliness, considerate and caring behaviour.'
– Dr Elizabeth Bryan, paediatrician and founder of
the Multiple Births Foundation

'When one of my sons decided to paint his entire room blue, it was not something I would have wished, hoped or aesthetically approved of! But if I wanted him to continue to make aesthetic choices and have responsibility for the environment he lived in, it was an important choice for him. We want our children to express their preferences with each other and outside the family, so we need to be sensitive to their need for self-expression.'

Problem-solving between siblings also takes practice and can result in creative solutions. 'Each child may come at a problem from a slightly different perspective,' explains Hugh Foot, Professor of Psychology at Strathclyde University. 'When they have to work on it together they have to share each others' perspectives on the problem to understand why the other person disagrees with them. It is what we call cognitive conflict, knowing where you're coming from and where the other person is coming from. That broader perspective on a problem can increase the chances of them finding an answer that satisfies them both.

'We all know what it's like. When you try to think through a problem yourself you can spend hours. You can get blocked, then you mention it to someone else, get talking and suddenly, "Eureka!" You've suddenly got a new perspective.

'I've just had a research team meeting and I'm sure none of us would have got as far if we'd been working alone, nor would we have seen some of the traps and problems inherent in our individual suggestions. The whole notion of research teams is brainstorming, with everybody pitching in ideas. Some are good, some are crazy, but it's a very important process because that's how to get fresh ideas. Sharing thinking is just as important in families.'

'Research indicates that the best teachers use around three times more statements of praise than criticism, and there is good reason why that may be so. We all tend to be better motivated by praise and reward than threat and blame. The recognition that comes through praise when it is genuine is at the heart of all successful relationships.'
– Professor Robert Fisher, Brunel University; director of the Centre for Research in Teaching Thinking

We all know how good it makes us feel when somebody tells us what they like about us or the things we do. Parental praise is a child's greatest boost and motivator, and we can use it to build our children's individual self-esteem and to encourage considerate behaviour between them.

Descriptive praise

'Descriptive praise is saying what we actually see, what the child has done or is doing and why we like it. "You've brought me the nappy, that's really helpful." "You've put the beaker back so it doesn't spill, well done." "You've given her a big hug. That's so thoughtful". It is much more effective than labelling the behaviour or the child as simply "good" or "bad".'
– Sarah Darton, health visitor

'Saying "because" and giving reasons is valuable not only in terms of developing children's emotional responses but also valuable to their cognitive development. We want them to see that there are reasons for things.'
– Professor Robert Fisher, Brunel University

Imagine you've painted a picture. One friend comments, 'That's nice'. Another says, 'I love how you've shaded the clouds. And the leaves on that tree look as if they're moving.' Who do you think has really noticed what you've achieved? Who would inspire you most to continue?

Non-specific praise, of the 'good boy', 'clever girl', 'lovely, dear' type, soon loses its currency. These phrases are used so frequently, and often so absent-mindedly, that they can suggest we've not been taking proper notice. They give our children little information about what behaviour we like or why we like it.

Descriptive praise, on the other hand, describes exactly what's been happening and why it is useful or appreciated. It shows we've been sufficiently interested and concerned to really take notice, and lets children know precisely why we would like to see such behaviour repeated.

Compare:

Descriptive praise: 'You remembered to do that without me even having to ask. That's so helpful. Thanks.'

Non-descriptive praise: 'Good boy.'

Descriptive praise: 'You kissed Laura and cheered her up. That's really kind.'

Non-descriptive praise: 'Good girl.'

'Rory was feeling poorly and Michael disappeared and came back with his rabbit, Rory's special comfort toy. I wanted them both to know how wonderful I thought that was, so I said: 'Michael has brought Rory's rabbit. That is so kind." I think it's really important to acknowledge the spontaneous kindness they show one another.' – Kate B.

Keep it genuine

'If praise is not meant and valid it undervalues any other good times.'
– Dr Elizabeth Bryan, paediatrician

Most children come with two sets of radar. One for the biscuit tin, the other for parental insincerity. They can spot both a mile off.

Simply turning around our language to make it more positive is not enough. We have to start seeing our children as they are – fundamentally ready to care and keen to please us, even though they sometimes need our guidance as to the best ways to do it. If we view one or more of our children as 'trouble', that's the message they will pick up no matter how much verbal praise we dispense. Faking it won't work; adjusting how we see and what we see in our children is much more effective (see Seeing my lovable child, page 155).

Look closely, and almost all children try to show interest in and kindness to their siblings sometimes. The efforts may be few and they might not be as we'd wish, but they'll be there.

'Even in patterns of repeated and negative behaviour, there'll be exceptions and moments when something new happens. That's the time to acknowledge and amplify those things. Children have the capacity to alter their views and alter their behaviours with siblings if you can get to the place where you explore other possibilities.' – Jim Wilson, systemic psychotherapist
and director of the Centre for Child Focused Practice at the
Institute of Family Therapy, London.

Keep it in proportion

'Constant or overblown praise puts a terrible pressure on the child. If every drawing has to be a masterpiece, they may never draw at all.'
– Kitty Hagenbach, child psychotherapist

'When parents are trying to be supportive of a child with problems, some do go a bit overboard on the praise. That child then gets a distorted view of how the rest of the world will see them. They can expect a very high level of adult attention and praise outside the home which they're not going to get. So it's a matter of getting the balance right – enabling the child to feel positive about themselves, and keeping it real and in proportion.'
– Corinne Abisgold, educational psychologist

If praise is over-the-top, it backfires. If a child does something kind or caring for a brother or sister, we can point out what it was and why it pleased us, but keep our responses proportionate to the deed. If we grossly exaggerate its merits, the child will at best think we've lost the plot and, at worst, doubt our sincerity. Once this happens, praise loses its currency and the child may begin to mistrust our responses and honest opinions.

If in doubt, look at the deed from your child's point of view. Is it something that would make them burst with pride or something they would accept as just about okay?

'Descriptive praise is an important skill, but like every other approach, it has to be used responsively. I used it a lot and I think it worked with one son but the next son hated it. He thinks it's like treacle. I think this is a terribly important point. To treat each child as a unique individual we have to be aware that what worked for one may not work for another.'
– Barbara Dale, counsellor

Praising one without crushing the other

'Once you've got more than one child it gets more difficult. I want to notice things my children are doing well and what I like and appreciate about them, and inevitably the one who's not being praised at that moment is

often aware of what's being said. That can sometimes feel like favouritism
or preferential treatment. It can be difficult to balance.'
– Sarah Darton, health visitor

'If they praise one, parents may try and restore the balance by praising the
other child as well. This undervalues a parent's pleasure and the child's
achievement. Each child is entitled to his moment of glory without having
to share it.' – Audrey Sandbank, Family Psychotherapist UKCP,
Hon. Con. Family Therapist for the Twins and
Multiple Births Association (TAMBA)

Once we have more than one child, praise requires extra sensitivity if
children are not to take our approval of one to be an implicit criticism
of the other. This is an especially hard balance with children of similar
ages or aptitudes, who compare achievements and parental responses
even more than most (see Twins and more, page 230), or with
children of very different needs and abilities, who may resent a
sibling's 'special' treatment (see Illness, disability and special needs,
page 217).

Praising all when we praise one doesn't seem to help. Praising each
child when they deserve it – and praising endeavour as much as
achievement, kindness as much as 'success' – seems a much more
constructive approach (see Letting each child shine, page 175). If
each child has enough personal praise, they'll be much better able to
cope when a sibling receives attention.

Beware material rewards

'There's a famous experiment in which children were given sweets as a
reward for doing a painting. It was found that by giving the children an
instant material reward the intrinsic motivation dwindled, they no longer
saw doing a painting as worthwhile or enjoyable in itself.'
– Corinne Abisgold, educational psychologist

Rewards are no substitute for genuine recognition and praise. Our
aim is for our children to get along and have fun together because
they want to, not because it may get them a gold star or an ice cream
from the corner shop.

Many teachers and many parents use reward systems and sticker charts. They are tangible evidence of adult appreciation – but it is the appreciation that counts. In a class situation, when a hard-pressed teacher has little time to communicate with each child individually, tokens and stars have a place. At home, they can work in the short term but tend to lose their potency over time and divert attention away from main aim – building better relations between our children through empathy and understanding, not Smarties.

If we want to use material or token rewards, it helps to keep them small, symbolic and used only to reinforce, not replace, clear statements of praise and recognition. Significant material rewards – a toy, perhaps, or an outing – are bribery. And bribery is a high-risk strategy because children tend to up the stakes and demand even better next time. In the real world, a bit of bribery may get us through the day or past the supermarket checkout. As an occasional, emergency measure, they have their place. But for our sake and theirs, it's best to keep them for emergency use only.

Establish family rules

'The original meaning of discipline comes from "disciple" and means learning; in this context the learning of self control.' – John Bristow, chartered psychologist and psychotherapist

To behave considerately towards brothers and sisters, children don't just need our warmth, example, encouragement and under-standing. They also need clear guidance on how to behave. This involves a set of clear, simple family rules. These are investments. Once our children are clear about the family ground rules they will find it easier to negotiate and avoid clashes. Family rules also make it easier for us to guide our children effectively and clearly before tempers flare: 'You know the family rule on this. Now I want to see you stick to it.'

Let's be realistic. All children need to push against the limits to learn how far they can go – with us and with their brothers and sisters. And some will push hard. It's our job to draw the line, and they won't

In the balance

Our approach to discipline is crucial to our children's relationships. Children who grow up in households where discipline is too lax tend to have problems getting along with siblings and other children.[11] If they have the sense that anything goes, anything will.

At the other extreme, harsh and hostile behaviour towards brothers and sisters is often seen in children who grow up in households where punishment regularly takes the place of discipline, and where harsh and hostile parental behaviour requires them to give way to greater force not greater wisdom.

In the real world, parental force is sometimes necessary. We may have to forcibly separate battling siblings, shout an ear-splitting 'NO!' to stop dangerous or threatening actions, or use our superior size and volume to control a rampaging brother or sister (see He Started It! page 83). But we should aim to use force very sparingly, only when absolutely necessary and only to keep our children safe. Warm, firm and educative discipline, supported by praise and positive attention, is much more effective in the long term than harsh, erratic or punitive action.

always like it. But if we remain clear, firm, loving and warm, each child will get the guidance and support they need.

The Guidelines

How well our children respond to family rules depends partly on how we establish them.

1. **Set:** Every family will have their own rules about expected behaviour between siblings. It helps if these are kept simple, clear and to a minimum. Talking in terms of 'family rules' will help children appreciate that these limits apply to all family members: 'No hitting in this family'; 'Family rule – no name calling' is far more helpful than vague pleas to our children to 'be nice' to each other or 'pack it in'. Children feel secure in a solid family value

system that protects them against the excesses of their sibling's behaviour as much as it guides them in how they are to behave.

2. **Explain:** Children don't just need to know what's expected of them, but why. Once they understand this, they can accept and adopt family rules as their own. This is the root of self-discipline.

    Of course, young children may not immediately grasp what is being explained, which is why rules will need to be clearly stated, repeated and applied. But over time, they will begin to understand why these rules matter. This is crucial. Rules merely imposed on children without such understanding are often broken or ignored as soon as we're out of the room.

3. **Remind:** Children may ignore a rule because they've forgotten it, they don't like it or they don't understand it. Most children will need reminding of rules again and again until the message finally sinks in: 'Remember, no hitting'; 'What's the family rule about that? Can you remember?'; 'It is not okay to hit your brother'; 'We don't hit, so how could you show that you're angry without hurting or frightening your sister?'

4. **Respond:** Transgressions should not be ignored, but we should aim to keep our responses proportionate, age-appropriate and constructive (see He started it! page 83). Harsh responses, including smacking and other physical punishments, can encourage children to obey out of fear rather than because they understand and agree with our family guidelines on behaviour. This increases the risk of them behaving badly if they think they can get away with it.

Explaining expectations

A five-year-old may seethe with indignation because he has to be in bed an hour before his older brother, or crushed if he's told off for flicking yoghurt while his baby sister, merrily spooning it on to the floor, 'gets away' with a milder admonishment. A young adolescent may fume because an older sibling is allowed to stay out or stay up later. Balancing the different needs of different ages while maintaining family rules of behaviour can be tough.

Some family rules work best when they describe the general principle rather than its specific application, so they have enough flexibility to apply to everyone, regardless of age. For example:

Family rule: 'We all have to have the sleep our body needs.'
Rather than:
Specific: 'Bedtime is 9.30.'

Family rule: 'If you know how to eat, eat properly.'
Rather than:
Specific: 'No messing with food.'

Encouraging older siblings to teach younger siblings by example can also reinforce family rules while increasing their understanding of the younger child's inability to abide by them just yet: 'I know she winds you up and even hits you sometimes, and that must be really annoying, but she's still young and has a great deal to learn. If we all show her better ways to behave, eventually she'll understand.'

Describing unkind or inconsiderate behaviour and why it bothers us is much more constructive and informative than labelling the child or children breaking family rules as 'naughty' or 'bad' (see The danger of labels, page 167).

Discussing the consequences of actions on people's feelings may also help children begin to understand how the same behaviour may be appropriate in some circumstances and not in others. A rowdy game of chase may be great fun in the garden when all participants are happy, but no fun at all if one child is tired, poorly or feeling vulnerable; splashing water on a little sister's tummy may make her laugh, but she may cry if she's splashed on the face; hiding your big brother's shoes may be great fun on a lazy Sunday morning, but a declaration of war when he's late for school.

The concept of appropriate behaviour is sophisticated territory, and understanding it takes time, relationship-building and clear parental guidance, but it is an important investment in families of two or more children when so many needs, wants and preferences have to be considered.

Building positive relationships: key approaches

Let the fun begin	Play helps each child feel good about themselves and about their brothers and sisters. It encourages understanding of siblings' feelings, the bedrock of considerate, positive relationships. We can encourage shared fun, intervene only if needed, and create opportunities for free play to unfold.
Appreciate property principles	Tackling toy wars constructively encourages consideration and cooperation between brothers and sisters. Teaching our children to take turns, respect siblings' possessions and negotiate helps them avoid disputes and search for solutions.
Encourage concern and cooperation	Talking about feelings helps develop our children's understanding of others' feelings and views. We can also treat our children as we would like them to treat each other; communicate positive and clear expectations of behaviour; give them opportunities to practice and display cooperation, and build their skills to problem-solve and compromise.
Acknowledge the good times	Descriptive praise is a powerful tool in promoting positive relationships. We can use it to highlight moments

	when our children show kindness, interest or consideration towards each other.
Establish family rules	To behave considerately towards each other, our children need our clear guidance as well as our warmth, support and understanding. Family rules will let them know what behaviour we expect – and why.

Key message:

We can strengthen our children's relationships for life. We can start now.

4

He started it!

tackling sibling conflict

'When you love your children, it really hurts when they are at each other's throats. I think it often hurts us more than it hurts them.' – Helen L.

'Optimal sibling relationships probably include a mixture of harmony and conflict, so the notion that everybody should act entirely positively all the time with their siblings is firstly not realistic and secondly probably isn't sensible either. Life involves competing for resources and sometimes it isn't fair. Children have to learn to cope with that.' – Dr Michael Rutter, Professor of Developmental Psychopathology at the Institute of Psychiatry, Kings College, London, and consultant physician at the Maudsley hospital

'Whether or not our children get on with each other is a chancy business, frankly.' – Peter Wilson, director of Young Minds

This chapter focuses on ways to intervene helpfully in our children's fights and disputes. The strategies explained here will help them in the heat of the moment, but their significance goes far beyond short-term troubleshooting. The way they teach children to settle arguments will also equip them to avert and resolve future rows for themselves.

Of course we can't eradicate conflict. Almost all siblings fight and there are good, healthy, developmental reasons why they do. Yet we *can* minimise unnecessary arguments and encourage our children to sort out their disputes without threats, violence or too much door-slamming. These skills will help our children live together more happily and build caring relationships inside and outside the family, for life.

Why are they fighting?

Understanding *why* our children are fighting helps us tackle their disputes more effectively. To do this we need to understand the nature of conflict between brothers and sisters, and to look beyond the behaviour itself to see what may be fuelling it. Are there obvious triggers or patterns? Is it a sign of a troubled relationship?

Conflict isn't all bad

'Our bullying study showed clearly that those children who were excessively shielded couldn't always fend for themselves.[1] Fighting and arguing with your sibling is quite a good preparation for surviving in the playground. It's one way children learn negotiation and survival skills.' – Adrienne Katz, founder and executive director of Young Voice

'It upsets me when they fight but they seem to accept it as part of life, like the weather.' – David I.

Disputes with brothers and sisters help children learn how to negotiate, deal with disagreements and resentment, practice humour and compromise and assert themselves. These are important skills – and home is the best place to learn them.

Sibling clashes as well as sibling warmth combine to give our children varied experiences of dealing with others. This boosts not only their resilience but also their understanding of other people's needs and feelings – inside the family and beyond[2] (see Caring and sharing, page 43).

Clearly, high levels of conflict can lead to relationship and behaviour problems (see If conflict goes unchecked, page 97). But when it is part of a mix, including warm family relationships and constructive parental intervention, it helps our children learn about each other and about life. This is a good line to remember next time someone tuts at them squabbling in the supermarket.

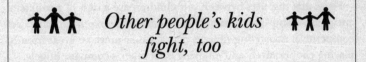

Other people's kids fight, too

Sibling discord is one of the most common and persistent child-related problems reported by parents,[3] yet because children tend to conduct their disputes in the privacy of their homes, it is easy to believe our own children fight much more than others.

If it's any comfort, reports from parents and professionals confirm that aggression and hostility, ridicule, sarcasm, name-calling and verbal abuse are all common behaviours between brothers and sisters. In one authoritative study, ninety-three per cent of seven year olds were found to fight with their siblings, and twenty-four per cent of these fought often.[4]

Close siblings still clash

'There is often real ambivalence between siblings. They can hate each other one day, love each other the next. They can be extraordinarily hostile towards each other and perhaps a few minutes later be very protective.'
– Dr Gavin Nobes, senior lecturer in developmental psychology

'Conflict is absolutely normal. Even physical aggression, which sometimes parents find very distressing, especially if they have been only children and haven't experienced it themselves, does not mean that children don't also enjoy each other's company, like each other a lot, miss each

other when they're not there. An unequivocal loathing between siblings is quite rare. They will usually get some pleasure out of being and doing things together.' – Professor Judy Dunn, developmental psychologist

Siblings who fight the least don't love each other the most. Brothers and sisters who argue and fight can still be close, loving and supportive. Indeed, their very closeness is why so many siblings wind each other up so effectively (see The big tease, page 87, and The brakes are off, page 88).

Fears that disputes between our children are a sign of a problematic relationship may prompt us to intervene inappropriately. Yet competitive, quarreling siblings may at other times be great friends, playing cooperatively and enjoying each other's company hugely.

Emotionally close siblings tend to spend more time trying to sort matters out between themselves (see One toy, two kids – what next? page 59). In one study, close siblings were found to fight most about property and power, while less close siblings argued most about betrayal.[5] But, significantly, they all argued.

The bigger picture

It is easy to get lost in the detail of which child did what to whom. We may get a much better view of what's happening and what may help if we stand back and look at the bigger picture. Are the children arguing repeatedly about the same issues? Could this be a sign of upset elsewhere in their lives? Is it our children's behaviour that needs most urgent attention, or our own?

Look for patterns

'When does a difficulty become a problem? There's a classic adage that goes something like "Difficulties are summed by the expression, 'Life is just one damned thing after another'. A problem is when it's just the same damned thing over and over again." It's a very important distinction. If behaviour is entrenched, repeated, if your kids feel it is something that won't go away, then it's a problem that needs tackling. Otherwise, it's a difficulty

The big tease

'My sister had a knack of doing and saying the most awful things. Once when my best friend came to call she wouldn't let me open the door. She just hollered through the letter box, "You'd better get away from here 'coz we're running live with nits and fleas!" I was mortified!'
– Cherie H.

'Because siblings know each other so well, they know exactly what is going to annoy their brother or sister. They are really good at teasing each other,' explains Dr Gavin Nobes, senior lecturer in developmental psychology. 'So closeness, familiarity and understanding is a double-edged sword. It is important for them to understand their sibling in order to cooperate and communicate well with this major figure in their life. It is also important in order to compete and conflict with them efficiently.

'It is like playing tennis. When you know the other player well, you can play doubles and cooperate efficiently as a team. You can play to each other's strengths and anticipate each other's moves. But when you play against them, you can compete well because you can exploit their weaknesses.

'Because of their familiarity and understanding, sibling children can cooperate and communicate with each other in more sophisticated ways than with anyone else. Because they know how to hurt each other, they can also tease, compete and fight more efficiently than they could possibly do with any one else, any one else in the whole world.'

that will pass or that they'll in all likelihood negotiate without our help.'
– Jim Wilson, systemic psychotherapist and director of the Centre for Child-Focused Practice, Institute of Family Therapy

Jotting down the time of day and what children are doing when arguments erupt may help us spot patterns and possible solutions.

Some of these may be relatively simple. Many children argue most when they are tired, bored, hungry or restless. Extra outdoor play may help calm active children who like to bounce on brothers and sisters. If children are picking fights to spice up their life, it's

The brakes are off

'A lot of parents are afraid of children fighting. Actually it's okay as long as they also have times when they get on as well, as long as there's a balance. It is all part of growing up and learning assertiveness skills within the family. Just like puppy dogs and baby monkeys, they fight amongst themselves and then they cuddle up when they need to feel secure. It is all part of life.' – Dr Sarah Newton, consultant clinical psychologist; specialist in children's psychological health

The intensity of conflict between our children can be alarming. 'Children have security in the knowledge that family relationships generally will continue even after conflict and that in itself may mean that the brakes are off in many sibling disputes,' explains Professor Hildy Ross, a research specialist in sibling conflicts.

'It also seems that sibling disputes often end without resolution, whereas friends are more likely to reconcile, compromise or resolve their differences. Again, that fits in with their understanding that the sibling relationship is going to continue whereas the friend relationship may not necessarily do so.'

Societal expectations also influence sibling behaviour, adds Hugh Foot, Professor of Psychology, Strathclyde University. 'Siblings are inevitably freer in their emotions and their physical contact with each other because they live together and are more intimate than they are with their friends. They will therefore enjoy excitements and joys together and demonstrate those more fanatically, but they will also fight more and be more extreme and more abusive than with their peers, partly because there are fewer social constraints on beating up your brother or your sister whereas social constraints are already beginning to be recognised at quite an early age in the way children interact with their friends.'

time to divert their attention to more constructive activities.

If they seem to be arguing repeatedly about the same issue they may need us to suggest possible ways to approach the problem (see When they can't sort it out themselves, page 112). If they seem stuck in roles, as either aggressor or victim, they also need our help. A child who is constantly picked on, teased or hit needs our protection. Without our intervention to break the pattern a dominant child may feel they have a green light to intimidate, and sibling conflict may descend into bullying (see Sibling bullying, page 117).

'When I'm tired I lose the plot, so I understand when my children do, too. They need extra help until they get the food or sleep they need. They need to be supported and babied a bit more.' – Kitty Hagenbach, child psychotherapist

'Bullying, aggressive and intrusive behaviour can occur in families. If you are sensing this then you need to make it plain that such behaviour is not acceptable. Make it clear that we all live together in this family and we need to work out our differences without resorting to vicious, nasty, destructive or persistent behaviour which breaches family rules of civility and conduct.' – Peter Wilson, Director of Young Minds

---

♟♟♟ *It's different for girls* ♟♟♟

Gender does seem to influence the nature of the relationship between siblings. In the early years, at least, hostility seems more common among children of different sexes.

'On the question of gender, I think the balance is coming out that there is on the whole, on average, more antagonism between a first-born girl and a secondborn boy,' says developmental psychologist, Professor Judy Dunn. 'It seems more fireworks are going to follow then, even more than two boys who you might think would express more aggression.

That balance may well shift when they hit middle childhood years but we just don't know enough yet. There haven't been enough longitudinal studies to have a very clear account.'

Look for roots

Intense sibling conflict can be a wake-up call that one or more of our children is struggling with life and needs our help (see Operation

Operation love

Stealing from siblings as a way to 'get at' brothers and sisters, or as an expression of need, is more common than we might care to admit.

'One of my sons became very devious and started stealing things. He had secret places to put things and secret places in his head,' says Amanda C. 'I made it clear that I knew he was doing it. I'd find the things under his bed. It lasted for about a year, when he was between five and six. It was mainly his sister's stuff, and maybe it was the only way he knew to fight back. She had made it quite clear she preferred his twin brother and thought he was a tiresome little idiot.'

The story sounds all too familiar to Marina F., a mother who discovered her middle child had gone on a stealing spree.[6] 'Over a period of a few weeks, my seven-year-old daughter stole £50 from her big sister, £20 from a friend and £60 from my desk. My partner and I had very serious words with her. Then we found a Gameboy in her underwear drawer that she'd taken from a child at school. We took it back and she said sorry, but didn't seem remorseful. That was the worst part.

'Since the short, sharp shock treatment hadn't worked, my partner and I decided to adopt Operation Love. It is a tried-and-tested remedy in our family when things go wrong and it involves lots of attention and affection being poured on to the capricious child.

'We were advised that stealing in young children is often a symptom of something else, a demand for attention or some perceived sense of injustice. That made sense. Our daughter was certainly suffering from having had a younger brother turn up after five years of being the youngest. And the group of boys she used to play with at school had recently spurned her.

'Nowadays, life has settled down for her and the thieving has stopped. I'm now inclined to think of it not as a big problem, more a blip on the landscape.'

Andrew Mellor, manager of the Anti-Bullying Network, offers a note of caution. 'An approach such as this [Operation Love] has to be genuine. If it seems forced or false, the child won't accept it. Our own experience tells us that, like all approaches, it will be good in some circumstances and not in others. I think that's an important message for parents. If it works, fine. If it doesn't, you haven't done anything "wrong". It won't work if the child senses that the praise and positive attention isn't for real.'

Love, page 90 and Kicking the cat, page 92). Disruptive or aggressive behaviour can be as much a sign of distress as tears or tummy aches. Perhaps a child needs our support in sorting out a problem with friends or at school. Perhaps they simply need more of our time and attention.

For most children, even negative parental attention is better than not enough, and undesirable behaviour towards a sibling is one sure-fire way of getting it. If this lies behind the children's disputes, the most obvious cure is large doses of positive attention and praise (see Acknowledge the good times, page 70).

'Some children will fight just to get our attention. That's the time we have to stand back and think, "Is this child constantly angry because he or she perceives they are not getting enough from me?" Whenever in our family things have gone awry and the children behaved really badly for a few weeks, I used to think, "I've really got to concentrate on this child, to try to understand what is going on here, something is going wrong and they're alerting me." When I woke up to it and gave them more attention, things generally fell back into place. If I'd just punished them for their behaviour I wouldn't have found the underlying reasons.'
– Adrienne Katz, executive director of Young Voice

Look at ourselves

'Few families are free of conflict entirely, and children observe what parents do in dealing with conflict between each other and other family members. What do parents do? When do they intervene? Do they divert negativity and find constructive solutions? These are some of the umpteen different ways in which siblings learn how to be with each other.'
– Professor Michael Rutter, child psychiatrist

'What we know about aggression in families all suggests that the more it is condoned or modelled by parents being aggressive to each other, the more likely it is to be displayed by the children.'
– Professor Judy Dunn, developmental psychologist

Our behaviour is a major influence on our children's behaviour towards each other. So we may have the power to modify their responses if we

Kicking the cat

'You could say that's what families are for. Family is a place where the pressures of other problems can be brought, and sometimes they are brought in an unthinking way.'
– Peter Wilson, Director of Young Minds

Siblings are often the nearest objects of aggression when a child is bored, frustrated or upset by something else entirely.

'I think that is true of everybody isn't it? The family is where we act out all our frustrations,' says educational psychologist Corinne Abisgold. 'Just as someone who loses their job may come home and kick the cat, we may bring our problems home and hurt those with whom we feel most secure. I think it applies to a marriage as well as to siblings. We bring our problems home and hurt those with whom we feel most secure.

'As a parent it helps to be conscious that dramatic changes in a child's behaviour towards a sibling may well be rooted in something outside the home, perhaps at school or in the community. It is exactly the same the other way round, of course. If parents are coming home and shouting at the kids the chances are that something is happening at work and their stress levels have shot up.'

Children need to express their feelings and can be encouraged to do so in less hurtful or provocative ways (see Exploring emotions, page 125).

'Can you say to your children, "If you've had a bad day at school let's think of something to help get rid of some of those feelings"? asks psychotherapist Pat Elliot. 'It can be a whole variety of things. Special time with you. Or a punch-ball in the garden. Or space and time to run around. Children often need to express their frustrations physically.'

If bad temper directed towards a sibling seems to have its roots elsewhere, it's worth reminding children that we are there to help (see Message received? page 187), and that taking it out on a brother or sister will only cause arguments which could make them feel worse. It helps to be clear that we recognise they are having difficulties, that we will listen and support as much as we can, *and* that it is not okay to be hurtful or inconsiderate.

have the power to modify our own (see How do we deal with disagreements? page 114, and The price of physical punishment, page 94).

- **Are we sending contradictory messages?**

   'It is very confusing to children if you punish them physically because they fight, or you shout at them to stop shouting. Coherence between what you say and do has a more powerful impact.'
   – Desa Markovic, family therapist

   'If a parent has self-control – staying calm as much as possible, not taking sides, making time to spend alone with each child and so on – children will model that. If the parent behaves in a way that doesn't seem to be contained or have boundaries, then their words and their actions are sending contradictory messages. Children can find that quite frightening.'
   – John Bristow, chartered psychologist and psychotherapist

   There's little point telling our children not to hit each other if they see us hitting or we hit them; talking about kindness and consideration for others will not cut much ice if children don't have frequent opportunities to see and experience its positive effects.

- **Are there marked and long-term differences in how we treat our kids?** Children who consistently receive more punishment and less attention and affection than their siblings tend to show higher levels of aggression and problematic behaviour and have more hostile relationships with their brothers and sisters.[7] Recognising our preferential treatment of our children isn't easy (see Facing up to favouritism, page 147), but essential if we want them to get on better.

- **Are we remembering our needs?**

   'Being the referee in the middle is exhausting. I feel like the rope in a tug of war.' – Mary M.

   If we're honest, we know how much our own emotional state influences our children's behaviour. If we are feeling stressed and irritable, we are much more likely to snap at them and they are much more likely to snap at each other.

The price of physical punishment

'I do have very strong views on hitting and I can't really think of a circumstance in which it would be acceptable. I would certainly never think it good advice for parents.' – Desa Markovic, family therapist

'In our recent reports on bullying and youth suicide, many of the children interviewed said they had been at the receiving end of adult violence.[8] That's telling us something. Too many of our children are being taught that violence is the way to get you what you want in life. It changes children's view of themselves and their priorities, and can damage relationships inside and outside the family.' – Adrienne Katz, executive director of Young Voice.

Children who are hit by their parents tend to hit back at others, including siblings, friends and parents. While it may stop misbehaviour in the short-term, punitive, harsh parenting tends to backfire. Aggressive parental behaviour and physical punishment over time increases the probability of children displaying aggressive and violent behaviour from childhood to adulthood.[9]

'Parenting style makes a considerable difference between what

The pressures on parents can be huge, and we can't hope to eradicate all stress from our lives. But by recognising the impact of our moods on our children's behaviour – and the impact of their behaviour on our moods – we may also recognise the importance of looking after ourselves as well as our children, of drawing the line when we've had enough, and occasionally prioritising our own needs for the benefit of the family as a whole.

'I found those times when I just couldn't help getting involved, screaming, shouting and getting right in the middle of things, usually just made it worse. Much worse. If you can look after yourself you are much more able to feel calm and resourceful, to be objective and see the bigger picture. When

goes on between siblings,' explains Dr Gavin Nobes, senior lecturer in developmental psychology. 'If parents are conflicting or aggressive, it will legitimise aggressive behaviour. It is very likely to increase aggression between siblings. We also know what helps. The available research evidence is quite clear about the need for parents to provide warmth, responsiveness, sensitivity, communication and firm but not harsh discipline. The emphasis of effective discipline is on positive things like praise and reward for good behaviour, rather than on negative things like punishment for bad behaviour.'

'Cultural differences matter much less than we probably think. The similarities far outweigh the differences. Barring physically abusive punishment, which does become a risk factor, what matters to children is that they are brought up in a loving atmosphere, where they are disciplined effectively, harmoniously and with respect for the individuality of the children. Whether they are, say, brought up by a buoyant, outgoing family or a quiet, relatively inhibited one is of very little importance, although this will influence the styles the children acquire. There are many different ways of showing warmth and concern, so there are many different routes to the same place.'
– Professor Michael Rutter, child psychiatrist

it happens you almost can't believe it – you are calm and gentle and straight and it works!' – Barbara Dale, counsellor

'I don't think you should pretend to be calm and collected when you are really upset. Honesty demands you sometimes have to tell children, "I'm really angry at that, don't do it. We'll talk about that later when I've calmed down a wee bit, at the moment I think I'm so angry I might say something I'll regret." That's perfectly reasonable. I think some people get the wrong message and think parents are to say nothing at all. Yet warmth involves genuineness and that may involve expressing genuine anger when that anger is perfectly justified.'
– Andrew Mellor, Anti-bullying Network

Effective action

*'When push comes to shove it's our job to help them sort things out.
Otherwise they'll just shove each other again.'* – Martin C.

*'I remember being in the sandpit with my brother and sister and them both
being very nasty to me and my mother just watching on and doing nothing.
I felt abandoned.'* – Brian D.

*'Parental intervention in escalating conflict can reassure children that
their parents are available to help and protect them when they are upset
or in danger.'* – Gene H. Brody, Professor of Child
and Family Development[16]

Knowing what may lie behind our children's fighting is essential. But
so is knowing how to tackle fights and disputes when tempers flare.
When and how we intervene in our children's arguments makes a
huge difference to their abilities to negotiate and resolve their
differences, both now and in the future. So what helps?

The heat of the moment

Parents used to be advised to let battling children get on with it unless
in imminent danger of bloodletting or breaking the furniture. Yet
new research makes it very clear that when parents intervene
promptly and constructively, *in ways which encourage children to sort out
their own disputes,* the number and intensity of sibling rows is reduced.
This has obvious long-term benefits for the children's relationship. It
also seems to boost each child's individual emotional development
and their capacities to problem-solve and negotiate generally.[17]

Precisely how we intervene will depend on the circumstances. Yes,
it would be simpler if one single and set response fitted every eventu-
ality but, in the real world, one-size-fits-all techniques often backfire.

Sibling conflict can range from minor squabbles to major on-going
battles and to be effective and constructive, we have to adapt our
responses accordingly. We also need to take into account the ages and
stages of the children involved. Little children will need much more
direct guidance and calm repetition of family rules before we can

If conflict goes unchecked . . .

Tackling conflict is not something we can attempt in isolation. It is dealt with separately and in detail in this chapter because it is an issue of such concern to so many families, yet every chapter in this book addresses issues that will help us support our children's relationships and reduce the risk of long-term and damaging conflict between them.

It's essential that we do. Chronically high sibling conflict has been linked to aggressive behaviour inside and outside the home,[10] and to academic difficulty and poor relations with other children at school.[11] Hostility and antisocial behaviour in a sibling is a known risk factor for the development of antisocial behaviour and delinquency in other children in the family[12] (see Growing pains, page 259).

Hostile and rivalrous feelings originating in childhood often persist between siblings well into adulthood.[13] Problems such as anxiety, withdrawal and low self-esteem are more common among children whose siblings were very hostile towards them in their pre-school years[14] and these feelings can continue through and beyond adolescence.[15]

expect them to fully understand what behaviour is expected of them and why.

But all the approaches outlined below adhere to three fundamental principles:

- **We are ready to intervene** when our children seem to be struggling or when a situation is potentially dangerous or overwhelming.
- **Our intervention encourages children to resolve their disputes constructively for themselves**.
- **The way we intervene takes into account the level of conflict**. Go in too soft when our children are at boiling point, or too hard in a low-temperature squabble, and they'll know we've little

understanding of what's going on between them – so they'll either take no notice or fight all the more. To intervene effectively, we need to check the heat.

Each approach also follows the same basic structure.

1. **Define the problem:** Sometimes the most immediate problem will be the disagreement itself; sometimes it will be the children's behaviour in response to that. By defining the problem, we make it easier for children to find a solution.

   Defining the problem: 'Okay, so you both want an orange lolly, but there's only one left.'
   Defining the problem behaviour: 'Someone's going to get hurt if you carry on.'

Who? Little me?

'We've got amazing information on children in the second year of life teasing their older sibling, and it gets more frequent as they get into their third year. It is exquisitely tailored to what will upset the other child, so if the older child has a special toy they adore, for example, it will be this that gets thrown out of the window. If you can keep your sense of humour as a parent, these instances of children knowing exactly what is going to annoy their older sibling can be very illuminating. They show quite how clever your child is at such a relatively young age.' – Professor Judy Dunn, developmental psychologist

Children as young as sixteen months have been observed aggravating, teasing or frightening their older siblings, at an age when psychologists once thought children had little grasp of the thoughts or feelings of others.[18] This is important for us to know, because it is all too easy for parents to presume the youngest is the victim, and to chastise the older child as the aggressor. Evidence now suggests the truth is often very different.

Younger children are frequently responsible for provoking disputes, and for escalating them into physical

2. **Describe the feelings:** Emotions need to be acknowledged and expressed so children are free to focus on constructive action: '*You both seem really angry about this.*'

   As well as acknowledging how our children may be feeling, we can also let them know how it is affecting us: '*You're both angry about this and how you're dealing with it is upsetting me, too.*'

3. **Search for a solution**. Whenever possible, our children should do the searching. To encourage them, we need to avoid judging or blaming any one child in the heat of the moment, even if it seems pretty clear who's at fault (see Who? Little me? page 98): '*How can you sort this out without shouting or hurting each other?*'

---

conflict. While the older child may be increasingly aware that they are not to hit back at their little brother or sister, little brother or sister may be hitting them with increasing regularity. By eighteen months, younger siblings tend to be more likely to hit back than burst into tears during conflict, and often strike the first blow. They also become more sophisticated in their strategies for attracting parental attention, often pulling attention away from their older sibling by acting the injured underdog, being cute or interrupting until they are heard.

Of course, it doesn't always happen this way. But it is best to be alert to the possibility, and to the dangers of making any snap assumptions about who is to blame when tempers flare and children fight.

'*It is very easy to make assumptions about what happens between your children, but so easy to get it wrong. My daughter, being four years older, would wind up her little brother verbally. He then turned physical and got the blame. She was giving him the ammunition to fire! I think you have to refuse to take sides or jump to conclusions; make it clear that you are not going to do so if you didn't see what happened, and then try and discuss it with each child after things have calmed down.*' – Christine Puckering, clinical psychologist and co-developer of the Mellow Parenting Programme

These are *not* soft options. We are making children accept responsibility for their actions and think hard about how they could behave better in future, and that can be tough. But it can also be very effective in turning around children's negative behaviour, right now and into the future.

These basic principles of effective intervention can be adapted to suit every level of conflict. Try imagining children's disputes graded on a thermometer scale – are they warm and quite likely to cool down again quickly; are they getting heated; are they hot and potentially dangerous or already at boiling point? Once we've checked the temperature, we'll know how best to put the principles into action.

Warm

'My children squabbled like billyo, you can't suppress it all and you really shouldn't try.' – Professor Hugh Foot, Professor of Psychology, Strathclyde University

'Children need to learn how to sort these things out for themselves and to grow up with their differences and conflicts.' – Peter Wilson, director of Young Minds.

Mild bickering, minor squabbles.

1. **Define the problem**: This is a very low-temperature dispute. These are often best ignored as they may soon blow over. If we repeatedly intervene at this level, our children will be slower to learn how to resolve conflict themselves, and we'll spend far too much time attempting to sort out their difficulties.

2. **Describe the feelings**: If it is irritating, say so. Perhaps move into another room, or ask them to.

3. **Search for a solution**: Let them first try to find it themselves.

'Children can enjoy puppyish play, even arguments. Why stop something they are enjoying? We want to reserve our interventions for when they are needed.' – Professor Peter Smith, researcher in children's social development

Telling tales?

'They are always telling on each other. He did this,
she did that. It goes on all day, from when they get up
to when they go to bed.'
– Paula T.

'The general culture tells us that parents don't like tale-telling, or
tattling, yet from our observations of families it is clear that
parents essentially accept and act upon the negative information
they get from their children about one another.'
– Professor Hildy Ross, research specialist in sibling conflicts

Children are often told not to 'tell tales', yet it may be important that they do. They sometimes 'tell' to alert us that they need our help. Parents also tend to act on the information given. So our children are being given a very confusing message: 'Don't tell, but when you do I may take it seriously.'

Perhaps a more constructive approach would be let our children know that:

1. It is important they come to us if they need our help, or if a situation is serious, hurtful or dangerous.
2. It is not okay if it's just to report a sibling's misdemeanour to get them into trouble.

We can discourage gratuitous tale-telling by refusing to jump to conclusions about who is to blame and by making it clear that we expect our children to sort out problems between themselves whenever possible.

'I think if you are refusing to take sides, children soon realise
habitual tale-telling is not going to get them very far. It's like
whinging. Usually the child who whinges a lot is the child who
has discovered that whinging works. If it stops being
effective, they'll stop doing it.'
– Christine Puckering, clinical psychologist and
co-developer of the Mellow Parenting Programme

Getting heated

Angrier disputes, name calling, arguments over toys, etc. A dispute is heating up. Our children now need our encouragement and guidance so they can sort it out for themselves.

1. **Define the problem**: The children's behaviour isn't extreme. The biggest problem is the dispute itself so that's what we need to define: '*Okay, so it's an argument over the Lego*'; '*Two kids, one trike. That's hard*'; '*So you want to play your CD and you want some peace and quiet.*'

2. **Describe the feelings**: Tentative phrases such as 'sounds like', 'looks like' and 'seems' are supportive rather than accusatorial and suggest that we're trying to understand what's going on: '*Looks like you two are angry with each other*'; '*Sounds like you're both getting upset over this*'; '*Seems as though this is maddening for you both*'. When children feel understood, tempers often calm.

3. **Search for a solution**: We can express our faith in the children's abilities to resolve the argument: '*I think you two could work out a solution that seems fair to you both*'; '*It's a tough problem. See if you can work out a way around it that you're both happy with.*'
   This may also be a timely opportunity to restate family rules: 'I'm sure you can work this out without hitting/screaming/calling each other names.' Then we should leave them to it, perhaps even leave the room. We can tell them to find us once they've worked out a solution.

> '*Giving the girls the responsibility to sort things out between them has helped. To be honest, their solutions are often fairer and longer-lasting than anything I could come up with. And I don't feel like the referee all the time.*' – Zoe D.

Hot

> '*It isn't okay to ignore siblings who are getting caught up in conflict. We need to acknowledge that it's having an impact on each of them, so that at the very least they know we're aware and available to help. Otherwise they may feel that it's the child who makes the most fuss who gets the most*

Name-calling

Our response to name-calling between our children will depend on the circumstances and our own family rules. As ever, it helps to give children room for manoeuvre: 'Sounds like names are being used here which are not allowed in this house. Neither of you is daft. I know you can work this out without using that kind of language.'

Encouraging children to consider the name-caller's intent may help them distinguish between affectionate teasing and hostile put-downs. If a child always presumes their sibling's worst motives, arguments will inevitably escalate.

Name-callers also need to know how to express their anger or frustration in less offensive or provocative ways: 'You know we don't have name-calling in this family. If you've a problem with your sister, tell her what it is.' (See The dangers of labels, page 167.)

attention. That's not going to help anybody.' – Cheryl Walters, Head of Research at Parentline Plus and Analytical Psychotherapist in private practice

Louder, angrier conflict with the potential to spill over into extremes. The line of permitted behaviour has been crossed or is about to be.

We now put firmer emphasis on the children's behaviour and the consequences of breaking family rules. We can also provide structured time for each child to say how they feel and how they might sort things out.

1. **Define the problem**: The most urgent problem now is not the dispute itself but the children's behaviour. The quickest way to address this constructively is to **state the risk in their behaviour and the family rule it's breaking**: '*Looks like someone could get hurt here. We don't hit in this family*'; '*Look, someone's already crying. In this family we try to solve arguments without upsetting each other.*'

2. **Describe the feelings**: We need to listen to each child and let them put their side of the story without interruption or judgement, even if there seems an obvious victim. Children who

♦♦♦ *The Friday night fight* ♦♦♦

'It was a Friday evening, my ten-year-old daughter had a friend playing and we were having a quiet drink when the house was rent with screams of fury,' remembers Doro Marden, Parentline Plus facilitator and trustee. 'Her twelve-year-old sister was doing an exercise tape in front of the video and didn't want to be disturbed and the other two wanted to be in the room too. Rapid escalation of the conflict ensued – scratching, shoving, obstructing, insults and appeals to outside powers (us).

'I tried to mediate (define the problem – "You want to finish your exercises, and you want to practise tap dancing here on the hard floor, what could you do about that?") but feelings and decibels were running too high for logic and I had to resort to peace keeping – physically separating the warring sides and removing the smaller one to vent her feelings elsewhere ("I hate her, I want to kill her, I want her to suffer and die slowly, I want to chop her up in little pieces." Me reflecting back the feelings – "You're really angry with your sister." Then more – "You're always laughing at me because I'm the youngest." Reflection: "You feel we don't take you seriously.") Eventually she calmed down.

'In the meantime the other sister was with her father tidying up some of the mess caused by the fight (jigsaw puzzle pieces everywhere). Eventually she came up with a peace proposal: "I'm sorry, let's be friends." Her younger sister refused and ate her supper away from the table before she felt able to reciprocate. The next day I was amazed to see them curled up in bed together reading and for a time after that they were much more affectionate.'

feel that their views have been heard and feelings acknowledged are much more able to control their tempers and manage their own behaviour.

When tempers are high, 'reflecting' back what our children are saying and feeling can also help them feel they have been understood (see Reflective listening, page 198, and The Friday night fight, this page). This may take the sting out of their fury. For example:

Child: 'I hate her. She says I'm lying but I never took her ball.'
Parent: 'Sounds like you're really angry with your sister.'

This may seem time-consuming, but is much less so than allowing conflict to escalate.

3. **Search for a solution**: Express faith in their abilities to work the problem through, but let them know you're available to help if they find it hard.

   If we offer solutions, we can also ask for some of their own: 'Seems to me you've got a few choices here. You could take it in turns, or move into different rooms where you won't disturb each other, or maybe you can think of something better?'

🚶‍♂️ *Focusing on the victim* 🚶‍♀️

This approach is best kept for those rare occasions when there is a clear aggressor and victim – perhaps we've seen one child hurt another. It is particularly useful for educating very young children not to hurt others, but can also be effective with children of any age. It denies the aggressor attention, while also making the victim feel safe.

If one child hits another, remove the child who's hurt, calmly explain why you are doing so, then focus all your attention on the victim. 'That must have hurt. Jamie needs to say what the problem is, not hit when he's angry.' You and the victim then move away from the aggressor, perhaps even leaving the room.

Once tempers have calmed, and there is less risk of a child associating negative behaviour with parental attention, we can begin to talk to each child about what happened and how difficult situations or emotions could be handled better in future.

'I think the more we make it boring and low-key for the aggressor, the more effective it tends to be. Some people try to somehow turn the situation round to suggest everything's fine when a child clearly isn't behaving well – "Oh, I'm sure he didn't mean it" – or to remove the aggressor, which gives him the attention he seeks and may encourage a repeat performance. Far better, I think, to focus on the victim so the aggressive behaviour is calmly and clearly rejected.' – Dr Elizabeth Bryan, paediatrician

'No matter how strongly we might feel that one child is doing wrong, it is crucial that all children receive time and attention to say what he or she thinks. This can be hard, especially if you feel angry, but the most effective intervention is to have that conversation. Maybe a child feels they weren't in the wrong. Maybe fighting was a result of desperately trying to assert their different view. Letting them express that is the most effective way to allow them to move on.' – Desa Markovic, family therapist

'I have to say that when I first started asking my two how they could sort out their arguments they just looked at me blankly. I think it was the shock. And when I come home from work, sometimes I just don't have the time or energy to talk things through, and we'll all resort to our old ways. But we're all learning.' – Rowena W.

Boiling

'When they are in emotional crisis, at boiling point, the key thing is to remain calm or the parent's state will add fuel to the fire.' – John Bristow, chartered psychologist and psychotherapist

'When they really explode I've got to get them apart and cooled down before there's any hope of peace. If I don't it just flares up again.' – Michelle B.

♟♟♟ *When Time Out rebounds* ♟♟♟

Time Out can help warring parties cool off and calm down, but can be a very short-term strategy if not followed up by some way for the children to express their feelings and opinions and work out better ways to behave together in future.

Once everyone has calmed down, each child can think of a way to put the situation right. This may take a while, but helps encourage a feeling of 'team' responsibility to resolve difficulties. Children who are merely banished to their bedrooms can seethe with such resentment and anger that they come out feeling more furious than when they went in, which helps no one.

'Time Out is crisis management, not a resolution of the problem. It

Dangerous, violent or hurtful behaviour. Talking about feelings must come later. In the full heat of sibling fury, our first task is to put a stop to dangerous or threatening conduct. Quickly:

1. **Separate**: Hopefully, we can do this with words. Sometimes we may have to do it physically. It's our job to keep our children safe, and if that's what it takes, that's what we need to do.

2. **Define the problem**: Their behaviour is the immediate problem, so again we **state the risk in their behaviour and the family rule it's breaking**. Try to stay non-judgemental, calm and *very* firm: '*This isn't safe. We don't hit in this house and you both need to cool down. Now.*' (See Focusing on the victim, page 105.)

3. **Search for a solution**: The immediate options for our children are clear – **Cut it out or time out:** '*Either go to separate rooms to calm down, or we can talk now about the things that are upsetting you both.*'

Time Out – sending children to separate rooms – can be the simplest way to interrupt aggression, but it is most effective if used rarely and as a means for children to cool down enough to talk issues through, rather than as a punishment in itself (see When Time Out rebounds, this page).

Whether or not we decide to use it, it is important to be clear about our intention to listen to each child's side of the story once tempers

just allows everybody to stop shouting or hurting each other,' says health visitor, Sarah Darton. 'I know one little boy who was continually sent to his room for lashing out at his sister. This was incredibly damaging because it wasn't followed by an exploration of what happened – what was he feeling that led him to hit his sister? What else could he do? Instead, he was just left seething, bitter and angrier than ever that he'd been banished without a chance to explain what provocation there'd been from his sister. He came out still furious, hating her and probably his parents.

'Problem solving has to come afterwards. If you are going to send one or both children away, it's so important to have a conversation afterwards about what it was about. If they don't have a chance to air their viewpoint, the resentment will stay.'

have cooled: 'Stop right now. Since you can't get along you'd better have ten minutes apart. You go to the kitchen, you to the living room, and I'll listen to each of you when you're calmer.'

What won't help!

By recognising unhelpful parental approaches, we're more likely to avoid them and save our energy for more constructive action. Common, but unhelpful, responses include:

- **'Who started it?'** They'll probably blame each other, especially when tempers are high. Inviting our children to fling the blame elsewhere rarely gets to the root of the problem, and is more likely to fuel tempers than calm them.
- **'Why can't you two play nicely?'** Children rarely know the answer. It's a mystery to many parents, so we can't expect our children to come up with a swift and satisfactory reply.
- **'No pocket money/Gameboy/television for a week.'** The threat of punishment and removal of privileges is sometimes necessary, especially to stop a raging child in their tracks. Yet it is only effective if used rarely and if followed up by constructive discussion (see Threats and promises, page 109). Without this, children can feel like victims. This will make them more angry or resentful, not less. Or they'll have heard the threat/had the punishment so many times before, it will have little impact.
- **'You two are always fighting!'** This doesn't leave much scope for improvement. Children tend to live up to their labels, whether applied individually or to their relationship with a brother or sister (see Kids don't fit in pigeonholes, page 159).
- **'Stop or you'll feel the back of my hand.'** Our aim should be to illicit cooperation from our children because they understand why it matters, not because they fear a clout (see Caring and sharing, page 43).
- **'Just pack it in!'** Sometimes the swiftest, most effective message is the shortest: 'Stop!', 'No!', 'Don't!'. But its effect is short-term, and will need to be followed up with calmer discussion to have long-term impact.

- **'But he's smaller than you/but she's a girl.'** We tend to champion the child we feel is most vulnerable. Yet younger siblings can goad big brothers and sisters from a surprisingly early age (see Who? Little me? page 98) and repeated reference to gender or age differentials may make a child feel their side of the story isn't heard. This will fuel conflict.

♦ *Threats and promises?* ♦♦♦

There may be times, in any of these situations, when your child or children aren't listening to a word you say. Then it's time to attract attention.

Some parents drop their voice to almost a whisper – the surprise can stop shouting children in their tracks. Most find it more effective to look and sound very calm, very firm and absolutely clear: 'We all need to talk about this and we all need to be quiet and listen. Now!'

We may sometimes find it necessary to resort to cruder methods. 'He's got a temper that can overwhelm him at times. Then, and it isn't very often, I have to almost jolt him into listening by threatening to remove his most precious possession – his Playstation – until he calms down,' says Paula C, mother of two boys. 'I've only had to confiscate it twice. Now he knows I mean it, the threat's enough to stop him in his tracks and I haven't had

to threaten it often. But when I do, it gives me a chance to be heard, to begin to calm things down and sort things out.'

Any threats of removal of privileges are best used very sparingly, as they can divert attention from the more important issues of resolving arguments and finding better ways to behave in future. They also seem to have most impact and meaning if related to the subject of the row. So, if children are fighting over who watches what on the television, for instance, they might lose TV watching time if they don't sort it out. If they are fighting over toys, these could be taken away for a time until they find a solution they're all happy with.

Whatever we chose, our aim should be to make the time and the peace necessary for our children to find solutions, rather than removing privileges merely to punish.

- **'I've told you time and time again . . .'** Sticking to an approach that clearly doesn't work in the faint hope that it might if we do it often enough will fray our nerves and do little to tackle the problem. Sometimes we have to ask ourselves, 'Does this help?' If it doesn't, it's time to look at alternative, more constructive approaches.

- **'Come on darlings, this isn't very nice is it? Be a sweetie and take your hands from his throat.'** It helps to be as clear and firm as we can. If we sound too lame or pleading, children won't know what to believe – our message or our tone. If we want our children to take us seriously, we have to mean what we say and say it like we mean it (see Clear messages, page 204).

What to do once tempers have cooled

'When the situation has calmed down the parent might take the child on their lap, so the child's environment feels supportive. Then they can attempt to help the child learn from what has happened, making a distinction between the behaviour of the child and the needs and feelings behind the behaviour: "I understand you're feeling very angry. If you feel like this how else could you respond?" What you say will depend on the age of the child, but even with quite a young child you can look at feelings and behaviours in a simple way.'
– John Bristow, chartered psychologist and psychotherapist

Once tempers have cooled, the real work starts. When our children are calm, they can begin to think through what they did, the effects that it had, and how they could behave differently with each other. And we can help.

We can reassure each child they are loved, that we will listen to what they have to say and help them work out ways of sorting out arguments without hurtful behaviour. We can also make it clear that positive approaches to problem-solving will help them, as well as help us and their brother or sister: 'I know you wanted the bike, but snatching it only starts a fight. How could you get your turn in a way that won't start an argument or get you into trouble?'; 'I know you felt it was unfair, but when you shout and scream it's hard for me to hear what you're saying. How could you get your point across in a way that's easier for people to listen to?'

Chatting with each child on their own may help them talk, or take less provocative delight in seeing a brother or sister 'in trouble'. If they seem unable to work out better ways to handle situations, we can suggest a few but leave the final choice to them. That way, they'll feel the decision to behave differently is their own.

When we see our children responding more positively to each other, we should let them know and tell them why it is so helpful to them and to us (see Descriptive praise, page 72). Positive attention is the surest recipe for continued considerate behaviour.

Making up

'It is quite common for siblings to claim, "I said sorry" as if that somehow made the original misdemeanour all right. If it matters to the parent, then it is something that should be encouraged, like please and thank you, but we have to accept that if children are forced to apologise, they may say it well before they mean it.' – Professor Judy Dunn, developmental psychologist

'Saying sorry can be a way of drawing a line under an incident, allowing kids to let it go. I think that's something we've all got to do, to let issues drop once they're dealt with, otherwise a child can feel like they'll never escape from past misdemeanours. And if that happens, where's the incentive to behave better?' – Helen O.

Little children can say sorry like an expletive. By early school age, many will have perfected the sarcastic 'Sor-ree'. Others will apologise with great ease and staggering insincerity.

Our children need to know how to apologise, and to realise it will be expected of them at school and elsewhere. Yet forcing an immediate apology can be counterproductive, especially when you, the child and the recipient know it not to be genuine. It may encourage children to hide how they feel, make them simmer with anger or stop them thinking fully about the consequences of their actions.

When we want our children to apologise, it helps to talk about the dispute and why we think an apology is appropriate. Better still, we can encourage them to suggest it as a way to improve the situation. If it's their idea, they are much more likely to mean what they say.

'I think children learn over time what remorse is and how to express it, but sometimes we try to force them to say sorry when they are still steamed up and angry. They're much more likely to come round a bit later, when they've calmed down and understand better what's gone on. Thinking of how the other person must be feeling is so important here. I am sure part of that comes with maturity but it is something we can encourage by pointing out if someone has suffered at the hands of another and encouraging and helping the child to make amends, whether it be verbally or non-verbally, perhaps by stroking the arm of someone they've hurt, making them a card or drawing them a picture.' – Dr Sarah Newton,
specialist in children's psychological health

When they can't sort it out themselves

'Our research indicates that there are benefits to parents becoming involved when their children are in dispute, but it is important that their involvement is respectful of the children and their abilities to contribute to resolving issues between them.'[19]
– Professor Hildy Ross, research specialist in sibling conflicts

'If my children really can't resolve an issue, I ask each one of them to tell me exactly what happened and how it was for them. Then I ask them what are they going to do about it. Usually by the time they've gone through that process they don't care so much about the argument. It is the process of both being heard that's so important – how horrible one was because he did this, and how horrible the other was because they did that. That's often all they need.' – Sarah Darton, health visitor

Tempers may have calmed, but if the dispute is long-running, recurring or a particularly bitter sibling feud, the difficulties won't be over. To untangle the problem sufficiently enough to see possible solutions, our children may need our active support and help.

A structured family discussion to help each child voice their opinions and suggest solutions may sound rather formal, but parents and others who've used it say it can be extremely helpful when all else has failed. The exact form of the discussion can be adapted to suit our children's ages and capabilities, but its elements will be familiar – defining the problem, describing feelings and searching for solutions. And throughout, our role remains the same:

- to mediate and guide non-judgementally rather than to impose solutions
- to focus on constructive discussion rather than blame-flinging
- to give each side the opportunity to state their case and suggest ways to improve matters.

By giving each child a voice and a choice, we give them back the power to address problems that are worrying them and the responsibility for sorting out their own behaviour.

Studies show this can have significant and long-term benefits. Siblings in middle childhood whose parents intervene impartially to help them work through problems display less conflict and more ability to reconcile differences up to two years later.[20] Many schools using these types of conflict resolution techniques have reported much-reduced incidences of bullying,[21] and children who use positive and calm approaches to resolve differences are generally more popular among their peers.[22]

All children need adult assistance to negotiate tough situations sometimes, but the approach is particularly helpful when

- One or both children have difficulty making their feelings or opinions heard.
- There is a wide disparity in discursive skills, because of differences in age, temperament or ability.
- Siblings feel alienated, emotionally 'estranged', or too negative towards one another to consider issues constructively without adult guidance.
- The responsibility of resolving a bitter dispute between themselves seems too burdensome.
- The children seem incapable of resolving a recurring problem.

'Getting to the bottom of things takes time, and some days that's just not possible. But add up all the time we waste with their squabbling and fighting when things aren't sorted out. I'm convinced this saves time in the long run.' – Karen T.

Like all approaches, it may seem strange at first but with a little practice it can become reassuringly familiar and extremely effective.

Nine steps to a solution

1. **Explain the groundrules**. Sit where everyone can see each other, perhaps around a table. Make sure everyone's present, calm and comfortable. Tell the children that for disagreements to

---

How do we deal with disagreements?

'How parents manage disagreements is much more important than where or how often they argue . . . Conflict between parents doesn't have to be damaging. Children may learn from their parents' techniques for handling and resolving conflict. In particular, children can benefit from observing parents when they demonstrate warmth, seek compromise, and use negotiation and humour as they resolve differences.' – Not in Front of the Children, One Plus One?[23]

How parents manage and resolve conflict in the family will influence how our children behave with each other.[24] If we handle disputes constructively and without hostility, stating our case and listening to others, we will give our children a lesson for life.

Children growing up in an atmosphere of extreme marital discord may develop emotional and behavioural problems and fight more with their brothers and sisters.[25] Yet, for the most part,

'disagreements between parents are a normal and necessary part of family life,' states *Not in Front of the Children*, a review of research into conflict in families, by the charity One Plus One.[26] 'Indeed, children may be more harmed if parents' ill-concealed attempts to suppress anger create a silently hostile environment.'

Psychotherapist Pat Elliot agrees. 'I think adult arguments are actually quite good in front of children if they can see there's a way of sorting

be sorted out, everyone needs a chance to speak in turn without interruption. We might want to remind the children about family rules. 'We don't hit in this house, so this discussion is to find a way of sorting out this problem without anyone getting hurt.'

2. **Acknowledge feelings**. 'You both sound really angry with each other.'

3. **Listen to each side**. Encourage each child to talk about how they feel, not simply what happened.

---

out issues without resorting to aggression. The sorting out may require a cooling off period – "Let's leave sorting this out until tomorrow, when we'll both be calmer" – but that's a useful lesson, too. Obviously not all issues should be argued about in front of children – we have to respect their age, understanding and vulnerabilities – but generally I think it helps them to see us have passionate disagreements, resolve them and be loving the next day.

'Unspoken conflict can be hard for children to cope with, for whatever the sweetness of the words, they pick up on their parents' feelings. I have worked with so many adults who say their parents would save their conflicts and arguments until the children had gone to bed. The children would hear raised voices and be absolutely terrified, but nobody would explain what was happening. It's far better to say, "Me and daddy are really very angry with each other because we want different things. So we're sorting it out." You've got to teach children how to cope with reality.'

How we resolve our disagreements with our children will also influence their attitudes to conflict with each other. Do they see disagreements as something to resolve, give in to or rage against?

'One girl I am working with has very low self-esteem and finds it very difficult to resolve arguments at school,' explains educational psychologist Corinne Abisgold. 'She is at loggerheads with her mother at home and she sees arguments as ultimately irresolvable. Falling out with friends during her stage of adolescence is common, but she really takes it to heart. Because she can't get beyond the arguing to the making-up stage with her mother, she thinks the falling out at school is probably going to go on and on, with little she can do about it.'

4. **Check back**. Reflect each viewpoint, to let each child feel they've got their point across: 'So, Helen, you say you wanted to use the CD player and Nicky, you say it's your turn.'

5. **Sum up the problem**. Can the children now agree the nature of the problem? If not, we can sum it up for them: 'It's hard when two people want the same thing. This problem keeps recurring, doesn't it.' If you are not sure about the root of the problem, ask them. 'Are your disagreements mainly about who's boss or have you any other ideas?'

6. **Invite solutions**. Let each child have a turn to suggest solutions and express your confidence in the children's ability to sort things out.

7. **Leave the room or stay?** Leaving them to it can be effective, but is not always appropriate, especially if you suspect one child wields significantly greater power through age, eloquence or temperament. If you believe one child may somehow force the other into compliance, it's best to stay put (see Another way to get my way?, page 117).

8. **Agree a solution**. Can they agree a way forward? If they seem to be struggling, we can suggest some ideas, making sure we offer a choice and leave the final decision to them.

9. **Review**. Fix a time to meet again and discuss how the solution has worked.

'When parents intervene and the kids decide how the issue will be finally resolved, the benefits seem to last and improve the children's ability to find resolutions over a period of time. They tend less often to arrive at a situation where one is a winner and one a loser. And two years later these are the same children and families who tend to reconcile their differences a little more than others.' – Professor Hildy Ross, research specialist in sibling conflicts

'Sometimes a more formal structure makes a lot of sense because otherwise one child may not get a word in. If they are used to that from an early age, it becomes an accepted part of life. It also shows that you respect there's a problem and that you respect both children's point of view. There's little more gratifying than being told you have asked an interesting question or raised an important point. It boosts children rather than squashes them.' – Dr Elizabeth Bryan, paediatrician and founder of the Multiple Births Foundation

Another way to get my way?

Children who learn basic conflict resolution techniques will know how to negotiate in ways that consider siblings' needs as well as their own. But that doesn't mean they'll always want to.

'Greater understanding between siblings certainly doesn't always mean greater harmony. Skills of conflict management are by no means always used to resolve conflict, but are sometimes used by children to gain their own goals,' says developmental psychologist, Professor Judy Dunn. 'Our analyses show that with age, children get more adept at negotiating and bargaining and avoiding direct confrontation, but often this new power is put to their own ends to get what they want.'[27]

So we shouldn't always take sibling 'negotiation' at face value. Neither should we assume that children will automatically transfer skills they have learned within one relationship to another. 'The same child can put their capacity to understand others to different uses in different relationships,' says Professor Dunn. 'A child can show great subtlety and interest in the well-being of a friend, trying to solve quarrels nicely and so on, and then behave very differently when faced with a sibling.'

When there are more than two children in the family, issues may sometimes be decided by majority vote. It helps to be alert to children clubbing together to 'exclude' or continually out-vote another.

When there simply isn't time to discuss and listen to issues at length, recognising the feelings of the 'loser' may prevent children descending into melodrama and stop 'winners' from gloating: 'Okay, so we're going to the park and not swimming because that's what most of you wanted. But I want you all to know that Julie is very disappointed. She really wanted to go to the pool.'

Sibling bullying

'My sister bullied me for years and my parents never seemed to notice how severe it was and how desperate it made me feel. Their lack of support hurt just as much as the bullying itself.' – Susan T.

'Bullying does take place between siblings and can be very, very damaging.'
– Andrew Mellor, Anti-Bullying Network

Sibling disputes are normal and generally healthy if handled constructively. One child habitually dominating or bullying another is neither. The extent of bullying within schools is now recognised; bullying within families rarely gets a mention but can be equally devastating for the bullied and the bullying child (see Behind closed doors, this page).

If we become aware of bullying behaviour patterns emerging, it is

✝ *Behind closed doors* ✝✝✝

'What should we be watching out for between our children?' asks Andrew Mellor, manager of the Anti-Bullying Network. 'One child consistently abusing another or a gross inequality of power, not necessarily related to age. Younger siblings sometimes bully older children. There may be a disparity in intellectual ability or merely a difference in character. Some children are more aggressive than others. If parents spot that they should pay careful attention.

'Bullying has many manifestations. Physical bullying is the most obvious, but is not necessarily the one most hurtful to victims. Verbal bullying, psychological bullying, being isolated, being threatened and humiliated, all these hurt.'

Professor Peter Smith, a leading researcher in children's social development, agrees. 'Bullying can have a catastrophic impact on a child's development and later life choices if it goes unchecked. Long-term victims are likely to have low self-esteem and feel depressed because they are not coping. That feeling may impact on their friendships and in later life those children may have difficulty trusting others.

'What is clear in our interviews

our job to help each child break free and find healthier ways to behave. We should aim to:

- **Liberate our children from their roles as 'victim' or 'aggressor',** not compound them by labelling them as the 'bully' or the 'bullied' (see Kids don't fit in pigeonholes, page 159).

Compare:

'Stop bullying your sister.'
And
'You know how to ask properly and how to be kind. So let's see it.'

'If unwittingly we start to label a child in the family as a victim or a bully, they will start to live up to those labels. I don't want to be PC about this. We shouldn't be frightened of engaging in conversation with children in case we say the wrong thing. But it does help for us to be aware of the problems labels can cause.' – Andrew Mellor, Anti-Bullying Network

with people who were victims for long periods is this lack of trust in relationships, because they felt let down by children who bullied them and by children and adults who didn't help. And they sometimes partly blame themselves because they didn't do anything effective to stop it happening.

'Children who bully over time also tend to carry that forward into adult life, and it has been shown to be a risk factor in later violence inside and outside the home. The research done on bullying children suggests that quite often they have experienced bullying or violence in the home – between parents, parent to child or between siblings – which hasn't been recognised and dealt with. Any of these patterns might be something that leads a child to think, "This is how you get on in the world. You've just got to be tough, violent and if you are bigger, take advantage of it."'

'Parents should remember, especially if they are dealing with a bullied child, that their relationship with that child can be a rock, to which a child adrift in a sea of bullying clings. It is very, very important. And sometimes a rock gets battered.'
– Andrew Mellor, Anti-Bullying Network

- **Make it clear to any child acting aggressively that we love them but will not accept such behaviour**.
- **Be direct** if children seem unwilling to address what's happening: 'I think your sister is pushing you around. When you're ready, let's talk', or 'I'm worried about the way you're treating your brother. You seem angry about something.' (See Message received? page 187). Even if they don't talk straight away, our children need to know we're ready to listen and help.

> *'The biggest ally of bullying is secrecy.'* – Christine Puckering, clinical psychologist and co-developer of the Mellow Parenting Programme

- **Talk about feelings**. This may help us intervene early without details of the precise course of events: 'You seem sad . . .'; 'You seem really angry right now . . .' (See Message received, page 187, and Exploring emotions, page 125.)
- **Give each child opportunities to form friendships** with children outside the family. This may help them break patterns of behaviour.
- **Ask what each child thinks may help**. What is the effect of their present behaviour? How do they think they might behave differently with each other? In bullying situations it's usually best to talk to each child individually and confidentially.

> *'If a child is stuck in a pattern of behaviour with a sibling, it may help to ask them what solutions they can come up with to help bring out better behaviour in their brother or sister. Without making them feel totally responsible for the situation, we can shift the emphasis towards finding a solution. It's almost looking at the issue from the other side and giving them a role that's very positive.'* – Dr Sarah Newton, specialist in children's psychological health

> *'We have to be careful not to expose the victim to the possibility of further ridicule or risk. If there's been an abusive situation and a gross inequality of power, I would be very wary of asking the children to talk in each other's presence. It may be that you need to act as the confessor and listen to all the points of view privately and individually, allowing*

them to express feelings, then focus on possible solutions. It is the
solutions that are important. And a solution rarely comes from
the simple imposition of punishment.'
– Andrew Mellor, Anti-Bullying Network

- **Help our children be assertive.** (See Assertive messages, page 208.) Advising a child to get their own back or hit back harder risks far more problems than it solves. The child may be hurt further or feel abandoned to fight their own battles. It also reinforces the idea that might is right. Yet talking about issues of self-defence, safety and standing up to siblings may help. This need not involve a physical response. Firmly stating 'No! You are not to hit me!' or finding an adult to intervene when they're scared are all positive steps and should be described as such.

'When is self-defence justified? This is a useful concept for youngsters to
consider. Self-defence is about using the minimum amount of force necessary
to defend yourself. If you use more force than you need, and start to punish
the other person, you have overstepped the line between aggression and
assertiveness. Children understand that this is unfair.'
– Andrew Mellor, Anti-Bullying Network

'For our children to feel okay about standing up for themselves we have to
be okay about them standing up to us. So we may need to address any need
we have for the child to be a pleaser, to be nice to everyone and say "Yes"
all the time. We need to accept that the child will sometimes say "No" to
us and we need to be comfortable with that.'
– Kitty Hagenbach, child psychotherapist

Tackling sibling conflict: key approaches

Look behind the scenes	Only when we've looked at the possible causes of conflict between our children can we judge what needs to be done to resolve it. What are the triggers? Is it how they behave towards each other? How we behave? Is it a symptom of other stresses in their lives?
Test the temperature	By evaluating the level of conflict, we can better assess how and when to intervene. Is the argument likely to cool down without our help? Getting heated? Hot? Or boiling with anger and aggression?
Act	Constructive intervention follows the same basic structure **Define the problem:** 'You both want the bike.' **Describe the feelings:** 'Sounds like you're both getting angry.' **Search for solutions:** 'How can you sort this out so you're both happy?' This should be adapted to suit the heat of the moment. Sometimes kids need to be separated before talking can start.

Talk	Once tempers have cooled, the real work starts. This is the time to encourage our children to think through what they did, the effects it had, and how they could behave differently next time. If a dispute is long-running or bitter, our children may need our help to explore issues and ensure the views and suggestions of each child in the family are heard.
Beware of bullying	Bullying between siblings can cause lifelong damage. We can help our children break free from destructive patterns and find happier, healthier ways to behave.

Key message:

Discipline is a tool to educate, not a weapon.

5

Exploring emotions:

understanding feelings in families

'My daughters are like bottles of pop. If they shake each other up, we can release the pressure by gently opening the lids, letting them get it all out. If we ignore the pressure, it can build up and explode at any time. And boy, can it explode!' – Fiona M.

'I think it can be very confusing for the child if they say, "I hate my brother", and you reply, "No you don't." The child is left questioning their own feelings or thinking "It must be bad of me to feel this, I shouldn't say it any more".' – Desa Markovic, family therapist

'This morning Helen accused us of loving her brother more than her because her fried egg popped and his didn't. She can read injustice into the way I pour an orange juice.' – Anna I.

The intensity of our children's feelings about each other can shock. They can be playing happily one minute and fighting the next; affection can transmute into full-throttle rage in a flash. Children may be close yet still treat each other with unbridled contempt. Most siblings really do hate each other sometimes.

Can you feel the force?

'The emotions our children arouse in each other are not things that come in a fairly predictable sequence, which you handle perfectly and which then go away. Life isn't like that. They are passionate, spasmodic and unpredictable, and the potential for them is always there.' – Sarah P.

'Siblings might hate each other or they might love each other, or they might be ambivalent as their feelings change from day to day or even from minute to minute. But very few are indifferent. Whether they're enemies or extremely close, most sibling pairs MATTER to each other. It is usually a very significant and intense relationship.'
– Dr Gavin Nobes, senior lecturer in
developmental psychology

Sibling relationships are as varied as the individuals who form them. Yet exploring common threads may help us understand why our children arouse such strong emotions and responses in each other. Once understood, we can help them appreciate and manage their feelings constructively. Most of the time.

The positive side of negative emotions

Strong negative emotions between brothers and sisters are often a sign of a powerful and intimate bond, as loving as it is maddening. Children who report jealousy and rivalry often also describe the bond with their brother or sister as warm, close and affectionate.

Negative emotions can be important in helping children recognise and assert their needs, and rivalries can be a powerful force in children's development of identity (see Kids don't fit in pigeonholes, page 159). They are also an unavoidable part of life. To grow into happy, healthy and resilient adults, children need to learn to handle anger, frustration and jealousy as well as experience love, joy and security.

'It is still a social taboo to be jealous. Yet if parents can acknowledge that such feelings are understandable, we will help children better understand their emotions. It is through that understanding that they will learn to moderate their emotions and behaviour.' – John Bristow, chartered psychologist and psychotherapist

Powerful and passionate

Siblings' intimate understanding of each other means the feelings each evokes can be powerful, passionate and often storm force. Even as adults, we may feel many things about our brothers or sisters, but true indifference is rare (see Growing pains, page 259). If we're getting on well, we feel good about that; if we are not getting on well, we can seethe in a manner disproportionate to the apparent provocation.

The lack of restraint between arguing siblings can be as shocking as their moments of closeness and mutual support are heart-melting, so it helps to remember that children often patch things up while their parents are still feeling battered and bruised by their battles.

It also helps to be alert to the positives in our children's relationships. These can be as profound and potent as the disputes but tend not to be as obvious or attention-grabbing. Our children may play together, talk to each other, comfort each other, support each other and spring to the other's defence if threatened, yet still not show their affection or appreciation of each other as openly as their anger or resentments. We can begin to counter this by showing more appreciation when they are getting on well, and acknowledging the importance of such times in family life.

Fast-changing feelings

Our children's emotions can be mercurial, switching from one to another with breathtaking speed. This does not mean their feelings are any less genuine, only that they can often recover or move between emotions very quickly.

'Children live much more in the present. An emotion at any moment can be totally overwhelming, huge, almost all there is. Then that moment may pass. A lot of the time we impose an adult frame – we would be shocked if adults were behaving in this way. But if you watch children, they can move through emotions very quickly. What can do the damage is when adults hook into a moment and make a big number out of it.'
– Kitty Hagenbach, child psychotherapist

How we respond to those feelings, help our children express them constructively and consider other people's feelings in their actions, will affect their ability to form healthy, happy relationships in childhood, adolescence and beyond.

Understanding children's feelings

'Mac had a blazing row with his sister and was hitting a tennis ball against the wall with such force that I asked him what was going on. He shouted back, one word with every hit, "I'm – imagining – the – ball – is – her – head".' – Rachel T.

'You've got to let the bad feelings out before there's room for the good ones.' – Andrew, nine

Our understandable urge is to clamp down on expressions of negative feelings towards brothers or sisters and tell our children they mustn't say or think such things. Yet suppressing emotions or denying their existence won't make feelings go away. Rather they can simmer and fester, ready to burst out another day with even greater force. Or they may become corrosive, eating away at a child's view of themselves and others, including their siblings.

The more we insist our children only express good feelings towards one another, the more powerful the bad ones may become. The more children believe certain emotions are unspeakable, the greater the risk of them bottling up their feelings, with potentially devastating effects on themselves and on their relationship.

We can teach our children to deal with their feelings more constructively. But to do this, we have to deal with them constructively, too. We can do this by:

- **Keeping perspective**. Kids fight, fall out, and say horrible things to each other. If we over-react by treating every misdemeanour as a capital offence, they may stop listening or lose faith in our ability to judge what's going on between them (see He started it! page 83).

- **Putting ourselves in our children's shoes**. This may help us understand our children's lives, feelings and actions a little better – and temper our responses accordingly. Can we imagine how it might feel to have built the brick tower of our dreams, only to have it trashed by a kid brother? How it might feel to be left out of games by an older sister? Frightened by a big brother? Or constantly goaded by a sibling who always screams for mum when challenged?

> *'Thinking about how the kids must be feeling, putting myself in their shoes, helped me manage my anger. It helped enormously, especially in stressful times.'* – Barbara Dale, counsellor

- **Staying calm.** If we are to help our children deal with their emotions and not be overwhelmed by them, we have to show they don't overwhelm us. This means not matching their behaviour, not shouting when they are shouting and not getting angry just because they are angry with each other.

  Of course this is much easier to say than to do, and there will be days when we're pushed beyond our limits, fly off the handle and behave in ways we wish we hadn't. We are human and fallible and our children need to learn to cope with fallible human beings. But the more we keep these times to a minimum, the more our children are likely to stay calm themselves and listen to what we have to say.

  Parents have suggested the following approaches, which have helped them when they were feeling overwhelmed or on the point of explosion:

1. **Walking away**. If the children are safe, leave the room and stay out until you feel calm enough to cope. Do something different – sit down with a magazine, do something for you. The loo seems a favourite place of sanctuary.
2. **Counting**. Simple but extremely effective. By the time we've got to 10, the peak of emotion may have passed. If it hasn't, carry on to 20!
3. **Breathing slowly**. Three deep, long, smooth breaths, inhaled and exhaled as slowly as you can manage easily. It soothes, and slows the heart rate.

'Our children need our love but they also need a sense that we can cope with all the storms of feeling that can fly between siblings. They need to know that we're there for them. That however bad it is, we'll get through and help them get through. At times of real difficulty in a family, people seem to say the most unforgivable things and yet they can be survived. Our children need to know we are on their side, and it is sometimes very difficult to be on two or more sides at the same time, but we can do this by being there and showing that we can manage and handle our children's feelings.'
– Desa Markovic, family therapist

- **Helping our children identify and express emotions and consider the feelings of others**. This doesn't mean we have to always agree with our children's feelings, rather that we recognise and respect that this is how they feel.

'It is very important to allow negative as well as positive feelings to be expressed, so our children can learn how to handle them. No child is going to feel happy all the time or comfortable all the time, and they have to learn how to cope with that.' – Kitty Hagenbach, child psychotherapist

Identifying feelings

'Giving them the language early on to express their emotions really helped, I think. My partner and I had talked about it all the way through the adoption process, and I was very keen that we gave them the language to express how they felt.' – Kate B

If children are to express how they feel about themselves, their brother, sister or life in general, they first need to know what those feelings are. Small children find it especially difficult to express emotions in words, so we can begin by doing this for them:

'You look sad. It's hard having to share mummy with another baby, isn't it?'
'Jo looks scared.'
'Looks like you both enjoyed that.'

Fantasy play allows children to explore their emotions and develop greater sensitivity to siblings' feelings[1] (see The importance of 'Let's

Children calling . . .

The following 'snapshots' of recent calls to ChildLine show the pain children experience if they believe their feelings about siblings are ignored or belittled by those they love.

- A twelve-year-old girl feels her mum loves her brother more than her: 'Mum hugs my brother but when I try to hug her, she says, "Don't crowd me".'
- A boy, twelve, tries to talk to mum about arguments at home but she has a headache. He told his sister and dad about his feelings but they called him a 'silly bastard'.
- A twelve-year-old girl feels her parents favour her sister, aged nine, over her. Her sister is 'allowed to get away with lies' and her parents say she had her turn when she was younger. Now she feels rejected by her parents and annoyed with her sister of whom she is jealous. 'I want my parents to listen to me like my grandparents do.'
- One girl said 'my wee sister does not give me peace. I have to play with her all the time. Mum does not understand.'
- A fourteen-year-old boy with a health problem is physically abused by his brothers. He's not allowed to play outside. 'I get angry and moody', and sometimes feels suicidal. His parents say he's cheeky and 'fakes' things.

Reproduced with the kind permission of ChildLine[2]

pretend', page 50). We can also help develop emotional awareness, concern and consideration in children of all ages by chatting about feelings in an everyday, light and relaxed way – how we are feeling; how a friend might be feeling; why the man on the television is angry; why the woman down the street looks happy; why the cat is frightened.[3]

Stories, paintings, videos, films and newspapers can provide endless opportunities to discuss emotions, issues, situations and choices without any heavy-handed or pointed reference to particular family members.

Fiction, drama, reading and mixing with other families enables our children to be exposed to a whole set of different ways to be brothers and sisters. As a parent certainly I found stories to be brilliantly helpful in exploring feelings. It helped give a light touch to something I might otherwise have done in a

rather heavy-handed and probably hopeless way.' – Mary MacLeod, chief
executive, National Family and Parenting Institute

*'There is quite a lot of evidence that if children grow up in families where
feelings are talked about and accepted in a real life sense, even very little ones
begin to get a grasp of how feelings affect the way people act. I'm cautious
about turning that into a simple rule of thumb because so many things feed
into what makes a child aggressive towards siblings, not simply that they
don't understand what is going to hurt the brother or sister. They may understand that perfectly well and that may bring extra pleasure in putting the
boot in. But in broad terms, understanding of feelings does help foster
consideration.'* – Professor Judy Dunn, developmental psychologist

Acknowledging Feelings

*'When one sibling says something rude, unkind or uncaring about another, we
tend to clamp down on the comment. Then the child comes up with something
else to show how he feels, we jump on it again and around it goes. I think we
need to do the opposite; we need to spend time with them so they eventually feel
able to express themselves in a less negative way. Rather than criticise and
repress the child, giving them time and space to express how they feel is healthier
and more effective.'* – Kitty Hagenbach, child psychotherapist

Acknowledging a child's emotions is the surest way of letting them
know we've 'got the message'. They then have less need to 'act out'
their feelings in their behaviour.

'It is hard when you're left out, isn't it?'
'You look worried.'
'It can be frightening when brothers and sisters fight.'

This often works like magic – the child feels understood, calms down
and begins to work through their feelings and problems.

*'My sixteen-year-old last night was trying to decide between going to one
college and another, less suited to her but where her friend will be going. She
began to get in a mood, stomping around. I said to her, "Your head and your
heart are pulling in opposite directions, aren't they?" And that was all that
needed to be said. Her mood improved dramatically. We can't work every-*

thing out for our kids and shouldn't try, but we can often acknowledge how it feels.' – Mary MacLeod, National Family and Parenting Institute

I know you're feeling miserable

We can't solve all our children's problems, nor should we. We can often support them best by showing we understand how they are feeling, then letting them work out new ways forward for themselves. This can encourage self-reflection and bring much wider benefits to their relationships in the long-term.

Child psychotherapist Kitty Hagenbach remembers such a situation with one of her own children. He was having problems with friends, but the same approach may be beneficial when trouble erupts between siblings, she says.

'I had an experience recently with one of my children who had difficulty with a peer group. He felt he'd been dropped and was having a very difficult time. Everything about me wanted to rush out to the other mothers and make it all right and yet I completely knew that it wouldn't be the best thing for him. So instead I supported him by showing that I understood he was miserable, that it was tough and that life is tough sometimes. Then he worked the problem through for himself, so what

appeared to be a very negative situation actually came out very positively. He realised that he had to make some changes to his behaviour that other children found difficult, thinking he had to entertain all the time, be in charge. He needed to moderate that, and he did. He's ten. He wasn't the same child after that because he found ways to act in a more mature way with his friends. It resulted in him being accepted back into the group, and at the age of ten the group is very important to children.

'A child is constantly changing and adjusting and we need to support them in that. We need to assess what they can manage on their own and to listen to them. They will tell us if they need our help. We also need to check whether we want to intervene for our own benefit – perhaps because we don't want to see the child struggling. In my case, it would have robbed my son of a chance to mature and to strengthen. He needed me to acknowledge how hard it was for him, then allow him to learn from his experiences.'

If an incident is serious or feelings go very deep, children may need our repeated reassurance and understanding before they can get a handle on their emotions. By calmly 'reflecting' or echoing back their feelings, we can let them know these have been recognised and also leave avenues open for further discussion (see Reflective listening, page 198).

> Child: 'I hate Jack. I wish he was dead!'
> Parent: 'I can see you're furious that he won't let you play.'

> Child: 'It's not fair! She's a witch!'
> Parent: 'You're really upset. Can you tell me why?'

Letting our children know we've had similar experiences may help them feel less fearful, angry or isolated and provide living proof that these problems can be overcome:

> 'I remember being really scared when my sister wrestled because she was so strong. When I told her how scared I was, she didn't do it so much.'
> 'Uncle David was left out of the football team when dad was picked. He says it was really upsetting. He felt a bit better when he found other sports he enjoyed.'

Negative emotions are often the most difficult to express, yet some children also need help to acknowledge and express positive feelings towards their brothers and sisters:

> 'Doesn't it feel fantastic when we can make each other laugh?'
> 'That was such a caring thing to do, and it made you both happy.'

This can help battling siblings develop a more balanced view of their relationship and its potential.

If we are not clear how a child is feeling, we can guess. Non-judgemental suggestions sound supportive and also give children the chance to correct us if we get it wrong:

> 'Looks like you are really irritating each other.'
> 'You seem happy.'
> 'Sounds like she's made you really angry.'

Offering a multiple choice can also help children identify their feelings and concerns:

What won't help

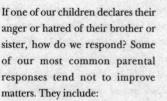

If one of our children declares their anger or hatred of their brother or sister, how do we respond? Some of our most common parental responses tend not to improve matters. They include:

- **'That's not nice':** It's not meant to be. A child confronted with such apparent lack of parental awareness may either clam up or find another way of making sure we get the message.

- **'That's not true':** A child told repeatedly to deny their feelings may eventually stop telling us how they feel or why. This can be the start of a serious and long-term communication breakdown.

- **'Don't be horrible/silly' etc:** This doesn't address the problem or the solution. Even well-intentioned ribbing – 'Oh, don't be daft, you're okay' – may be frustrating or devastating to a child trying to express a very real concern or emotion. If used regularly, labels such as 'silly', 'horrible', 'naughty', 'unkind', etc., can stick and colour a child's view of themselves and their 'role' in the sibling relationship (see Kids don't fit in pigeonholes, page 159).

- **'I know you love her really':** It may well be true, but it doesn't mean the negative emotion isn't genuine. This may also prompt a stormy denial, which won't do much for sibling harmony.

- **'How dare you say that!'** For safety's sake, and to build a rich and honest relationship, our kids need to know they can tell us anything, even things we'd rather not hear (see Message received? page 187). Getting angry may stop their expression of anger/ hatred/fear, etc., but it won't stop the feeling.

- **'Okay, no pocket money':** Punishing children for their 'bad' feelings may make them feel bad about themselves and encourage repression of emotions, a volatile and potentially damaging mix.

- **'She'd never say that to you':** That may be right. But it may also be wrong. We're not witness to all that goes on in our children's relationships and putting one child on the moral highground is a dangerous tactic. Snap judgements and declared favouritism are among the quickest and surest ways to fuel sibling conflict (see Who? Little me? page 98, and Facing up to favouritism, page 147).

'I can see you're fed up but I'm not sure if it's because you've had a bad day at school, you're tired or something else is bothering you.'

'If kids aren't forthcoming about how they feel, why not just hunch it? If you get it wrong they'll most likely tell you: "I guess that must be very upsetting" or "I expect you're pleased about that. Am I right?" "What do you think?" We can offer views tentatively and allow ourselves to be corrected. If you can do that with your child, the chances are that you can live with perspectives and possibilities instead of absolute truths and certainties. That's a big thing as a parent. That's not to say there's never a need to be firm and direct. That's a vital skill for parents. But so is knowing when to use a light touch.'
– Jim Wilson, systemic psychotherapist

Expressing feelings

Feelings don't disappear if dismissed or ignored. Yet our children need to know they don't have free rein to show how they feel in whichever way they choose and that normal family rules apply:

'I know you're really angry, and you know hitting's not allowed in this house. How else could you let him know how you feel?'

'I can see you're fed up with waiting and you know it's not okay to snatch things. How else could you get what you want?' (See Caring and sharing, page 43 and He started it!, page 83)

We can suggest different ways of venting emotions if our children seem stuck for ideas. They may like drawing pictures, they may prefer to use words or they may need to get physical – running, jumping, thumping the bed; some children attempt rational discussion, some specialise in Neanderthal-style grunts. Most need to do all of these things sometimes.

Ignore any advice that your children 'should' use any particular means to express themselves. What matters most is that they do it somehow, that they are encouraged to use constructive means which don't hurt the feelings or bodies of brothers, sisters or anyone else, and that each child does it their way.

'I tried to follow advice we were given at the adoption agency about giving children ways to express their anger – giving them a pillow to punch and things like that – but it didn't work. What does is to open the back door and let them jump on the trampoline. I don't even say anything now, I just open the door. We can talk once they've had a good bounce and calmed down.' – Kate B.

'I have two boys, one who's very fiery and the other who holds it all in. The fiery one sometimes needs to make a hell of a mess and be destructive. He has a real need to get this energy out and will tear up newspapers and the like. We leave it for a couple of hours to calm down, then he and I clear it up, maybe chatting as we're doing it. My other son tends to get sulkier. Then I need to find time to be with him, not to talk about it directly but just help him to gradually open up. Drawing can be a very good way, too. You can get lots of feeling into a picture. I was once presented with a picture of a broken black heart. It was devastating to receive because it was a very powerful message about how angry and sad one of the children was. But it was important that he did it. It really alerted me, I thought, "My God, I've got to pay attention to this."' Kitty Hagenbach, child psychotherapist

Explaining feelings

Brothers and sisters can behave in troublesome or disturbing ways, and we can help foster greater family understanding if we explain why this may be. This doesn't mean making children feel responsible for their siblings' well-being – children expected to act as little parents may grow to be adults who prioritise others' needs but fail to respond to their own. But a gentle, sympathetic explanation about a sibling's struggles can help children respond with more understanding:

'Bill's fallen out with his friend at school so is feeling a bit low and touchy. Today's not a good day for winding him up, okay?'

'Gemma's had a rotten day and needs a bit of peace and quiet. We all feel like that sometimes, don't we?'

It's surprising how helpful it can be to simply point out the causes and consequences of our children's actions. These may seem obvious to us but can be harder for kids to grasp. Talking and thinking about

♟♟♟ *Feelings in bereavement* ♟♟♟ *and other times of emotional turmoil*

'My sister's death is still with me, more than 25 years on, perhaps because it seemed so against what I thought was the natural order of things, perhaps because it had such an impact on my parents and my family, which now has a quiet grief at its core. Did anyone listen to how I felt? Not after the funeral, I don't think so. There's this presumption that kids just bounce back, isn't there?' – Mark T.

Siblings may respond very differently in times of family crisis. Recognising how each child feels is crucial if we are to support them as unique individuals.

Pat Elliot, a psychotherapist specialising in bereavement and parenting, works with many adults who, as children, experienced the death of someone close. Their stories have lessons for any of us wishing to help our children cope through hard times.

'We need to allow and understand differences in our children's emotional responses,' she explains. 'One child may be very angry and another very sad, and they each need to be allowed to move through their grief in their own way and at their own pace. We all have wounds in our growing up. Healing them involves someone significant in our lives seeing and recognising them. Once that happens, we can begin to move on.'

Children often feel guilty, confused or 'bad' about their strong feelings, or unwilling to burden a parent with their thoughts about a crisis that affects the whole family, she explains. This can have repercussions for the rest of their lives. 'If, as is often the case, there is little communication between adults and the children, grief becomes a very lonely place. This can persist into adulthood, so the child becomes an adult still unable to discuss these feelings with family members or others.'

Pat ran a group in schools for children who felt they wanted to talk because they'd lost someone close. 'Several children wanted to grieve grandparents, yet the parents hadn't even been aware their child was affected by the death in any way.

Children often move in and out of grief and most other emotions very quickly, looking sad one minute and playing happily the next. This does not mean the child's grief is any less real or in any less need of acknowledgement and support.'

Explaining to our children how emotional turmoil may cause dramatic changes in behaviour may help put any escalation of sibling conflict into perspective. Discussing the different ways people may express their feelings can also encourage greater tolerance of brothers and sisters behaving 'inappropriately' in a family crisis.

'With a young child, it helps to go back to concrete examples, such as, "You like sausages and he likes fish and chips and that's how we are, nothing good or bad in either way, just different,"' Pat Elliot suggests.

'When they are bereaved, people of any age often feel they're going mad, because their behaviour changes and their feelings are so intense. Reassuring children that this is temporary and that many people feel this way can help them feel less isolated and less fearful: "Sally's died and we all feel odd and different. You're being very different now, so's your sister and so am I, and we can find ways to help each other through."

'You can also say, "I understand how hard this is and it's still important to behave properly at school" or whatever, so you offer them understanding and some sort of boundary to their behaviour. It's not a matter of just letting it all hang out, but of helping a child deal with their feelings in a way that's most helpful to them.

'Physical activity can help a child express some of their turmoil. They also need our physicality, our cuddles and our holding, and our understanding of their need to sometimes regress, to be more babyish if that's how they find it easiest to express their emotional needs.'

If a child dies and is idolised by the parents, remaining children in the family may compare themselves unfavourably. This can burden them for life. 'Even if the dead child is newborn or stillborn, you can still explain to the surviving sibling that their brother or sister would have grown up to be a normal child, with temper tantrums and trying moments, so the child left behind doesn't feel burdened by the image of this lost, perfect baby,' says Dr Elizabeth Bryan, paediatrician and founder of the Multiple Births Foundation.

Pat Elliot agrees: 'I was talking to

a little girl, six years old, who exclaimed, "But Peter was naughty, too! I remember!" I have another client, an adult, who's been compared negatively with her sibling who died, and at other times told, "You're just like her". So she had no sense of having ever been seen for herself. This need for recognition as a unique individual is a big issue for parents to be aware of.'

Brothers and sisters will not always be willing or able to support each other. 'If they are already close and affectionate, a critical incident often brings them even closer together, but if the relationship is rivalrous and hostile it may exacerbate the conflict,' explains developmental psychologist Professor Judy Dunn.

To help them cope through tough times, children and adults are often best supported by someone who will listen, answer questions honestly and accept their feelings. This may be someone outside the immediate family, who has perhaps had similar experiences.

them encourages greater emotional awareness and more constructive behaviour.

'She's not going to listen now because you shouted at her. Wait until you can speak calmly, then people will take more notice of what you have to say.'

'You knew your sister was feeling sad, and you played quietly so she had a chance to tell me all about it. That was so kind.'

'We can enhance any good qualities and skills our children may have to help each other by making opportunities for them and praising a child for helping and caring. Even a child of four can put their arms around a child who feels miserable and feel heroic for doing it. You can say, "Look, you stopped him crying, you are able to do this. Aren't you wonderful?" The child can sense that they are needed, valued and they are effective, which makes them more likely to try it some other time.'
— Adrienne Katz, executive director of the youth charity, Young Voice

'Children who have lost a sibling can feel as if there's an angel child they have to live up to. That's a big burden. They may keep trying to achieve and achieve and achieve in order somehow to match the status of the child no longer there.' – Corinne Abisgold, educational psychologist

'When a loved one dies, anger is sometimes directed towards the dead person – "Why did they leave me?" If the person or child who has died is seen as an unacceptable object of anger, children direct their anger elsewhere, perhaps towards friends or a teacher at school, or towards each other. A bereaved child may show behaviour changes, loss of concentration, daydreaming, tearfulness, fearfulness of who else they may lose in their world. It is important that teachers and other adults they may come in contact with are made aware of their situation, or they may misinterpret the signs.' – Audrey Sandbank, family psychotherapist

'But I just don't like him'

'It is absolutely normal, understandable and to be respected if you don't happen to like your brother or sister. Certainly anything parents or others do to push it in these circumstances runs the risk of further alienating them.' – Dr Elizabeth Bryan, paediatrician

'At the end of the day, if our children are really not getting along, it's sometimes best to accept it. If, because of their different personalities or interests, it's just not going to happen maybe it's better to let them go their different ways, go to a friend's house while the other has a friend home, that sort of thing, so they have more time apart and less time together, which could make things worse. They may have a more compatible age and stage later.' – Eileen Hayes, writer and parenting adviser to the NSPCC

Even if one of our children feels close or affectionate towards a brother or sister, there is no guarantee their feelings will be recipro-cated. Most siblings go through times when one seems particularly indifferent or hostile, and learning to cope with that is an important lesson in life that most children seem to manage.

Yet problems can arise if the emotional 'mismatch' becomes embedded and lasts (see Growing Pains, page 259). We can't force affinity, but we can try to reduce the impact of rejection by encouraging friendships outside the family and looking for other ways to boost each child's confidence and self-esteem (see Feeling good, page 144).

You may want me, but your brother needs me right now

'Hopefully, your children see that you are there when they need you, and that when their brother falls over and scrapes his knee you are there for him. Sometimes you have to put the demands of one child before another, one child wants a story and another needs help with homework. You have to decide who needs your support most at that time.' – Sarah Darton, health visitor

We can't be everywhere and do everything at once, so sometimes we have to assess our children's emotional needs and focus on the child who needs us most urgently. If each of our children knows we understand and respect their feelings and will listen and support them when we can, they will more readily accept times when a sibling has to take priority:

'I know it's hard to wait, but your sister's worried about her homework and I want to give her some help.'

'Sam's really sad and I need to find out why. As soon as I've done that, we can read your book.'

Occasionally prioritising our own emotional needs (remember them?) will help our children appreciate that other people's feelings matter, too:

'I'm too upset/tired to concentrate right now. Give me a few minutes, then I'll help.'
'I've had a horrible day, and I'm feeling too grumpy to deal well with arguments. I

Asking the indifferent child to feign affection will most likely rebound. Even in the unlikely event that the child agrees, their siblings will spot the insincerity. Yet we can attempt to maintain family communication (see Message received? page 187) and ask them to ensure their feelings don't spill into thoughtlessness or intentionally hurtful behaviour. Asking them to imagine how their brother or sister must feel may help.

need you two to sort this out. I know you can do it.'

Understanding the difference between needs and wants, and discussing this within the family, can help us all negotiate the minefield of children's often competing demands:

'I know you want me to help but Jack really needs me right now. He's hurt his knee. I'll be with you as soon as I can.'

'I know you want to go to the park, but Jess really needs a sleep. If we go later, we'll have a better time.'

A child having the abdabs over the contents of his lunchbox may be less in need of urgent attention than the child sitting in a corner, undemanding, quiet and withdrawn. Our role as parents is to attend to the child with the greatest *need* at that moment, not the child with the most obvious *want* or loudest protest, and to ensure that, over time, all our children receive the one-to-one attention they require to flourish. A child may *want* to stay up until his older brother or sister goes to bed, but what he *needs* is a good night's rest. A child with obvious problems or disadvantages may actually be in less urgent need of our concerned attention than their 'well' sibling who has coped without it for too long (see Illness, disability and special needs, page 217).

'When one child is struggling, they will need more support and the other children will need to be made aware of that: "I still love you, but right now so and so's having a lot of trouble and needs my time and attention." That's life. If we provide too perfect an environment for our children they won't grow strong and learn to cope. In that sense, they need to learn that other people have needs that sometimes have to come first.' – Kitty Hagenbach, child psychotherapist

Sibling relationships, like any others, shift and change as children move through different ages and stages and anything we can do to maintain links, however tenuous, may make it easier for our children to pick up the threads again later.

'We know that around ten-to-twelve-years-old there is a lessening of the negative and positive extremes of sibling relationships, so there tend to be fewer fights and less intense pleasure in the company of the sibling, so my guess is the intensity of any mismatch will decrease then, too.'
– Professor Judy Dunn, developmental psychologist

'It can feel like being in a nightmare, but I think you have to tackle it honestly and straightforwardly: "Your brother is different and wants to do different things, and you need to respect that even if you don't like it." Even if one child feels the other is a nerd, say, they have to respect they are part of the family and you could expect them to be kind and caring and to put themselves in the other one's shoes – "How would you feel if it were you? How can we help him?" – without forcing them together.'
– Cheryl Walters, psychotherapist and
Head of Research at Parentline Plus,

Feeling good

'Something that is becoming clearer, the more time I have with my boys and the more people I talk to, is that one of the strongest things you can do to support the relationship between siblings is to support your relationship with each individual child. If each child feels of value and acknowledged then they are going to be in a better position to act constructively and positively with their brother or sister.' – Kate B.

'Home is where we can give children the armour of self-esteem that will equip them to cope with life.' – Robert Fisher,
Professor of Education at Brunel University

If we want our children to feel more positive about their siblings we must also help them feel more positive about themselves. Boosting each child's self-esteem will help them develop the security and

Self-esteem and success

'It is very important that parents are conscious of their children's concept of self. We know from research that self-esteem at the age of ten is probably the most powerful predictor of success in learning and life.' – Professor Robert Fisher, Brunel University

Confidence and high self-esteem help children have more positive relationships with brothers, sisters and others throughout life. A sense of self-worth has also been linked to lower levels of antisocial behaviour, lower teenage pregnancy rates and lower levels of alcohol and illegal drugs misuse. One recent study suggests it can even boost earning potential.[4] 'There is now clear evidence that children with higher self-esteem aged ten get as much of a kick to their adult earning power as those with equivalently higher maths or reading ability,' says Dr Leon Feinstein, research director at the Wider Benefits of Learning Research Centre.

'Most important seems to be the nature of the relationship between the parents and children. The effect of parental hostility on self-esteem and anti-social behaviour was overwhelming, much more important than even the absence of a parent, the nature of the school or the parents' social class. The most likely explanation is that the quality of the relationships formed by parents and children helps them develop the psychological attributes with which they can achieve success.'

To boost our children's potential in all aspects of life, self-esteem needs to be developed alongside an awareness of other people's feelings and needs. This crucial combination should be the aim of any parent wanting to nurture positive relationships between their children. Professor Robert Fisher of Brunel University explains: 'What we are after is self-efficacy, the combination of self-esteem and understanding. Children need to develop a sense of their own worth, but it is also important to help them become sensitive to and understand other people, because it is other people who are going to be the source of success and happiness in their lives.'

confidence to deal with their emotions and manage their behaviour, to consider other people's needs, grow in independence and resilience, accept life's challenges and cope better with its knocks and disappointments (see Self-esteem and success, page 146).

This is not something we can 'bolt on' to our relationship with our children with the help of any one technique or strategy, almost as an added extra. Self-esteem is something that develops over time, through a child's experiences of feeling valued. It is not only nurtured by a child's family relationship; family and social circumstances, temperament and life experiences also play their part. Yet we can boost our children's sense of their unique and individual worth by:

- **Loving them unconditionally**, for being themselves.
- **Not comparing them** with brothers or sisters or encouraging competition between them (see Kids don't fit in pigeonholes, page 159).
- **Showing interest** in their home life, school life, friendships, passions and pastimes.
- **Recognising their individual qualities, strengths and achievements** (see Letting each child shine, page 175).
- **Taking care not to burden them** with responsibilities or challenges they are not yet ready to handle (see Children as childminders, page 282).
- **Recognising and respecting their feelings and opinions** (see Message received?, page 187).
- **Praising behaviour we like** (see Acknowledge the good times, page 70).
- **Making it clear that we love the child**, even when we don't like their behaviour (see He started it! page 83).
- **Spending time** with each child, one-to-one.

Exploring our feelings as parents

'At any one time, I may find one of my kids really easy to get along with while things feel more strained with the other. And they notice it, my God they notice it! Then it changes, and I may feel closer to the other. These rhythms are a part of family life.' – Sarah Darton, health visitor

'Sometimes we don't like our children, and then we have to be honest with ourselves: "Why do I prefer this child? Is it their behaviour or do I find their temperament difficult?" That will help us see more clearly how to make a real connection, a greater closeness, with them. It also helps to be honest with the child. We have to be careful not to say, "I don't like you when you are like that", but we can say, "I don't like it when you behave like that" and "If you were to express your needs and feelings differently I'd find it easier to listen".' – John Bristow, chartered psychologist and psychotherapist

Many of us will sometimes feel a closer bond with one of our children. This uncomfortable fact is rarely admitted but is so common as to be almost inevitable. It needn't cause any long-term damage if handled sensitively, with care taken to help each child in the family feel noticed, loved and valued.

We respond differently to our children because they are different people at different points in their and our development. And it is essential we recognise our children's differences because only then can we be sensitive to their individual needs (see Kids don't fit in pigeonholes, page 159). The danger lies when this translates into clear, entrenched and long-term preferential treatment.

'Clearly children are treated differently, and I think all of us who are parents are aware of that. We try to treat our children equitably, but they are different individuals, and it would be ludicrous to suppose that we respond to each of them in identical ways. We don't and we can't.'
– Professor Michael Rutter, child psychiatrist

Facing up to favouritism

'Without question, differential parent-child relationships are associated with adjustment problems in children from an early age. Children are extremely sensitive to how their parents treat them and their siblings.' – Professor Judy Dunn, developmental psychologist

'The difficulties come and the rivalry begins when one child feels more loved or accepted or more "right". As soon as a child feels the other child or other children in a family are favoured then they begin to act out ways of getting

attention or, even worse, to withdraw and go into themselves.'
– Kitty Hagenbach, child psychotherapist

'In many cases just being conscious of these issues can be very helpful. Being aware at least gives you an option to attempt to deal with situations.'
– Christine Puckering, clinical psychologist and co-developer
of the Mellow Parenting Programme

Favouritism happens, and the affinity we feel with a particular child may be rooted in many things – their gender, birth order, health, temperament, even looks. Particular problems faced by one child may make us more attentive to their needs for a time. We may feel more drawn to children of a particular age or stage, and any one of our children may be a better or worse 'fit' with the rest of the family. A book-loving child, for example, is likely to prompt a very different response in a family whose members read little than in a family where reading is a common pursuit held in high regard. We may simply feel closer to or even like one child more than our others for a time.

If we aim to be responsive and loving towards all our children when we can, temporary imbalances tend to even up and our children are generally able to cope (see You may want me, but your brother needs me right now, page 142). What hurts, and what can shatter sibling bonds, is when children interpret differences in our behaviour as an indication that they are less loved than their brothers or sisters.

Recent research makes clear what in our heart of hearts we already knew – that an obvious and long-term imbalance in which one child receives less attention, affection and more punishment than any other in the family will make that child feel less loved or favoured.[5] They may then display their distress and resentment in withdrawn, destructive or aggressive behaviour. This can fuel extreme hostility and conflict between siblings, and their relationship may never recover. So what can we do?

'Favouritism? I think it is common and almost inevitable. One child will resonate more than another for various reasons. I can't really see how that can be avoided. What we can guard against is this being too unfair for the other children.' – Peter Wilson, director, Young Minds.

'The quality of the sibling relationship is determined by no single factor. Rather, the fit between individual children's temperaments and the characteristics of the larger family context will influence their relationships with others in the family. The matches or mismatches that are created by the meshing of particular child characteristics with particular parent and family characteristics are significant.'
– Gene. H. Brody, Professor of Child and Family Development[6]

- **Be honest with ourselves**

'Most parents, if they are honest, have some favourite aspects of a child's character and it's hard not to show that. But we have to work at it. It's awful if a chid just KNOWS you prefer another. That's when we need to search out the positive qualities in each.' – Eileen Hayes, writer and parenting adviser to the NSPCC

'My dad didn't like my brother. Loved him, but didn't like him. Me and my dad did everything together. I ate, slept and breathed my dad. Weird.'
– Marc E.

Facing up to our feelings, and recognising how they may be influencing our different responses to our children, is an important first step towards correcting imbalances in our relationships before they become entrenched or one child seems to monopolise family favour.

'All parents need to be alert to the fact that often they will favour one child above another, maybe they're the baby, maybe they're the only girl or boy, maybe they just have a sunnier disposition or whatever. That's when we need to take a back-step, be fairly objective and say, "I haven't sat down and spoken to this child for too long." It's a very deliberate attempt to make sure we give attention as much as possible on a one-to-one basis to each child so we are not forever saying, "I've got no time because I've got to do this". Making time for each child is essential.'
– Dr Mandy Bryon, consultant clinical psychologist, Great Ormond Street Hospital for Children

Through a child's eyes

'A mother told me the other week how one of her children had turned round to her and said, "Why don't you look at me the way you look at my brother?" It was just the subtle look on the woman's face, that kind of glowing parental pride, and this child didn't feel he got that. Whether he did or didn't is another issue, but the child didn't feel he did and that's what hurt.' – Corinne Abisgold, educational psychologist

'Most experiences have no meaning other than our interpretation of them. Clearly, some experiences are damaging, whatever you think about them, but by and large the same situation may be very different according to how it is experienced by the child. So the realities of how they are treated is important, but so are the stories they tell as to what that means to them.'
– Professor Michael Rutter, child psychiatrist

How a child *perceives* their treatment within the family will shape their sense of self-worth, just as much as actual unfairness. This should alert us to the importance of children's feelings about preferential parental treatment, even if we don't share their views.

A recent Young Voice study into bullying in Britain found a marked difference in the percentage of children who said they had experi-

• **Watch and listen**

Most children at some time moan that 'it's not fair'. Often they mean 'I don't like this' or 'I don't want it this way'. But sometimes their grievances are legitimate and their protests may alert us to genuine imbalances.

We need to listen (see Message received? page 187), consider whether any negative behaviour may be fuelled by a genuine need for extra attention, and ask ourselves whether our children have good reason to complain. Does one child have a better deal? Even if one child is not loved more than another, is one child shown that love more clearly? Does one child genuinely *feel* less loved,

enced unfair or unequal treatment at home (65 per cent of bullied children vs 36 per cent of those not bullied).[7] 'The difference was very strong, very apparent,' comments Young Voice executive director, Adrienne Katz. 'The parent may believe they treat all children fairly, and other siblings may think they do, but it's the child's perception that counts, because that's what colours their view of the world, that's the lens through which they see things.

'We have to take into account their perception. And when we do we can take action, talking these issues through with them, demonstrating to them that they can shine in other arenas. Gender was also an issue in that many respondents in the study implied that family rules were different for boys than for girls. That's interesting, and I think as

parents we should take note.'

Child psychotherapist Kitty Hagenbach agrees with Katz's emphasis on the child's view of unfair treatment. 'This is a very real problem for parents. It is sometimes very hard to know why a child feels they are not treated as well as their siblings, but if they do, they do, and it's no good saying "No you don't" or "You shouldn't", "That's not how it was", or "I've always treated you the same and after all I've done for you this is how you repay me."

'The most positive thing we can do is just be aware of their feelings and keep working at affirming good behaviour, affirming their strengths and affirming our love. There are no easy answers, but I think that's the best way to go.'

and thus need more reassurance (see Through a child's eyes, page 150)?

'The best response to "It's not fair" is to listen, I think. It came up the other day. The nineteen-year-old was moaning about the sixteen-year-old, saying, "How many holidays is she having this year?" I listened to his perspective and how he felt about it, then I pointed out that she'd organised her trip abroad and that he could do the same. Then we explored how he could do it and he decided to set up a special savings account. By listening to how it felt for him, he was then able to move on and be constructive.'
– Barbara Dale, counsellor

- **Who do you remind me of?**

> *'In every nursery there are ghosts. They are the visitors from the unremembered past of the parents.'* – Selma Fraiberg et al, 'Ghosts In The Nursery'[8]

> *'Check out with yourself if and who your children remind you of. Clearly if a child looks and speaks like your father, you will be aware of it, but if your eldest goads your youngest as you were goaded by your brother, your response may be far stronger in defence of your younger child than is fair. Maybe you will be blind to the youngster's behaviour because of the similarities between you.'* – Carol Ann Hally, health visitor

Our children may display characteristics that remind us of others, and how we respond to that – with pleasure, irritation or apprehension – will depend on our feelings towards that person as well as our feelings for the real child.

If we are aware of treating or responding to one child very differently, it may be helpful to ask who they remind us of. Who do they look like? Sound like? Evoke memories of? If we had problematic relationships with our own siblings, does this affect how we respond to interactions between our own children? Are we presuming the same of them rather than allowing them freedom to develop their own, possibly more positive relationship?

Examining our responses and memories is crucial if we are to avoid reproducing echoes of our own childhood conflicts in our children.

> *'I think it is a common experience to re-live your own experiences of where you were in the family. I had one mother who said to me that she felt very guilty at being pregnant because of what she was doing to her firstborn. She was a first child and interpreted her child's experience as her own. It helps to explore these issues and to recognise that our children's experiences may be similar but they may also be very different. By making the separation between oneself and one's child, parents may begin to look at things more constructively.'* – Christine Bidmead, RGN RHV, Training Facilitator, Centre for Parent and Child Support

> *'Even as adults, when your relationship with your sibling has moved on, you may still be left with an almost ghostly trace of your childhood sibling*

relationship, and this can be triggered by your own children, for good or for bad. These triggers may be quite unconscious, but lead to powerful feelings that are irrational in the new context but understandable when their history is known.' – Christine Puckering, clinical psychologist and co-developer of the Mellow Parenting Programme

• Positive action

'I fell out of love with my daughter. She irritated me. I'd get snappy and jump down her throat over little things I'd probably ignore with the rest. I couldn't tell you why or how, but it happened, and I knew things could only get worse if I didn't sort it out. I tried to notice the good things she did and to rein in my temper. We'd go swimming once a week just on our own, too. That helped. And I do love her now. That's an important thing to say, that things don't get stuck and stay that way, that they can move on and get better.' – Fiona M.

'One practical thing we can do is to make sure we have time alone with each of our kids, especially the one who is feeling unloved. We can try to make it especially nice when we're together to try to shore up their shaky sense of security.' – Professor Judy Dunn, developmental psychologist

It may be that we find one child's way of responding to situations more difficult to handle. Perhaps they whinge or sulk, perhaps they shout, get stroppy or crumple in the face of adversity. Different responses will elicit different reactions in different parents. But if we find one child's style of response particularly hard, we are likely to react to it more negatively, which may prompt negative behaviour in the child – and the downward spiral begins.

Most of us will be aware of times when we have become 'stuck' in a negative cycle of action and reaction with one of our children. Recognising the pattern is the first step towards breaking the chain. If the child is old enough, talking about more effective ways to express their needs may help (see Message received? page 187). Far more importantly, changing the way we relate to the child may bring changes in the child's behaviour.

'The thing is to try to make opportunities to cement the relationship that you find hardest, to make opportunities to be with that child, doing things that

child likes without the presence of the other child in competition.'
– Christine Puckering, clinical psychologist and co-developer
of the Mellow Parenting Programme

Spending more one-to-one time with any child who feels less loved is the simplest and most effective way of helping them feel more valued. Special days and outings can help, but so can simple activities such as reading, playing or shopping together. What matters is that we have opportunities to be on our own together and rediscover pleasure in each other's company.

If each parent has stronger bonds with different children, try 'swapping' them over and spending special time with the child with whom you feel less connection. Putting ourselves in our children's shoes, imagining what it must feel like to be them, and recognising the basic needs that often lie behind trying behaviour can help. So can taking time to remember moments when they melted our hearts (see Seeing my lovable child, page 155).

What can we find to celebrate and enjoy in our less-favoured child? Do we notice and praise their special qualities, their moments of warmth, their efforts and accomplishments? (See Acknowledge the good times, page 70, and Letting each child shine, page 175) Do we recognise and respond to their individual needs?

Children don't need parental perfection. What they do need is our love, care, respect, understanding, and our ability to recognise when family bonds are becoming distant or troubled. Positive action and clear signs of parental regard and affection for each of our children can boost their resilience through tough family times, help us reconnect with them and help them reconnect with each other.

'It is vital that each pair in every family builds a separate relationship. A stepmother, for example, who has a visiting stepchild, can ensure she has ten minutes' time alone with that child every visit. Even if the child isn't receptive, you could, say, take a walk to the newsagents and ask what they did at school. You may not even get an answer, but what you are doing is building a relationship and demonstrating you are interested, demonstrating that the door is open and that if and when the child is ready, they can step in. I think that needs to happen with every coupling. Relationships don't just happen. You have to build them.' – Cheryl Walters, psychotherapist and Head of Research at Parentline Plus

Seeing my lovable child

'I found my first child very hard work,' says Sue W. 'I did lots of parenting with my head. Because I was a nursery nurse, I thought I must know what to do and I did get it "right" in terms of what I "did", he didn't have any major problems, but in my heart of hearts I knew my relationship with him wasn't as it should be. When I had my second, when he was two, I described it to a very close friend. I said I loved Issac but I was in love with Luke. With the little one it was a different feeling really from the minute he was born, and I felt this intense bond.

'I didn't really make a shift in my relationship with my first until he was getting on for six. I found it very difficult not to get at him for getting at his little brother, who was very easy, incredibly affectionate, and had lots of hearing problems so I felt very protective. I knew that something should be different, so I went on a parenting course.

'That helped me let go. I used to feel if I gave him an inch he'd take a mile, that if I let up for a minute in terms of keeping control of the day, you know, "Get your clothes on now; I said now!" – that the world would fall apart. The course encouraged me to let go of that and have more faith that things would turn out okay, to set limits but to be less rigid.

'The other thing I remember vividly was doing a visualisation exercise, imagining your child lying in bed. First you imagine your child with the label "naughty" and think about how you feel. Finally, you imagine that child as "lovable". It sounds ridiculous but I suddenly thought, well of course he is, completely lovable. It sounds so simple but at the time it pulled me up and I thought he's just a little boy and he is lovable. It was a turning point. Now I really feel I love them both desperately.'

Exploring emotions:
key approaches

Understand feelings between brothers and sisters	They can be intense, volatile, unpredictable, fast-changing and, sometimes, shocking: 'I hate her!' They are a result of the closeness of the brother-sister bond. Negative emotions are *not* a sure sign of a problematic relationship.
Acknowledge how our children feel	Acknowledging children's feelings is the surest way of letting them know we've got the message: '*You seem a bit sad. Are you feeling left out?*' They are then less likely to 'act out' their feelings in their behaviour towards each other. Identifying and acknowledging each child's feelings in any situation helps them feel respected and understood as an individual.
Encourage constructive expression	Feelings don't disappear if dismissed or ignored. Yet our children need to know they haven't free rein to show how they feel in whichever way they choose. Normal family rules apply.
Help each child feel good	Children who feel better about themselves generally behave better towards brothers and sisters.
Explore our feelings as parents	We will have different bonds with our different children. We should take care this does not translate into overt

and long-term preferential treatment.
A child who feels less loved or
favoured will resent their siblings,
possibly for life.

Key message:

Feelings about siblings shape relationships for life. We need
to handle them with care.

6

Kids don't fit in pigeonholes:

identity and individuality

'Children are different and grow up differently and we have to recognise each one for who they are. This is not always easy because we all have our own aspirations and our own preferences and histories. It is a tough job being a parent, to be impartial and to approach our children with fairness.'
– Peter Wilson, director of Young Minds

'My children are all so, so different. How they turned out to have such different personalities and interests never ceases to amaze me.'
– Charlotte G.

'My mother pigeonholed us constantly. As the youngest of four, there weren't too many holes left by the time I came along. I had to squeeze in where I could.' – Karen T.

If we put our children in pigeonholes, we may blind ourselves to their true natures and needs and fuel resentment between them. Our desire to be fair may translate into attempts to treat all of our children 'the same'. On the other hand, comparing them to each other or assigning them 'roles' within the family – the 'naughty' one, 'cheeky' one, 'sporty' one, 'funny' one, 'responsible' one – also stops us seeing each child's true worth, needs and potential.

Both can have a devastating effect on a child's view of themselves and of their brothers and sisters, from early childhood to adulthood. And both can be avoided if we are alert to the issues and recognise each child as an individual, unique and distinct from their siblings, and free from stereotypes.

Separate and special, not 'the same'

'We were a "musical family" so I had to learn the piano like my sisters and brother. I was never much good, but that's what my parents expected us all to do. I'm sure they thought it best to offer us all the same opportunities, but I hated it.' – Angela B.

'You can't love them equally, you have to love them uniquely, and it's much easier to say it than it is to live it.' – Sarah Darton, health visitor

We want to be fair, we don't want to show preference, we want to short-circuit the potential for rivalry, so we may attempt to treat our children equally in all things – from the attention we give them each day to what we expect of them in life. Yet this won't help our children and it won't help family relations.

It may prompt children to feel they are not recognised or fully appreciated for who they are, and that we do not fully understand their particular problems or individual potential. This can spark great hostility towards brothers and sisters.

If, on the other hand, we generally respect and respond to each child's strengths and needs when we can, each child will feel more secure and valued. This security helps them feel less touchy or slighted when a brother or sister needs attention (see You may want me, but your brother needs me, page 142). If we celebrate each child's unique qualities, enthusiasms and abilities, each will feel valued in their own right. This will help temper jealousies and rivalries fuelled by a sibling's 'success'.

Being alert to each child's uniqueness also reduces the risk of us viewing our children as 'types', with set personalities and attributes (see The danger of labels, page 167). Children's needs and strengths are fluid and change as they grow. Our role is to recognise and respond to these changes, and through this to show each child they are loved and valued for being themselves.

'It's about having a unique relationship with each child, which hopefully is equal in its weight and importance, but different because each child's needs will be different. Everything isn't always fair, and it's healthy for children to understand that.'
– Sarah Darton, health visitor

Exaggerating differences

'Siblings in a family exaggerate their differences for the same reason that species in an ecosystem evolve into different forms: each niche supports a single occupant.' – Steven Pinker, How The Mind Works[1]

Children often use their siblings as a measure of who they are, who they are not and what they want to be. This may help strengthen a sense of shared family, cultural or racial identity (see My brothers and me, page 162); it may also heighten children's sense of individuality and difference within the family: if their brother is this, then they'll be that; if their sister has achieved at a certain level, their sense of their own achievement will be based partly on how they measure up against that.

Parents will notice how often children seem to divide up characteristics and attributes between them. This phenomenon, particularly noticeable between same-sex siblings and the first two siblings in a family,[2] can mean that one child is very sporty while another shuns physical pursuits, that an older child displays a flair for maths at school while the younger shows a distinct and purposeful disdain for the subject, that one child delights at rapid fire jokes while another develops a more understated, dry wit.

As siblings grow, the differences between them tend to increase. This is partly due to their different experiences of childhood (see Why are siblings so different? page 165). Yet they also tend to accentuate

🚶🚶🚶 *My brothers and me* 🚶🚶🚶

Newspaper columnist and writer, Gary Younge, grew up in the mainly white English town of Stevenage. Being the youngest of three brothers in a black family had a profound effect on his sense of identity and his understanding of prejudice.

'Growing up in an overwhelmingly white town, having brothers meant that your experience was only unique outside the house. In most other places you would be the only black person there.

'Without brothers I imagine it would have been difficult to make sense of people's prejudice, fears or support. With them, particularly as the youngest son, I knew that it was the world that was weird and not me.

'As youngsters, we were always expected to stick up for each other. If we were out playing and there was trouble then either we all stayed out and dealt with it or we'd all come in. As a single parent my mother had to rely on that. And as the mother of three young black boys she knew that we had to rely on that. I don't remember it ever being explicitly stated but it was always implicitly understood, that if we didn't back each other up then no one else would.'

their differences as each searches for their own unique identity and place in the world – their own 'ecological niche'. After all, there may be very good reasons for taking up the piano instead of the cricket bat if your brother is already a star turn on the pitch.

The urge to define and measure ourselves and our accomplishments by comparison with a sibling can last a lifetime. It is a natural and inevitable process of growing up with brothers and sisters, and does have positive consequences. By dividing up the turf, children may reduce the risk of turf wars; emphasising difference is one way of avoiding rivalrous clashes and painful comparisons.

Yet it can be damaging if allowed to go too far, obscuring children's views of their own potential pleasures and capabilities. Different does not mean opposite; not right now isn't the same as never; and one child's enthusiasm need not mean another's disenchantment (see Chalk and cheese, page 163).

Chalk and cheese

'My children started skiing at the same time, but my daughter decided to take a slightly different track and take up snowboarding rather than compete directly with her brother. I didn't feel it was a bad decision. In a way, she decided to develop her own areas of interest and skill and avoid direct rivalry and competition. For her, I think it was a positive process.' – Christine Puckering, clinical psychologist and co-developer of the Mellow Parenting Programme

Children's sense of their own identity is greatly influenced by how they view their siblings. This is a natural and often positive process, but can be damaging if a child begins to consider themselves 'less' than their brother or sister, confusing 'not the same' with 'not as good'.

Desa Markovic, a family therapist, explains: 'Emphasising difference is a way of establishing identity. Sometimes it may not feel safe to be similar or to have the same interests and ambitions as your siblings. Perhaps the idea of competing brings discomfort? Perhaps it would not feel safe to lose? Or to win?

'Some children have not learnt to trust that they would be appreciated for who they are and what they do, so they become "good" at stealing, lying or other socially undesirable things. Some children feel their siblings have all the good and there is nothing left for them.

Or they admire their siblings so much they believe they can never be their equal. This can lead them to do something totally unrelated to their sibling's interests, or to feel they can never do anything worthwhile.

'The process of finding difference is not necessarily problematic. Sometimes it works well and children, by trying to find something different and special, develop skills and abilities and feel able to make choices unique to themselves.

'Yet sometimes the idea of difference is taken to mean "either/or", for example, "If my brother is good at music, it means I can't be." It would help us all to consider difference in a more complex, constructive way, so our children can show interests in similar areas if they wish, thinking, "How can we both be good in the same area in our different ways?".'

Comparisons Hurt

'Parents can bite their lip and avoid direct comparisons: "Why can't you be more like X", "If X can manage, why can't you?" That's extremely important to a child's sometimes shaky sense of their own worth.'
– Professor Judy Dunn, developmental psychologist

'Sometimes parents, with best intentions, want to give their children a "push", or compare them with others by saying: "How come your brother/sister can do it and you can't?" However well-intentioned, this can be heard as a criticism and rejection; perhaps all children need to hear is: "I will love you anyway".'
– Desa Markovic, family therapist

We can compare our children with the very best of intentions, wanting to make each child feel special, encouraging each child to achieve more or attempting to boost a child feeling low – 'You are so much better at this than X'; 'X did it so I know you can, too.'

The damage this causes to sibling relationships can be lifelong. Comparisons can solidify over time into family 'labels' for each child (see The danger of labels, page 167), which can distort children's views of themselves, and their brothers and sisters. At best, comparisons make a child feel judged in relation to their sibling rather than in their own right, a sure-fire recipe for resentment and increased sibling competition.

Many parents who have reflected on times they were compared to someone close, even favourably, admit that it made them feel uncomfortable. The process can continue well into adulthood, with elderly parents making direct comparisons between grown-up children, often with the best of motives. The consequences have lessons for us all.

'When I phoned to tell my mum I'd passed my degree, she said she was delighted and so relieved because I'd got the same grade as my brother the year before, so he wouldn't feel bad. It took the wind out of my sails. As a parent myself now, I completely understand how concerned she was for us all, but I would have so liked that moment to have passed without reference to him.'
– Susan K.

Why are siblings so different?

'Brothers and sisters who grow up together are often surprisingly different from each other. Recognition of this has led to some of the most exciting recent work in psychology and related sciences. It tells us that siblings' different experiences of life must be particularly influential in making them the people they are. Parents treat their children differently, sometimes overtly, sometimes subtly, and it is likely that this has a profound effect on children's development. So will siblings' different peer groups and the different ways siblings treat each other.'
– Dr Gavin Nobes, senior lecturer
in developmental psychology

We are often astounded by the differences between our children. Psychologists have been, too. Recent research into the differences between siblings has prompted a re-examination of the factors that influence children's psychological and social development – what moulds them into the very different people they become.

- **We are not the same parents with each of our children**. Conventional thinking used to be that each parent had a single child-rearing 'style', responding to each of their children in a similar manner. We don't. We may stick to basic ground rules – no physical punishment, for example – but we respond differently to each of our children, and each child's experience of us as parents is unique.

We respond differently because our children are different – they arrive in the world with different temperaments, sleep needs, feeding requirements, etc. Their wants, needs and responses will be different throughout their lives, and evoke different responses in us.

Whether we realise it or not, our own deep-rooted ideas, concerns and expectations – about girls, boys, first children, later children – will also prompt different responses. Mothers, for example, tend to hold boy babies for longer periods of time and talk to girl babies more. So from our very first days together, we will respond in a significantly different way to each child in the family.

- **Each child will respond differently to the same event**. Family life is not the same for each

> '*Although siblings have common or shared experiences in families that encourage supportive relationships, they also have non-shared or unique experiences which make them different from each other. They may also interpret shared experiences in unique ways. For example, a mother may lecture both of her children regarding good manners; one child may agree to improve whereas the other child may take it as criticism and feel rejected and resistant.*'
> – Victor G. Cicirelli, Professor of Developmental and Ageing Psychology, Purdue University, USA.

child. Imagine two teenagers from the same family at a Sunday lunch or other get-together. A heated political discussion ensues. One child may be thrilled at the cut-and-thrust of debate; another may hate it, counting the minutes until they can escape the hot air and hot tempers. It's a simple example, but the same applies throughout children's lives. Siblings may be in the same place, at the same time, witnessing or taking part in the same event, and feel very differently about it.

- **Each child will have different experiences**. Children in the same family will also have separate and very different experiences. They will have different friends and take part in different activities. Crucially, they will have different siblings: each other. Each child's development will be influenced greatly by how their brother or sister prompts them to think, feel and behave.

- **They may accentuate their differences**. Children often accentuate their differences as a way of defining their individuality.

All these factors go to create what psychologists term siblings' 'non-shared environment',[3] their unique and individual experiences of life inside and outside the family, which will make the innate differences between them greater as they grow.

Developmental psychologist, Professor Judy Dunn, explains: 'Children may come from the same family physically but not psychologically. Careful studies are showing that both the positive and negative things that we do as parents can have a very different impact on different children.

'Some children are much more vulnerable than others, some are more resilient, for example, and part of a parent's sensitivity about what is going on between our children is to recognise these differences. It becomes a different family world for different siblings.

'Any parent who has more than one child will know that not only are her children different from each other but also that they react to things differently. Instead of thinking about children's environment on a family-by-family basis, we need to think about it on an individual-by-individual basis.

'The message is not that family influence is unimportant, but that each child's experience of that family will be different. And this has led to a huge shift in our research and understanding of human personality development.'

'Just because our children come out of the same womb doesn't mean they have much in common at all, frankly. In any family you can have an extraordinary ragbag of people. The challenge for parents is to show their love and understanding in all the different ways that those different people need.' – Peter Wilson, director, Young Minds

The danger of labels

'The importance of allowing children to be individuals doesn't mean you have to make them opposites. So often our children's characteristics are well within the "normal" range yet we treat them as if they're at opposite ends of the spectrum. If it just so happens that one child is more energetic or tidier than the other, it doesn't mean that the other is absolutely untidy or lazy. I am convinced these labels have effects on children, that they may live up to what is expected of them.' – Dr Elizabeth Bryan, paediatrician

Labels are generalisations about a child's characteristics, abilities or role within the family. They can begin at birth and are extremely common, especially in families with more than one child.

A mother may say her new baby is anxious and never sleeps, while her first child was 'a dream'. A baby who had a difficult birth may be greeted as 'a survivor' or 'a fighter'. A baby with colic, say, may be labelled 'difficult' or 'a nightmare'. These negative and positive descriptions can influence how family members respond to each child and thus the sorts of people those children grow to be.

If labels are used often, they tend to stick. To sense their potency, it may help to think back to our own childhoods. Were you labelled the 'funny' one, the 'good' one, the 'sensitive' one, the 'problem', the 'peacemaker', the 'responsible' one, the 'moody' one or the 'easy' child in the family? How did that label make you feel? Did it help or hinder recognition of your needs and potential? Were labels attached to your brothers or sisters? Did they expand or limit people's view of each child?

'Parents recognise differences between their children from the very beginning – this one sleeps; this one's fractious; this one never stops feeding. At the same time as being fascinating for the parent, it also gives one a set of tramlines along which to propel the child, so the very fact of identifying difference sometimes means the child becomes categorised as "easy" or "difficult" or "sweet" or "a trial".' – Mary MacLeod, National Family and Parenting Institute

Most of us will have been labelled as children to some extent, and most of us will label our children sometimes.

- **To chastise:** 'naughty' boy, 'bad' girl, 'You two are a nightmare!'
- **To boost:** 'clever' girl; 'good' boys; 'pretty' girl.
- **To compensate,** often for our own fears and vulnerabilities: 'You're a fighter'; 'You're so sweet'; 'Don't be a drip.'
- **To release** emotion and frustration. Labels can be used like expletives: 'You clumsy girl!' 'You idiots!'

They can be a hard habit to break, but it makes sense to try. If applied too often, labels can:

- **Crush, confuse or scare.** Children who think their parents dislike them, rather than their behaviour, may develop a dangerously low opinion of themselves (see Labels for life, page 172).
- **Become self-fulfilling.** Children repeatedly told that they, rather than their behaviour, is the problem will find it hard to see how they can improve the situation. Their label – 'stupid', 'lazy', 'nasty' – may become part of their view of themselves so they behave accordingly.
- **Communicate nothing constructive.** Labels don't tell children precisely what it is that we dislike or approve of in their behaviour, or how they could do things differently.
- **Fuel or even create bad feelings between siblings.** Children with a

low sense of their own worth are far more likely to feel rivalrous, resentful and hostile towards their brothers or sisters.

Even positive labels can have negative consequences. A child told repeatedly that they are a 'good' girl or 'responsible' boy may grow to believe that our love is conditional upon them being so, which may severely limit childhood fun and freedoms.

A child repeatedly praised for being a 'clever' boy may grow to fear failure and parental disappointment, and so avoid risks and challenges. A brother or sister told 'You're so good, I'm sure you'll play with little Fred' may feel manipulated and resentful. All labels, critical or complimentary, may hinder a child's ability to flourish as an individual.

'When my mother was dying and my dad needed help, he called on me. He told me he'd asked because I was much more in tune with mum than my sister who, he said, could be overbearing and bossy when they needed sensitivity and peace. I didn't need to know that, and it made a hard situation harder. I wanted to help but I didn't want it to be used or viewed as some kind of league-table rating.' – Mike M.

✝ *Children calling . . .* 👪

The following 'snapshots' of recent calls to ChildLine indicate older children's concerns about comparisons with siblings. School pressures were a particular worry.

- A sixteen-year-old girl felt depressed and neglected, and 'mum shouts at me for not coping'. 'My GCSEs start tomorrow and they always compare me with my sister who has passed ten GCSEs.'

- A seventeen-year-old boy has failed his end-of-year exams and doesn't know how to tell his parents. He feels they 'constantly nag me to work harder and longer hours; they are always comparing me to my brother.'

- A girl, aged sixteen, feels pressured by work and college. Her mum and stepdad pressurise her to earn her own pocket money, and she feels exhausted. She feels neither they nor her sisters understand studying, and she feels like an 'oddball' for wanting to do well at college.

Reproduced with the kind permission of ChildLine[1]

Labelling our children's relationships carries similar risks. Comments such as 'They're a nightmare together', 'You two are always arguing', 'Typical brothers' and 'They've got nothing in common' can feed a shared but distorted view of insurmountable difference and become a self-fulfilling prophecy.

If squabbling siblings is part of the family 'mythology', or how we think things are bound to be, our children may grow up to share that belief, drifting apart with little incentive to repair the relationship. Conversely, constant references to our children 'getting on so well', regardless of what's really happening between them, are almost certain to inspire thoughts of revolt.

'Even positive labels attached to the relationship, such as "You two are so good" or "You two always get on well" are constricting, setting up situations in which each person might feel deprived of the choice to be different. Negative labels also give a very restrictive view of the potential of sibling relationships. There can almost be an expectation of conflict. We need to move beyond this narrow focus which expects "sibling rivalry".' – Desa Markovic, family therapist.

'I was the eldest and the "sensible" one, the one to be relied upon to look after the younger ones and I didn't think it was quite fair. As a health visitor I have seen older children doing far more even than I ever did and I think to myself, they are being robbed of their childhood. They need to go out and play. I don't ever remember being irresponsible, which is not quite how childhood should be.' – Christine Bidmead, RGN RHV, Training Facilitator, Centre for Parent and Child Support

Every family member will benefit if we rip up family labels. So how do we begin?

1. **Comment on the behaviour, not the child.** This is the first and most crucial step. At its simplest, it requires us to stop thinking in terms of 'good' or 'bad' children, and to start focusing on the behaviour we like or dislike: 'The bedroom's a mess' rather than 'You two are so messy'; or 'Good homework' rather than 'Good girl'.

'On the helpline we find that many parents will say my child is this, that or the other, as if the child themselves is bad, rather than the behaviour. I think

🏃🏃🏃 But aren't kids born 🏃🏃🏃 that way?

Research has shown how genetically-based personality traits are evident often from birth. But biology isn't destiny, and pigeonholing a child as any set personality 'type' can cause lifelong damage to them and to family relationships.

Yes, the temperaments of some brothers and sisters may make for a potentially explosive, affectionate or supportive mix, yet whether they actually explode, love or support will be influenced by how we encourage understanding, communication and the handling of disputes within the family.

Take one personality trait with a genetic link – shyness. The scientist who discovered the genetic component of 'shyness' also found that if parents provide warmth and gentle but firm guidance, previously inhibited children can overcome their 'innate' reserve.[5] So whether children born with a predisposition to be shy actually become shy will depend on what we parents do. Our children's genetic predispositions are not a set of inevitabilities but a set of possibilities, which we can magnify or minimise by the way we support each child and their relationships within the family.

'A fundamental point in understanding siblings is to look at the whole family system – how parents influence siblings, how siblings influence parents, how siblings influence each other. All these are interconnected.' – Dr Gavin Nobes, senior lecturer in developmental psychology

it is very important to let a child know that certain behaviour isn't acceptable, but to avoid labelling them. Labelling children can do huge damage to their self-esteem.' – Cheryl Walters, Head of Research at Parentline Plus, and psychotherapist

2. **Describe what we see and feel.** This takes the process one step further, so not even the action is labelled. If we describe exactly what we see and feel, and don't resort to labels, we give our

children much more useful information. For example, 'The bathwater is all over the floor. I'm upset because it's dangerous as well as messy' is much more instructive than 'That was naughty.'

Equally, 'You're taking turns with the truck. I'm impressed,' gives children more instructive information for future use than 'Good girls'.

To reduce the risks of labels in the family, we also need to:

Be alert to children's use of labels

'It pushes my buttons, I must say. I tell my boys that just calling somebody "Stupid" isn't very helpful. "If you're really cross with your brother tell him what he's done that you don't like, what did he actually do?"' – Sarah Darton, health visitor

---

Labels for life

'If academic achievement is applauded within the family, and a child is praised as the "bright" child, they may put all their energy into being so, often at the expense of other feelings and interests. They may become developed intellectually but not as all-round people, because that's what's been admired and that's what they've received "Brownie points" for. Labels can encourage children to be one-faceted. Positive or negative, they can have the same self-fulfilling and limiting effect.' – Kitty Hagenbach, chid psychotherapist

Family therapist Desa Markovic is working with a woman who was labelled as the 'good' girl in her family. This left its mark in adulthood, as Desa explains. 'This young girl, attractive, tall, charming and able, was very unhappy in romantic relationships and unhappy about herself. Her image of herself was as a dull, unattractive, unexciting woman with no sex appeal. During our conversations she described her sister as "exquisite", "gorgeous", an "extraordinary woman", "attracting attention immediately" and "getting noticed".

'As children, my client was considered the "good" and "clever" one and the sister was the "pretty" one. When I asked her if she could describe herself independently of her sister, the

If children are labelling themselves, we can show them a more realistic and constructive view:

Child: 'I'm stupid.'
Parent: 'You're finding that hard. We all have things we find tricky. When you're ready, maybe we could look at it together.'

Child: 'We're always fighting.'
Parent: 'You are arguing a lot at the moment. How could you sort things out so you get along?'

Child: 'I'm bad.'
Parent: 'You don't like what you did. How could you make it better?'

---

question itself was a revelation. She'd never thought of herself other than in relation to her sibling and the sister was always the attractive, exciting, favoured one. So she could never be attractive herself. It is a striking example of how sibling relationships can have an enormous impact through life.

'This idea then intrigued her and she decided to talk with her sister. The conversation revealed that her sister felt my client was the preferred child, because she felt she had no brains, she wasn't clever, was just nice to look at and nothing more. It was a very touching conversation. My client said to her sister, "I hated you all my life because I couldn't be like you," and the sister told her, "I hated you all my life because I couldn't be like you".

'I don't wish to blame the parents. I do believe they did this out of the best intentions – noticing the best qualities in each child and emphasising that – "Look how pretty you are", "Look how clever you are", but the same story went on being told, and by other family members as well as by people outside the family such as friends, teachers and children at school. Over time it became fixed as almost the only thing worth mentioning about them, affecting how they viewed themselves and each other.

'Maybe it would help if parents were just aware of the risks of something being emphasised, no matter how beautiful, to the exclusion of other characteristics. Maybe it would help to think, "What am I not seeing and what am I not noticing in my children and in their relationship?"'

If we notice teasing and name-calling between our children, taking the child doing the teasing to one side and pointing out that it is hurtful and unfair may help: 'We try not to name-call in this family. Tell her what it is that bothers you and ask her not to do it, but don't call her names.'

If we hear self-deprecatory, sibling-idolising comments, it's time to step in with a smattering of parental support and perspective:

Child: 'She's so brilliant at school.'

Parent: 'She did well in her English exam. We're all good at different things, and that's one of hers. Remember the artwork you brought home last week – it was fantastic!'

> *'If one of my sons is upset at being labelled by the other I might ask, "Do you really feel like that?" He'll say "No," and I'll say, "Well, perhaps you could just ignore it then, perhaps it isn't really your problem but his. He's feeling unhappy and taking it out on you".'*
> – Kitty Hagenbach, child psychotherapist

Retract and apologise

> *'Most of us will label our children sometimes. When it happens, it helps to be honest, to retract the comment and apologise.'*
> – Kitty Hagenbach, child psychotherapist

We all make mistakes. If we label our children, as most of us will sometimes, it helps to apologise and explain how we could have handled the situation. 'Sorry, kids. That was a daft thing to say because it didn't tell you what I was upset about or why. What I should have said was . . .'

If nothing else, it will give our children an illustrative lesson in how to say sorry and turn around a difficult situation.

Celebrate difference

> *Families where children succeed, but in very different ways, are often ones in which the basic foundation is acceptance and celebration of whatever each individual brings within the family. The parents celebrate each child*

for who they are and what they bring and don't get caught up in the anxieties of expectation.' – Corinne Abisgold,
educational psychologist

The most powerful way we can teach respect and acceptance of difference is by showing respect and acceptance of our different children (see Building tolerance, page 176).

We can encourage our children to accept and respect difference without exaggerating it, to recognise that no one person has a monopoly on any particular trait and most of us are a mixture of many, and that all of us are good at some things and not so good at others. Appreciation and acceptance of difference will help them be more resilient to the mockery of siblings and others; more able to resolve their disputes constructively; more disdainful of labels others might attach to them and more understanding of their own needs and strengths.

They will then recognise that people have different abilities and aptitudes and that everyone has something to offer. They will also realise that just because their brother is a fantastic footballer, or their sister an ace swimmer, they are not inferior as a person. Just different, and excelling in different ways.

'Parenthood is an exceptionally anxious business. The average parent is worried sick about something. Yet listen to people who have been successful and many will say, "Well, my mother just accepted us all for who we were and there was always the sense that we would be okay. All right, you weren't good at some things but you will be good at something else." It's an attitude, an outlook of appreciation and confidence, and it's incredibly powerful.'
– Corinne Abisgold, educational psychologist

Letting each child shine

'Children can give up trying if it's constantly rammed down their throats that they should live up to a siblings' achievements. They may not take this out on the sibling, but it can have devastating effects on the child and possibly on the sibling relationship.' – Eileen Hayes, writer and parenting adviser to the NSPCC

Building tolerance

If children respect their differences, they are in a much better position to resolve disagreements with consideration and without aggression. They are also more able to accept themselves. But how do parents build such tolerance and respect?

'It can begin by us showing respect for our children,' says family therapist, Desa Markovic. 'To give the message in what we do and say, "You are different. You may have different ways of expressing yourself, different habits, needs, personalities and different ways of being. I appreciate those and do not value one more than the other.

To respect difference, to be tolerant, to be able to empathise and understand others is important for all sorts of situations in life, in creating flexible relationships and warm connections with people.

'As parents we also need to ask ourselves: "How tolerant am I of differences in other? How much appreciation am I showing of different views? How can I show more?" Are we respecting our children for their differences to us – their different taste in food, music, spending time, expressing themselves?

'We can allow our children to disagree with us; helping them to

'I find it very annoying when Margaret plays the violin in front of people and they say how good she is, while I am sitting there feeling jealous.'
– Multiple Voices, Twins and Multiple Births Association[6]

Siblings compete. A pre-school child may burst with pride because he's the biggest, fastest, tallest, strongest and 'best', even if his 'opponent' is still in nappies. We all know children who want to be first served, first dressed, first to choose the biggest, first in the queue, even first down the stairs. It's a pain for the parent and an even bigger pain for the sibling demoted to 'second' place.

We can help a child understand they are not masters of the universe, and the sooner we do, the less risk they run of being taught the same lesson less gently by other kids (see Caring and sharing, page 43).

Yet the forces that may push our children into pigeonholes of

articulate their views in ways that do not have to cause conflict. Having healthy discussions and debates, being open about what we think without expecting our children to always think the same; being interested in what our children think and having equal interest in their opinions whether they agree with us or not; allowing them to question and explore; trying to understand them and giving them the right to state their views without being dismissed or criticised, all these things will help.

'We also need to think about acknowledging the differences in our children as they grow and change over time; acknowledging that their needs change as will our relationship with them.'

Experiences of different lifestyles can also help children accept differences in each other, suggests educational psychologist Corinne Abisgold. 'I think it helps children to experience being around different people with different value systems in order to see that there are different ways of living a life. My mother used to have the house really tidy, and of course I loved to go round to a house that was a huge happy mess. It is important for children to see that there are different ways of doing things, and of being happy, and that they are not necessarily "right" or "wrong".'

'winner' or 'runner-up', 'success' or relative 'failure' are present throughout their lives, outside the home as well as in, and we can't shield them from all comparison and competition even if we wanted to. As they move through school, they and others will be tempted to compare their grades and achievements with those of their brothers or sisters. They may also become more conscious of how each child in the family measures up to parental expectations. Accepting and supporting each of our children as individuals may require us to take a close look at our ambitions and dreams for them all.

Our children will each succeed at some things and be less good at others. For them to flourish, take pleasure in successes and not be crushed when they find things hard or when a sibling does 'better', they need our genuine acknowledgement and support. We can offer these by:

• Seeing each child's special qualities

'Doing, not just saying, is incredibly important. Telling your child you are interested in and appreciative of what they are doing is great, but we have to also show that through our actions. It's part of our job as a parent to watch them and notice them and to show we are enjoying it.'
– Corinne Abisgold, educational psychologist

'As a parent, one wants to find ways to reward all children. Research in schools is showing that children do better when there is a wide range of positions of responsibility, rewards and privileges than at schools where these are given to a narrow range of children considered the "star" pupils. There are very few children who haven't got something they can be reasonably good at. It may be social, academic, in sports, music. They don't have to be brilliant, but they can feel good about doing a good job. In exactly the same way in families, I think one needs to try to respond to the strengths of each child in their own way.' – Professor Michael Rutter, child psychiatrist

Every child shines at something. Our role is to spot those aspects, abilities and achievements that make each child feel special. It helps to look beyond the obvious – they may be great at making people smile, throwing a ball, sharing, trying their best, listening, sorting out arguments with their sister, being a friend, praising their little brother's efforts.

Appreciating special skills, while not defining children by them, will have a marked impact on their sense of worth and potential. Ultimately, our aim should be to make each child feel special just for being themselves (see You're special because you are you, page 179).

It is never safe to assume our children know what we are thinking and feeling; each will need to be told that we love them very much and are very proud of who they are. Supporting what we say by what we do is also essential if children are to take us seriously. Praising a child for her efforts at netball may give her a boost; watching her play will boost her further still. Admiring a child's painting may make them feel good; putting it on the wall will make them feel great. Ackowledging their kindness is important, but remembering to mention it to grandparents, partners or other loved adults will make them feel extra special.

'I was talking to somebody last night who had just seen one of her sons in a school play. She was astounded how good he was and felt guilty because

he'd said: "I want you to be proud of me for once." For years, he'd been taken along to sports events and practice sessions because that's what his brother excelled in, and he hadn't quite found his own niche. It is important to grant each child the opportunity to shine.'
– Carol Ann Hally, health visitor

You're special because you are you

'Grandad was the only person who really accepted me for who I was, the only person I really felt at home with.' – Carol M.

Love involves acceptance. Children who feel accepted and loved for being themselves are much more likely to have a secure sense of their own worth and develop positive relationships with their brothers and sisters.

'I used to go and stay with my grandma. She has no expectations of me and all I had to do was walk through the door and her face lit up. Just me being there was all she needed. That was so powerful to me as a child,' explains educational psychologist, Corinne Abisgold.

'Extended families can also be important in giving children that feeling of acceptance and worth. I grew up in a Jewish community and when I went to a wedding or a big event, everybody would look at me and want to say Hello because they knew I was so and so's grand-daughter, so and so's daughter, I was this person's niece. Just being who I was meant I had a place in the community that was mine by right, and no one could take that from me.

'A lot of children have lost the opportunity to experience that nowadays. Of course, a community may bring its own pressures, perhaps about achievement, about the role of boys and girls, but as a child I simply felt being me was celebrated.

'How do we address that? I don't know, but perhaps we could start by being aware that achievement has become a substitute for the acceptance of children for being who they are. Perhaps we should look at how many traditional communities celebrate the life of a child not because of how clever they are, or how skilled, but because they *are*, by simple virtue of them being.'

- **Ensuring pleasures are open to all**

'If children see their parents absorbed and enjoying an activity, they know the enjoyment's for real. We've somehow split ourselves away from our children in our society and they don't see enough of adults enjoying themselves in what they are doing. If a child sees a parent enjoying drawing, cookery, reading, or whatever, it doesn't have to be sold to them. They can see the pleasures.' – Corinne Abisgold, educational psychologist

Enjoying pursuits for the pleasures they bring, rather than the praise or success we may achieve through them, is a powerful lesson for our children. As ever, the examples we set are important. If our children see us only celebrating achievement rather than enjoyment, they're unlikely to be convinced. If we make it clear that we know we're not the world's greatest cook/gardener/DIY fiend/swimmer/car mechanic, but still find great pleasure in the activity, they are more likely to try pursuits where they are not assured of success. Crucially, they're also likely to feel less crushed if they don't perform as they wished or when their sibling does it better.

- **Learning about learning**

'Every child needs to understand that we learn by what we get wrong, and that if we get things right all the time we are not yet learning.' – Corinne Abisgold, educational psychologist

All children need to know it's okay to make mistakes, as they are an essential part of learning. Children with competitive or high-flying siblings need to know this more than most. We can remind them that different people learn in different ways at different speeds and at different times, that nobody is good at everything and everybody is good at something (see Seeds of success, page 181). This may sound obvious to adult ears, but to a child burdened by the fear of never being as 'good' as a brother or sister, it can be a revelation and liberation.

Seeds of success

'When you have more than one child, with different gifts and strengths, it becomes very important to not only value them for themselves in their own right but also to help them to value those aspects of their intelligence that are differently developed,' says Robert Fisher, Professor of Education at Brunel University.

'Because children are different we need to value them differently. Schools have a tendency, particularly in large classes, to treat children as a corporate group. At home we have the opportunity to treat them very much as individuals. The task of parents and teachers is to help them see where their individual strengths lie and help them to use and value the full range of their abilities to respond to the world intelligently.

'Some children have skills that schools recognise as important, such as verbal, mathematical and scientific intelligence. Other capacities are less readily recognised in an academic setting – a child may display social intelligence, the ability to communicate well, get on with others and be aware of their needs, or they may have leadership skills which enable them to help and to think for themselves and benefit from what others say and do, or display non-academic forms of intelligence such as visual intelligence, or skill in physical movement.

'Within any loving relationship or household, where a child is not experiencing success we have to manufacture opportunities for them to achieve the satisfaction of doing well. We need to give children tasks they can succeed in, something they find slightly hard to do but which is within their area of competence. We can also measure their own success and performance rather than measuring them against other children, particularly siblings, which may enhance feelings of rivalry or inferiority.

'We also have to help all children see that failing and getting rebuffed and not having what we want all the time is an inevitable part of life and that there are constructive ways to face the problems they have. It is only through overcoming failure that children learn to become risk-takers and have that positive outlook that is at the heart of creativity and success in any sphere of human activity.'

- **Remembering brothers and sisters aren't teachers**

Although children may guide other children's learning in creative and effective ways, siblings don't make great teachers.[7] As well as the sometimes suspect 'teaching' methods used, one sibling presuming the superior role over another, even when their differences in age and ability would seem to warrant it, is a recipe for discord.

Occasional support, help and explanation can have positive effects on our children's relationships, building bridges of communication and respect. The problems arise when these roles are repeated so often they become a fixed family hierarchy.

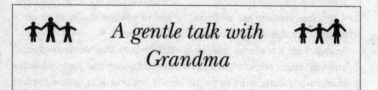

A gentle talk with Grandma

One of your children has a glowing school report. At their grand-parents', the child is showered with praise while his brother or sister squirms at the dreaded question, 'And how did you get on?'

In situations such as these, says paediatrician Dr Elizabeth Bryan, prevention has to be better than cure. 'School reports are so individual that they should be discussed with each child in private and only shown to other children at the wish of the owner,' she says. 'You may then want to share each child's achievements quietly with their grandmother or aunt, but not in a group situation because inevitably a less sensitive relative will make comparisons between the children or say something crushing.'

It is our job as parents to alert relatives to the dangers of comparing siblings' achievements. 'And some need educating from the start,' says Dr Bryan. 'It may be appropriate to raise the issue with teachers, too. Raising it after a problem has arisen really is too late for the child. It also puts you, the parent, in the difficult situation of having to be overtly critical. Far better to talk and avoid comparisons from the beginning.'

• **Seeing what makes each child proud**

> *'We need to encourage our children to look at what they are doing*
> *and monitor their own feelings about it, rather than always looking for*
> *adult praise. In the worse case scenario, a child always looking for*
> *positive adult feedback rather than how they feel about it themselves may*
> *be the child who tries to make other children look stupid or who copies*
> *other children's work.'* – Corinne Abisgold,
> educational psychologist

Encouraging each of our children to monitor and judge their own
progress is a useful way to focus on the positives of effort and personal
achievement. Without being judgemental, we can ask children what
they felt best about and what they enjoyed, rather than what they
achieved, did 'right' or got 'wrong'.

If a child, unprompted, tells us about a particular accomplishment,
they're clearly proud and we can respond by sharing and enjoying
their triumph: 'You must be so pleased!' Praising without reference
to anyone or anything else, especially brothers and sisters, can
encourage a reticent or considerate child to admit pleasure in their
own abilities (see Acknowledge the good times, page 70). This will
help each of our children shine in their own way.

Identity and individuality: key approaches

Respect each child as an individual	Every child is unique. We need to respond to each as an individual, distinct from siblings and stereotypes, and from his, her and our past.
Avoid treating them 'the same'	Our children have different experiences, different strengths and vulnerabilities. They will need us at different times in different ways.
Beware comparisons and labels	Pigeonholing children or judging them in relation to their brothers and sisters stops us seeing each child's true worth and potential. They can crush a child's sense of worth and fuel sibling resentments.
Celebrate difference	By encouraging our children to tolerate and respect their differences, we will help them clash less often, be better equipped to compromise, and cope better with the ups and downs of their relationships as they grow.
Let each child shine	By appreciating and acknowledging each child's individual interests, skills, accomplishments, gifts and strengths we help each experience 'success' in their own terms. This reduces the risk of damaging rivalries and resentment.

Key message:

Appreciating each child's unique qualities boosts the brother-sister bond.

7

Message received?
family communication

'Once the kids start speaking to each other again, they can generally sort things out. It's when they're not talking that the trouble really starts.'
– Angela G.

'Children can be without a voice in families. When one child feels less able to state their case because of lack of confidence or opportunity, they can feel isolated and ignored. As parents, we can create the security they need to be able to say things.' – Clare Beswick, early years and childcare consultant

To have a healthy and fulfilling relationship with each other, our children need to communicate and to consider each other's views. To treat and support our children as individuals, we need to know them, and to know them we have to listen to what they have to say. To help them negotiate life's ups and downs, our children need to listen to us, at least occasionally.

Good communication lies at the heart of happy, healthy relationships. And it runs in the family.

Time to talk

'A very high percentage of parents call the helpline to find out how to talk to their children, to their partner, to their children's teachers. They feel they don't have the skills to talk, to communicate, and ask, "How do I say this?", "How do I approach this?" It is absolutely vital that each family member has the opportunity to voice their opinions and say how they are feeling. We all need to think about how we talk as a family and how we create a safe enough environment for difficult things to be said.' – Cheryl Walters, psychotherapist and Head of Research at Parentline Plus

'We need to stay in open communication with our children, as what was true yesterday might not be true today. They are changing so quickly.' – Kitty Hagenbach, child psychotherapist

Constructive communication with children doesn't come in neat packages at convenient times. If children want to tell us something urgently, they will, whether we're about to step under the shower or fly out of the door on the way to work. Sometimes it will be possible to stop and listen – and it makes sense to do so when we can (see The power of listening, page 191). Opportunities to really hear and respond to what our children have to say are reduced dramatically once we have more than one child, so it helps to grab them when they arise.

At other times, life gets in the way of the best of intentions. We won't be able to stop on the spot if we've got to get them to school, pick up their sister from Brownies or take their little brother to the loo. Dismissing or ignoring a child with something important to say can leave them crushed, yet most children will cope if we explain the situation and our willingness to listen as soon as we can: 'I really want to hear this, but I'm late for work already. Let's make sure we talk tonight'; 'I want to chat this through once I can concentrate properly, because I know it's bothering you. How about after I've finished cooking?' Booking in a time to talk often helps, but will only work long-term if our children know we'll stick to our side of the bargain.

'We need to make that time to sit down for five minutes and listen to what they have to say and not keep putting them off. We all do it sometimes – "Tell me later" or "I can't listen now, can't you see I'm busy?" – but to a child "later" can mean nothing or never. That's why being specific can help: "I

Tuning in and chilling out

'When a child won't answer a question, it's time to stop asking them. As parents we can want desperately to get through to a child. The irony is that the more you try that, the less likely you are to succeed. The tip is to wait for opportunities, and to focus on establishing a safe enough environment to talk.'
– Jim Wilson, systemic psychotherapist

'We have so little loose time in our society, but that's when children say and do things that are most revealing. All this bussing children around to different activities, classes and clubs worries me a lot. If we're always dashing around doing something, we're denying them the chance for relaxed, unstructured time to let conversations unfold and for them to learn how to be comfortable with that.'
– Corinne Abisgold, educational psychologist

Communication can't always be planned, but we can create opportunities for relaxed time together with our children. 'It's not all about intense one-to-one verbal communication, it's also about providing opportunities for family bonds to develop,' says counsellor, mother and long-term foster-parent, Barbara Dale.

'For our family, the special time is meal times. We always have main meals around the table, without the TV on. We like food and that's an important part of our lives, and it gives us time and space for reflection, for argument, for discussion. That can be very productive and exciting. Good links come when families do things they enjoy together in an environment that encourages communication – it might be swimming, playing, running down a hill, going for a walk.'

Mary MacLeod, chief executive of the National Family and Parenting Institute, agrees:

'Communication can't only be planned. It has to be about seizing moments or being able to respond when there's an open door. That means adults having freedom from preoccupations, and that can be very hard to achieve, especially when the adult is going through a particularly tough time, perhaps experiencing bereavement or loss or going through issues such as separation.

'It's not always easy by any means. But the importance of unstructured time with our children is clear. Different children may want it at different times, in different places and in different ways, and being able to respond in ways the parent and child find comfortable is a constant challenge. But having relaxed times with each of our children, even cuddling in front of the telly, is hugely helpful.'

Kate, mother of two adopted sons, very consciously built time and space into the family week so relationships could develop. 'In the early days when they first came to live with us, our youngest would get into rages so we tried really hard to help him express all that anger and confusion and give him loads and loads of cuddles, but also we gave him a place to be quiet.

'In our lounge we put blankets and pillows in a big heap and we'd just go and sit in there and chill out a bit. We might go with a book but when the book was finished we'd just stay together, being calm and maybe I'd stroke his hands and feet. I think touch is so important with children. Those calm times really helped build a bond and gave us the calm space and time we both needed.'

Recently, she's decided to back pedal on the children's activities. 'We've stopped rushing around so much, and that seems to help,' she says 'It's given the boys a space to work out their own relationship. A lot of my friends rush from one thing to the next and I did get into that for a while, but in the end it was clear they were missing time just to chill out at home. I guess it's about allowing them the chance to build bridges, with us and with each other. They may not cross them immediately, but they know they're there when they need them.'

can't stop at the moment but at nine o'clock when Daniel's gone to bed we
will have time to look at your homework and talk about your day." That
really seems to help when parents feel pulled in so many directions.'
– Clare Gibson, Contact-a-Family

Finding times to be relaxed in each child's company is also crucial if lines of family communication are to be kept open, particularly if a child is finding it hard to talk about issues that concern them. In busy family life, unstructured, calm times can be one of the hardest things to achieve, but it is one of the most important investments we can make if our children's voices are not to be lost in the rush.

How we make those times will depend on our circumstances and our children's temperaments. Some children like cuddles and chats, some find it easiest to talk while doing other activities, while travelling in the car, or having a soak in the bath. How we provide opportunities for conversation to unfold matters little; what matters most is that we do (see Tuning in and chilling out, page 190).

'Boys especially may feel less skilled in language and become self-conscious
about saying what they think or feel, especially if the rest of the family finds it
very easy. How can you explain to your parents why you should be allowed to
do something if they are much better at telling you why you can't? In family
discussions it may be easier to say, 'I don't know', 'I can't remember', or even
to say nothing than look foolish in front of others. Some children prefer to
have their say later, on their own, when they feel safe and have had time to
think things over.' – Audrey Sandbank, family psychotherapist

The power of listening

'It seems to me that the new parenting myth is that all you have to do is talk
and then it is easy. Talking is just part of the process. Listening is just as
important, having the capacity to listen and to hear what is said without
becoming defensive. To be able to think through whether there is some validity
in what is being said, because it may not be the whole truth but may carry
some truth. Listening well is something for every member of the family
to learn.' – Cheryl Walters, psychotherapist and
Head of Research at Parentline Plus

'One family I knew stopped going on holiday together because their two teenage boys were literally at each other's throats, they'd punch and hit and hurt each other. It was very extreme, really awful for the parents, and not a lot seemed to help, I have to say. But one thing that did was to try to make sure the boys felt heard before it got to that stage. So much physical violence comes from anger and frustration and if you can get in there quick, help them express that and really listen, it may not erupt so aggressively.' – Sarah Darton, health visitor

'She's less eloquent, less socially skilled. Her brother can chase rings round her, but that doesn't mean what she has to say is any less important. I have to make sure she's heard.' – Amanda C.

Some of the most important things for our children to communicate to us are the hardest things for them to say. And sometimes the child most in need of being heard is the one who finds it hardest to express themselves verbally, or who makes their need for attention less clear.

We can encourage our children to talk by the way we listen to them. This is much harder than it sounds and takes a good deal of practice, but stay with it. If we can listen well, our children will know they can turn to us whenever they need our love, guidance or understanding. Importantly, they will also learn how to listen to each other.

'You can't force a child to tell you anything and we have to resist the temptation to want to fix everything right away. What we can do instead is to offer children safe, unthreatening opportunities to talk, where we're not probing or asking very direct questions. If we keep making those safe spaces, our children will know that they can come to us and talk when they are ready.'
– Kitty Hagenbach, child psychotherapist

To listen well we need to:

- **Show we're listening**

All children need to know we're listening to what they're saying, but how we do that will depend on the child and the circumstances.

Sometimes it's best to stop everything else we're doing, to look at the child, perhaps even get down to their height if we're towering above, and show in our responses and expressions that we're paying full attention.

At other times and for other children, this approach may be too intense. Adolescents and boys in particular often find direct eye contact intimidating, especially if they're finding it difficult to talk. They may feel more comfortable if we listen while doing some activity together (see 'Sideways' communication, page 206). We can still show we are paying attention through our responses; low-key remarks such as 'ah-ha', 'okay', 'hmm', etc., shouldn't interrupt their flow but will signal that we are taking notice.

> *'Listening, really listening, is one powerful way a parent can show*
> *how much they value their relationship with that child.'*
> – Andrew Mellor, Anti-Bullying Network,

- **Avoid interruption**

Interrupting a child, even with well-meant suggestions, corrections or pronouncements, may stop a child in their tracks. As a family, we should practice listening to each other without butting in. Only then will each child have a chance to have their say (see Helping children listen, page 194).

- **Respect silence**

We may feel we are helping our children by filling the gaps in their conversation with suggestions, 'helpful' observations, even to end sentences that seem beyond their grasp. Yet children may need that quiet time to form their own thoughts and ways of expression. Filling the gap with our thoughts may make a child clam up or simply tell us what they think we want to hear. Being heard in respectful silence without interruption, by adults who respond only to show they're paying attention, can reassure a child that what they have to say matters enough for us to wait for it.

👫👫 *Helping children listen* 👫👫

'*Siblings can often have a better understanding of the problems younger children face than do their parents. They not only realise why and when children feel insecure but can help them through difficult situations.*' – Professor Judy Dunn, developmental psychologist

If we can encourage our children to respect and listen to each other's thoughts and feelings, they are more likely to behave considerately towards each other and, as they grow, find support and understanding in their sibling relationships.

As a first step, they need to learn to let their brother or sister get a word in edgeways. Taking turns at speaking, and being quiet when others speak, sounds so simple but can be so hard for children to achieve. Young children may be bursting to say their piece. Older brothers or sisters may presume the right to speak first, loudest or longest. The less articulate or confident child in the family may feel overwhelmed and think better of expressing an opinion at all.

Simple turn-taking games help young children appreciate that their 'go' will come round if they wait – and often faster than if they attempt to 'push in' (see Caring and sharing, page 43). As our children grow, we can be very clear about the right of all family members to have their say, praise any signs of respect for the needs of others to be heard, and call a halt when the cacophony becomes unbearable.

We can also help each child understand the benefits of listening. Our aim is not for them to simply 'follow orders' and listen

• **Avoid interrogation**

Helpful listeners rarely ask questions – they can focus too much attention on the 'surface' problem and not enough on what may lie beneath. Such restraint is hard, especially for parents. There may be information we want or need to know. Yet it's often more effective and supportive to request this later. We are likely to discover

because they have to, but to understand that by listening they may see a situation more clearly *and* have a higher chance of others listening to their point of view.

Perhaps the most powerful lesson, as ever, is the one we provide by our own behaviour. If we want our children to listen, wait their turn and not interrupt their brothers and sisters unless absolutely necessary, we should listen and wait for them.

'I call it the poison hour, that time, usually early evening, when everybody's tired and everybody wants to be heard at the same time. That's when I need to get in between them and say, "Right, you first and then you. One at a time." Someone I know tape-recorded a mealtime and the number of interruptions by all of them was quite astonishing. It certainly made the family more aware of how much they break in and how much more they need to respect what's going on for others.'
– Doro Marden, Parentline Plus facilitator

'We can help children listen to each other, and it needs to be done in a fairly structured way. When they are small you can encourage them to take turns and help them understand that if everyone shouts at once nobody hears a thing. It also helps if they see you taking turns and listening with other adults and not letting children interrupt whenever they choose. But there comes a time when you have to stop and let them put these things into practice for themselves and find out what happens if they don't. Learning consequences of behaviour is a powerful and necessary lesson in life.' – Eileen Hayes, writer and parenting adviser to the NSPCC

more of import or interest by encouraging a child to disclose their feelings and fears rather than pressurising them to respond to our concerns.

If absolutely necessary, questions are best kept open-ended, encouraging a child to discuss issues further if they feel ready. Closed questions tend to invite one-word responses – yes or no – which can kill conversation stone dead.

Compare:
Open question: 'You look upset. I wonder what happened?'
Closed question: 'Were you horrible to Jamie?'

Open question: 'Tell me the best thing that happened today.'
Closed question: 'Did you enjoy yourself at Daniel's?'

> *'Children find being questioned very difficult. Asking a child why he
> is looking so sad is probably going to get a "Dunno" or a shrug in reply,
> but if you can say, "I wonder what's going on today?", use an open-ended
> question or more creative ways of communicating with a child, it can be
> very helpful. Children are so used to hearing direct questioning of the who,
> what, why, when, variety that they tend to just switch off.'*
> – Brenda Meldrum, Head of Training, The Place To Be

- **Avoid judgement**

A child may stop speaking if we seem to have made up our minds. Often the root of an upset between brothers and sisters lies far beneath the problem or statement initially presented to us, and it may take time and patience for the full story to unfold. Judgements, even of the apparently supportive variety – 'I think you did right', 'Next time you should . . .' – are best avoided if we want a child to carry on talking.

- **Allow children to problem-solve**

Allowing a child to talk through a situation may be enough to help them see it more clearly. Children can be very resourceful at solving their own problems when given the opportunity and our active help when they're struggling (see Searching for solutions, page 67, and When they can't sort it out themselves, page 112). The more practice they have, the easier it will be for them to reach compromises and resolve disputes with others, including their siblings.

- **Pay attention to body language**

Most of our communication takes place without words. Children know this but adults sometimes forget. By being alert to all the ways our children can show how they are feeling – their behaviour, posture, gestures, tone of voice, expression and so on – we are more likely to get the message. We can also display our understanding and rapport by 'echoing' or 'mirroring' a child's body language – sitting if they are sitting; leaning our head on our hands if they are doing the same.

> 'Most parents can use their powers of observation to understand what's happening. We watch the child's body language and demeanour – is he standing upright and looking straight at you or is he bowed down? What emotion is his body expressing? This can be a very powerful way of understanding what's going on for our children.'
> – Brenda Meldrum, Head of Training, The Place To Be

- **Allow children to be open and honest**

For our children's well-being and safety, they need to be able to tell us anything and know that we will listen. But we cannot expect children to be open and honest about how they think and feel if they believe that doing so will get them into even more trouble or upset us too much (see Exploring emotions, page 125). Times for listening should be reserved for just that if we want our children to open up. Parental judgements and discipline can come later, if necessary.

> 'We are trying to help people understand that listening can be painful, that you may actually hear things you don't want to hear. It helps to keep hold of the broader picture of why we're doing this, why listening matters in families. It can be painful, but it is very important.' – Cheryl Walters, psychotherapist and Head of Research at Parentline Plus

Knowing our limits

'When you think about the huge anger and envy children can feel towards their sibling, it must be terribly difficult sometimes to talk about this to parents. Often, another person like a grandmother or trusted family friend is better able to listen to what parents would find too hard to hear.' – Brenda Meldrum, Head of Training, The Place To Be

'Sometimes grandchildren feel able to confide things in grandparents, or teachers, or family friends, that they wouldn't want to divulge to parents. In that period of mid-adolescence in particular, when children tend to be most distant from parents and most often have periods of conflict, they often feel more able to talk about relationships, sexual matters and so on with someone who doesn't have the parental disciplinary role. The important thing is that they are talking to someone.' – Professor Peter Smith, Professor of Psychology at Goldsmiths College, University of London, and Head of the Unit for School and Family Studies

- **Use 'reflective' listening**

   'This stops me getting quite so wound up when they're saying things about each other, and it helps take the sting out of their tempers.' – Angela G.

This is a skill used by counsellors and other professionals to encourage children to open up and talk when they seem reticent or troubled. Parents can use it, too. It is best kept for times when sibling wars have broken out or one child seems distressed or withdrawn. Use it too often and it may lose its impact but if kept for times of need, it can be incredibly effective.

It has two basic steps:

We may not always have sufficient calm, control or emotional reserves to listen to our children in a useful way, especially in times of stress. Often, our children are at their most needy when we have least to give.

If our children have a trusted adult outside the immediate family to whom they can turn, they will still feel 'heard' and valued. Talking outside the family may also help children view their own situation and behaviour more objectively and constructively.

For some children, finding someone who will listen is, quite literally, life-transforming. The charity Young Voice conducted a recent study into bullying in Britain.[1] 'It was clear that boys who bully often haven't learned or practised how to control their chaotic feelings. They often didn't want to upset their mothers so bottled things up until they were too much to bear,' explains Young Voice executive director, Adrienne Katz.

'They tended to have dual feelings towards mothers, one feeling of protectiveness, and the other that their mother was constraining and controlling and didn't understand how it was for them. This mix of anger and protectiveness created huge tension. When boys had an emotionally supportive relationship with a man, the risk of depression tended to be reduced. Crucial to that supporting and protective relationship was whether the child felt able to talk and whether he was listened to.'

1. At its simplest, this involves 'reflecting back' the child's words without extra comment, so they feel understood and able to carry on talking and thinking.

   Child: 'I hit Joe.'
   Parent: 'You hit Joe?'
   Child: 'Yup . . . He was being a real wind-up and called me an idiot.'
   Parent: 'He called you an idiot . . .'
   Child: 'Yes . . . He's always calling me names.'

2. The next step is to 'reflect back' the gist of what a child has said, rather than simply the words. This may help clarify matters in the child's mind, helping them understand a situation better and helping us all get to the root of the upset without intrusive – and possibly counterproductive – questioning. The technique is most

useful when listening to one child at a time, but it can also help clarify and untangle sibling disputes when two children are bursting to speak at once.

Child: 'She never lets me in her room. Ever. And she's slammed the door on me again.'

Parent: 'You're sad because she doesn't want to play with you at the moment.'

Child one (Sarah): 'She took my pen without asking, then left it out so it's all dried up.'

Child Two (Rachel): 'But that's no reason to hit me.'

Child One: 'I hate her! That's the last time she's ever coming near my things.'

Child two: 'I didn't know it was her pen and she really punched me. Right here.'

Parent: 'Seems like Sarah's angry that you don't respect her things, and Rachel's upset because you hurt her rather than told her what the problem was.'

If it feels appropriate, we can 'reflect back' children's underlying feelings. Save this for those times when you're sure what those feelings are, or choose tentative phrases such as 'sounds like', 'looks as if', 'I imagine', and so on. 'You look sad' feels much more accepting and less challenging to a child than 'What's the matter?'; 'Sounds like you two are getting angry' will generally leave the door open for more constructive discussion than 'Stop it!'

Reflecting feelings can also be a useful way to show our understanding without appearing to take sides.

Child: 'It's so unfair. Michael got picked for the team and I didn't. And he's younger than me. I wish he'd never been born.'

Parent: 'That's really hard. It must hurt.'

Let each voice be heard

'We're not talking perfection here. I mean they still fight and argue and fall out. But they do talk to each other about things that have happened, problems they have. And I'm sure they have a good moan about me.' – Martin P.

'Parents should be sensitive to the views and needs of siblings, maintaining communication to learn what the children are thinking and respond accordingly. Children need explanations when there is a difference between them, and need to understand the importance of supporting and helping each other. They also learn by imitation, taking their cues by how the parents treat each of the siblings.' – Victor Cicirelli, Professor of Developmental and Ageing Psychology, Purdue University, USA

Equipping our children with the skills they need for life means encouraging them to talk as well as listen. Happy, healthy sibling relationships can only be built if each child has a voice within the family.

Asking opinions

Chatting through even simple issues as a family can teach our children the basics of effective communication. Asking their views can help each child feel they have important contributions to make: 'How do you feel about that, Sam?'; 'Okay, now everybody's said what they think except Helen. It's important we know her view, too.' (See asking Elizabeth, page 202) Once family interactions on this level become second nature, children should find it easier to chat through problems and disputes (see Searching for solutions, page 67, and When they can't sort it out themselves, page 112).

'It helps enormously to include children when discussing family matters, provided the subject is appropriate for them – how much television to watch, what to do together at the weekend, and so on. This is how children can learn that the family is a team and that we need to support each other. As well as meeting individual needs, they learn that the unit also has a function and a dynamic and that they have responsibilities in keeping that going.' – Kitty Hagenbach, child psychotherapist

'I sometimes encourage families to have at least one hour a week when they sit down together and talk through events and issues, a bit like circle time at school but in the home setting. Realistically, some families have no time in the week when they're all together. If, say, one parent is reluctant and thinks it's all a load of rubbish, the chances of it working with

*them present are slim. But we can still engage with whoever is willing
to join in, leaving the door open for others to participate should they wish.'*
– Dr Sarah Newton, specialist in children's psychological health

---

Asking Elizabeth

'I make the assumption that children have within themselves a repertoire of resources and opinions,' says systemic psychotherapist Jim Wilson.

'One young woman I saw – let's call her Elizabeth – suffered from anorexia. She was always described as having anorexia and all the conversations in her previous therapies were about her treatments. Then, in one session when her mother and father were talking about their marital difficulties, I noticed that Elizabeth was keenly tuned in, so I moved her to sit beside me to ask her what she thought her parents could be doing to improve the marriage.

'She was quite taken aback, (a) that somebody had consulted her and (b) that we had talked to her personally as a resourceful person who could be helping somebody else. We need to be careful of the mindset that some children have nothing useful to say.'

Welcoming questions

Our task is to keep family communication channels open, and not risk shutting them down by fobbing off questions as irrelevant, inconvenient, embarrassing or none of the children's business. Open communication *with* our children encourages better communication *between* our children, which in turn reduces the risk of all-out sibling battles.

Precisely how we respond to questions will be determined by many things, including our culture, religion and opinions, and the child's age and stage, yet, as a general rule, if a child asks a question, they're ready for the answer.

It helps not to give unrequested details. If children want to know more, they'll usually ask supplementary questions, and unnecessary or inappropriate details can often confuse.

It also pays to be honest. If we're not sure how to respond at any particular moment, we can say so. 'I'm not sure about that, let me think' and 'I want to answer that properly and haven't time right now. Let's talk after school' are still positive responses, leaving open the possibility of future communication.

We can build in opportunities for children to question and be prepared for them to ask the same question many times, especially over issues they find hard to comprehend or accept. They may need time to grasp what is being communicated to them, or need more information as they grow and their understanding develops.

> *'Children can't necessarily take in everything we say just once. So for everything we're trying to educate our children in – sex education, considerate behaviour, understanding about death, everything – it helps to say it many times and in different ways, and to leave ourselves open to questioning. Raising associated subjects, discussing events in the news or what happened at school, all these things will help a child feel they can approach us and share with us what they think and feel. If we make ourselves available in this way, a child will ask when they need to and when they're ready.'* – Pat Elliot,
> psychotherapist specialising in bereavement and parenting

Checking the volume

Shouting is infectious. Most families have their moments – the pre-school rush is a favourite. But the less we shout, the less our children will shout at each other and the more talking will become the family 'style' of communication.

When shouting does erupt, it helps to explain that there are more effective ways of getting a message across: 'Joe, I can see how angry you are. I think you should tell Amy how you feel, not shout. That way she'll take more notice.'

It's a lesson we might learn, too. Instructions shouted from the next room or down the stairs are much more easily ignored by kids with attitude than are calm, direct instructions from a parent standing close by. In real life, this isn't always possible, especially when we've other children to attend to. But when the issue is important, we may save our breath and our tempers if we:

- Stop shouting ignored instructions
- Move to same room as the child
- Stop what we're doing and look at them until we have their attention.

Then we can say what it is we want them to hear with greater confidence that they'll take some notice.

Making connections

'If talking seems difficult between siblings, try "doing" instead, finding some shared activity or enterprise they could engage in, be it creating or constructing something or planning an outing, something where the pressure isn't on from outside to actually speak words. If you share an experience, the language will generally follow. And let's remember that words are only one way of communicating. Touch, facial expression, shared pleasures, there are all sorts of ways of communicating thoughts, feelings and wishes.'
– Dr Sarah Newton, specialist in children's psychological health

We can support communication between brothers and sisters if we can encourage them to spend time together doing things they enjoy (see Chocolate cake is good for kids, page 69). Every child will have a special interest or pastime. Talking about that, and using language and stories connected with it, can help children feel easier about conversation generally (see 'Sideways' communication, page 206).

Sending clear messages

Communication in families can become muddled. We will communicate more effectively with our children and they will with each other if messages are clear.

Matching messages

If our words, actions and expressions don't convey the same message, children won't know what we're trying to say. Smiling sweetly while asking our children to please take their hands from around each other's throat is unlikely to elicit immediate cooperation. Looking disinterested or distracted while telling a child we are listening is unlikely to convince.

For children to fully understand what we are saying, the messages sent by our posture, tone of voice, facial expression and so on, need to match.

The same is true of interactions between brothers and sisters. A scowled and begrudging 'sor-ree' is unlikely to pass as an apology. Limply pleading 'I want you to stop that' is unlikely to halt a rampaging brother or sister in their tracks (see Assertive messages, page 208). It may help to talk with our children about the different ways we can communicate, and how much more effective their communication can be when their body language, tone of voice and words send the same message.

> 'I'm not really a forceful person and my children just ignored me when
> I asked them to stop fighting or squabbling. They'd just carry on until
> I really blew my stack. A friend of mine is much more forceful from the start
> – when she says no she means it and her kids know it. I'm trying to do
> it more like that – let them really know when enough's enough, not
> gruffly but firmly. It means I don't have to lose my temper so often.'
> – Kim D.

'I' messages

Children can pick up our bad habits. If we hide statements in questions – 'Why are you lot making so much noise?' rather than 'I need some peace and quiet' – our children are more likely to avoid straight communication with brothers and sisters. 'How come you've got my car? Who said you could have it?' is much more likely to spark a row than 'That's my car. Next time ask before you borrow it.'

Clear, constructive communication encourages all family members to express how they feel about a situation and what they want done about it. Confused, indirect or blameful statements merely increase tension, put children on the defensive and make positions more entrenched.

'Sideways' communication

'Much of our "talking" is done with sideways glances, sideways communication,' explains Jim Wilson, a systemic psychotherapist and director of the Centre for Child-Focused Practice at the Institute of Family Therapy. 'Some things you need to confront, but I think there is also an art in offering things without lecturing. I notice with my son, for example, that we can do much more talking when we are trying to figure out how a computer works than if we sit down to have an attempt at a serious conversation.

'As parents, we can look for the key moments of connection with our children. Say a child is interested in footy, you might find you can talk with them about whatever the matter is through some kind of analogy about their favourite football team. Let's say the issue is anxiety about not achieving as much as a sibling appears to be doing, the connection might be around football teams, about different players' particular skills, about losing games and what they need to get them through. It's a question of spotting and working with the resources in the child's life and then trying to connect with those.

'Sometimes we might offer a narrative, a story, and make suggestions that way. One child I saw was badly traumatised through witnessing her mother's physical abuse. She was a wee girl of six. I was able to connect to her much better by telling her a story that another young child had told me. I was able to say, "This is what she told me" rather than "This is what I am telling you". It's a rather simple technique but I found it really helped.

Compare:

Constructive: 'I feel upset when you don't let me have a turn.'
With
Blameful: 'You never let me have a turn. You're so selfish!'
or
Constructive: 'Kids, I'm tired and I need you to stop fighting. Right now!'
With

'When they're ready to talk, you'll see it in the child's eyes, in their availability and in their posture. They are not going to come up and say, "now I want to talk about my brother" or "now I want to talk about failing my exams".

'I was working with a girl recently whose brother had died in a car crash. As I was talking with her and asking her questions I could see she was looking at her watch, and the more questions I asked the more she backed off. Eventually I started to tell her a story about the death of a brother and his presence in the family. It was a child's version of the film *Truly, Madly, Deeply*. As I was telling the story, walking round the room rather than staring at her, her posture changed, she sat forward and her eyes lit up. I didn't want to notice it too much so I just kept telling the story, and that made the connection. I didn't say to her, "Do you think that story is a good story?" That would have been too direct. Sometimes we need to make the setting possible for the child to volunteer things, for the conversation to emerge.'

And sometimes we may need to communicate 'sideways' without words (see Beyond Words, page 210). Jim Wilson explains: 'This girl later set out a scene of her family unit as she saw it, very simply, using coins to represent family members. I said, "Where would you put your dead brother?" and she picked up a pound coin and put it right next to the coin she'd chosen to represent herself. I asked, "Is he in the family more now than when he was alive?" and she said, "Yes". She had picked up the coin that had the biggest denomination, and placed it right next to her. I don't think we could have found that meaning by simply talking. It was much more than she could have expressed in words.'

Blameful: 'You're driving me nuts.'

'I' messages – stressing what 'I' see, feel and need rather than what 'you' have done – can make children feel part of the solution rather than the problem: 'Kids, I'm fed up. There are toys all over the floor. Help me clear them up.'

'I'm scared when you two run ahead like that because you could get hurt. I want you to walk next to me.'

Some parents find it helpful to think of constructive 'I' messages in four parts:

1. **State the feeling** ('I feel . . .')
2. **State the behaviour** ('. . . when you . . .')
3. **State the effect** ('. . . because . . .')
4. **State the solution** ('How can you help?' or 'I would like you to . . .')

For example: 'I feel frazzled when you two shout because it's horrible to listen to and solves nothing. How else could you sort this out?'

> *'I found this approach so helpful. It helps children understand our needs and feelings, which can get overlooked otherwise. It doesn't create more bad feeling, it doesn't dump on them, and it motivates them to consider us and sort things out.'*
> – Barbara Dale, counsellor

Assertive messages

> *'She can't stand his whinging. If he starts whining and moaning, she caves in every time. And he knows it.'* – Lisa M.

> *'My daughter was in absolute awe of her brother, hero-worshipped him, and I think it's only when he left home at eighteen that she actually began to think, "Now what do I feel about such and such? What do I want?" I can't remember her contradicting him or insisting on her way ever. Not once.'*
> – Alison T.

> *'She could tie him in knots in an argument, so he'd revert to pretty brutal methods to get his point across. Like jumping on her and holding his hand across her mouth or screaming so he didn't have to hear what she was saying. That's why we've tried to show him different ways of saying things firmly.'* – Laura P.

Some children seem to back down, give in or simply assume second place behind their brother or sister. Such behaviour is often applauded by adults, who may see it as a sign of thoughtfulness, generosity or affection. It may spring from all these things, yet over time it may also fuel resentment and anger and lead to more rather than less sibling conflict.

Some older children find it difficult to voice concerns or express what they want or need, especially in the company of a demanding younger sibling. Others find it hard to resolve disputes without resorting to force or threats. Some younger children follow their older brother or sister's lead and rarely venture their own thoughts or suggestions. Many children (and many adults) would benefit from learning how to express their views and assert their needs constructively, and how to recognise the difference between consideration of others and keeping quiet or caving in.

This will not only help foster mutual respect and dialogue between siblings, but will also benefit them in other relationships. Helping our children value themselves and their decisions has been linked to higher resistance to peer pressure and reduced risk of early drug misuse,[2] so the impact spreads far beyond home life and childhood years.

A first step in helping our children stand up for themselves without resorting to force or threat is to explore the differences between aggressive, passive and assertive behaviour. Older children may understand the concepts, while younger children may grasp more by considering concrete examples.

Very roughly, responses to difficult situations can be divided into three groups:

1. **Aggressive:** Uses unnecessary force or threat. Tends to make situations worse not better. Often occurs when a child presumes their needs are more important than anybody else's.
2. **Passive:** When children don't stand up for themselves or what they believe to be right. Often occurs when a child presumes their needs to be less important than anybody else's. Tends to make situations worse, because it doesn't resolve underlying problems and can lead to low self-worth and simmering resentment. And simmering resentment, as we know, tends to lead to explosive anger.

Beyond words

Children often use play to explore and examine situations they find hard to talk about or even put into words. We can sometimes help them (see The importance of 'Let's pretend', page 50).

Jim Wilson, a systemic psychotherapist, often encourages children to use symbols rather than words to enact situations. Through this technique, called 'mini-sculpting', children use objects to represent family members and other significant people in their lives, exploring circumstances and feelings more easily and playfully than they might in direct conversation.

'Two brothers came to see me after being moved from foster home to foster home because of their fighting,' he explains. 'They brought conkers along to one session, and we thought these would be good to use as symbols, one conker representing each brother, to explore when they felt closer or further apart from each other, and why and when they fought.

'At later sessions, they introduced their "parents", represented by felt-tip pens, moving the conkers and pens around to enact how they each felt divided loyalties and had very different perspectives on whether mum or dad was to blame for the marriage split.

'As the scenes progressed, with the pens and the conkers, they started challenging the scenes the other had created. They were challenging each other's perspective on the situation. I said to them, "Guys, is it possible for you to have two different stories and still remain together?" That was when the penny dropped that it was possible to live with different perspectives and opinions. Before that, they felt they had to have one jointly-held perspective, one version of events, and they'd beat each other up in an attempt to get it: "It was mum's fault." "No it wasn't, it was dad's." "It wasn't, it was mum's." That was underlying their constant arguments.

'Through the "mini-sculpts" they began to volunteer their respective views on why the parents split and they ended up in care. They began to tolerate and discuss their differences, without fighting to prove their particular version was the absolute truth. I don't think these two brothers would have reached that point of understanding and tolerance if we had attempted to communicate only with words.'

Brenda Meldrum, of The Place To Be, agrees. 'Children often can't express through words what they are feeling, but they can through paint and toys and dolls,' she explains. 'One child I worked with, an eleven-year-old, was referred because he was scared of being bullied at senior school. His father was caretaker at his primary school and his mother a dinner lady so he'd never left his parents before. He was really frightened.

'He elected to draw a picture of his family but he didn't put himself in it. That made me wonder what he thought about himself as a family member. The adults and his sister figured very large, his father was huge, but he thought of himself as having little significance and little worth. When I asked him to put himself in the picture he was very small, next to his dog.

'It transpired that his sister was going through a really big crisis with an eating disorder and there were major problems within the family that were making him feel very unhappy. First, though, we had to work on his fears of being bullied. He chose puppets to play with and we did a puppet show. I had two puppets, one of which was injured in the school playground and the other was a friend. His puppet was the vet and the two puppet friends made an appointment to see him.

'As the vet, the boy said, "Now look here, little man, who did this to you?" My puppet didn't want to tell because it was secret and the vet said, "But you can tell me." The injured puppet told the vet a name.

"Now look here, little man," the vet said. "This is what you've got to do, you've got to go along and see your teacher and get support." So through the puppet play, the child had organised his own responses to being bullied and worked out that he could find a strategy to cope. And when a child feels they are coping with something difficult, their self-esteem increases.'

We must try to resist the temptation to 'lead' the play or dissect children's creative work, because we then risk setting the pace and the agenda, rather than allowing children's own thoughts, feelings and fears to unfold at a pace they feel comfortable with.

'It helps to accept what's going on rather than to question it,' Brenda Meldrum explains. 'Supposing you see a child drawing a picture with a very sad face, a direct and intrusive question would be: "I wonder why she looks sad?" A more helpful response would be to say, "Oh dear, she looks sad." We adults may want to discover what's really going on but the best and most constructive approach is to let children's play and its emotional content develop at its own pace. As the play therapist, my role is not to impose my own meaning but to see what story the child is bringing, how she constructs events, what she thinks about things. And I think parents can do this, too.'

3. **Assertive:** When a child knows their needs matter and other people's do, too. Involves them standing up for their rights while recognising those of others. They state their wishes clearly and firmly if necessary, yet do not hurt other people's bodies or feelings unnecessarily to get what they want or need. They listen to other people's points of view. This tends to make situations better, because all those involved feel understood and respected. They don't need to find ways to 'get even'.

As ever, we can show our children how to respond assertively by doing so ourselves. Compare:

Assertive: 'I'm tired and I need you two to help by getting to bed without mucking about. So let's go.'

Passive: 'Please go to bed.' . . . Half an hour later: 'Please go to bed . . .'

Aggressive: 'Bed! Now! Or you'll feel the back of my hand.'

Discussing different situations and responses with our children may help clarify the issues.

One child wants to use a sibling's toy. What's the best way to get it?

1. Take it without asking, snatch it or shout 'Give me that'? **(Aggressive)**
2. Play with something else? **(Passive)**
3. Ask calmly and *confidently*: 'May I play with your truck?' **(Assertive)**

A younger child has burst into tears because it's their brother's turn to roll the dice in a board game. What should the brother do next?

1. Snatch the dice or call the younger child an idiot? **(Aggressive)**
2. Let the child keep the dice so the game ends? **(Passive)**
3. Explain calmly and clearly: 'I'll have my turn quickly, then it'll be your turn again.' **(Assertive)**

'Helping children understand the difference between assertion and aggression is key. Aggression is abusing your power to hurt another person. Assertion is using your right to defend yourself against something you don't want to do. It is stating your own feelings; saying what you want

without riding roughshod over other people's needs. Children can understand these concepts, and parents can teach them by engaging them in discussions in language they can understand. Children are much more sophisticated than we tend to give them credit for.'
– Andrew Mellor, Anti-Bullying Network

'The flashing light comes on for me if a child is subdued or submissive. This was often in the background of extremely bullied people. The quiet people don't make waves, they don't make trouble, they are not always throwing a tantrum, they are not always screaming and yelling, and they are the ones more likely to stay too quiet for too long until one day they have a crisis. We must help these kids develop initiative and help them discover and assert their feelings – "What do you think?", "How do you feel about that?", "If you want that, how could you get it?"'
– Adrienne Katz, executive director of the
youth charity, Young Voice

Family communication: key approaches

Watch for moments and make time to talk	Communication with children doesn't come in convenient packages. We need to seize opportunities when we can. Spending relaxed time with our children and creating spaces just to be quiet will help conversations unfold.
Spend time just listening	Listening is key to family communication. We need to listen to our children and encourage them to listen to each other. 'Reflective' listening lets children know they have been heard, encourages them to talk further and helps them find solutions to their problems.
Let all voices be heard	Every child in the family will need to express their feelings and views. We can help by encouraging family discussions and asking opinions, educating all children in turn-taking, and talking 'sideways' to children who find direct communication hard.
Make connections	We can make connections with each child, sometimes focusing our communication on their individual interests and activities. We can foster communication between our children by encouraging shared activities they each enjoy.

Send clear messages	Muddled communication lies at the root of much family conflict. We will communicate better with our children – and they'll learn to communicate better with each other – if our messages are clear, assertive and constructive.
Go beyond words	Children often communicate without words – through play, stories, art, symbols. We should let them.

Key message:

Good communication runs in the family.

8

Extra pressures:

illness, disability and special needs; twins and more; divorce, step-families and family change

Some of this information relates to very specific situations; most contains messages for us all. The circumstances it addresses – disability and special needs; twins and more; divorce and family change – raise issues of interest or concern for every parent of more than one child: dividing parental attention; supporting children with different needs; the development of identity and supporting our children through tough times. And one message comes through loud and clear – the child in most urgent need in the family is very often the child who attracts or demands least attention.

Illness, disability and special needs

'Siblings often feel quite invisible.' – Francine Bates, chief executive, Contact-a-Family

'Harry took up so much of my parents' attention because he had to. He was very ill so I came second for most of that time. That was hard. But I knew what was going on and I never once doubted their love.' – Adam T.

'My brother Jamie's got a thing called Down's Syndrome. That means he finds some things harder. He annoys me when he does stupid things, but he's fun sometimes and he's got a heart of gold. A boy down the playing fields calls him names and we've had some really big fights, but my friends aren't nasty. My dad says we're all different and Jamie's just different in a way you can see from the outside.' – Kyle, aged ten

Having a disabled or ill brother or sister or a sibling with special needs does not, in itself, tend to harm sibling relationships. Some children are distant and hostile, some are extremely caring and close, most move somewhere between the two – and the rates tend to be the same as among 'well' brothers and sisters (see How do you feel about each other? page 219). The lack of difference may surprise many.

What will come as little surprise to those who've read previous chapters of this book are the factors that seem to encourage a close and affectionate sibling bond – how parents respond to each child's needs, and the degree to which the family situation and the feelings of each child are acknowledged and discussed.

Wide differences in the nature of conditions, the requirements of care, family circumstances and children's individual temperaments and behaviour mean the range of experiences among families is vast. A child who is aggressive or violent, for example, will have a very different impact on their siblings and their family than one who is generally passive and calm. Yet there are many common threads of need and experience. By exploring these, parents and others may gain a better understanding of what will help each child and how best to support the relationship between them.

The well sibling

'One child whose sister had cystic fibrosis said, "Whenever my grandmother rings, if I answer the telephone the first thing she asks me is "how's Susan?" Never how are YOU? And I'm not supposed to feel bad about that".'
– Dr Mandy Bryon, consultant clinical psychologist,
Great Ormond Street Hospital for Children.

'One child said, "They never ask about me, they never ask how I am, they always ask how's my brother." The neighbours, even the shopkeepers, would

How do you feel about each other?

Parents often worry that conflict between their children is due to one child's disability or need for particular attention. Yet recent studies suggest that levels of conflict between brothers and sisters when one needs special care are no different to the general sibling population.[1] What seems to help their relationships most is what will help all siblings – family communication, emotional support and responding to each child's needs.

'At the start of workshops we ask people to think about their own brothers and sisters, about their feelings and emotions for each other, and then we write a list of the feelings between well siblings and children with special needs. The lists are the same,' explains Clare Gibson of Contact-a-Family, a charity helping families caring for children with a disability, special need or rare disorder. 'Of course disability has an impact, and of course some children find it harder to deal with than others, but the feelings between siblings are astonishingly similar, whether one child has a disability or not.'

Dr Mandy Bryon, consultant clinical psychologist at Great Ormond Street Hospital for Children, agrees: 'When I studied the impact of chronic illness, I asked two groups of siblings what each thought of their brother or sister.[2] In one group, a sibling of each pair had cystic fibrosis. In the other, the children were all healthy,' Dr Bryon explains.

'Each group showed the same rate of aggression, disagreement, companionship, teaching, empathy and so on, so the illness itself didn't alter the type of sibling relationship they might have. When I looked at differences between those children who reported a positive sibling relationship and those who had a negative relationship marked by aggression and disagreement, those whose relationship was negative were much more likely to have families where the illness wasn't spoken about. The difference was quite striking.'

*ask how her brother was doing but nothing was asked about her. She felt
like she wasn't important any more.'* – Tricia Sloper,
Professor of Children's Healthcare, Social Policy
Research Unit, University of York

The impact of being the brother or sister of a disabled or chronically
ill child is lifelong. Studies show, for example, the degree to which a
child's choice of friends and, later, partners and spouse, is influenced
by people's ability to accept and befriend their sibling. It is often a
matter of 'love me, love my brother/sister'.[3]

Whether the impact is largely positive or negative depends partly
on the degree of disability and on family size – the smaller the family,
the greater the responsibilities the well sibling may have to carry. Yet
what seems to matter most is the degree to which we, the parents,
support each child.

*'Every member of the family is affected when there is a particular focus on one
child, whether because of their behaviour or because they are physically ill,
have developmental disabilities or mental health problems. There will
inevitably be an impact.'* – Dr Sarah Newton, specialist
in children's psychological health

*'It was assumed that I didn't have a problem because I was healthy and my
sister was so ill. It seemed indulgent for me to talk about my worries, because
my parents had enough on their minds, so I kept a great deal to myself as
I was growing up.'* – Jennifer C.

One of the most startling conclusions of recent research is that a
healthy child will often suffer more psychological problems than their
ill or disabled sibling. Yet because their needs are less obvious, few if
any adults may respond.

Most poignant and painful of all testimonies from 'well' siblings are
those from children who felt they didn't matter or weren't seen. Lack
of attention from parents or other loved and trusted adults can, over
time, lead a child to feel they have no status, importance or place in
the family.

*'What has come out from my study and from other research is the degree to
which support tends to focus on the disabled child and not on the sibling,*

and that in fact more problems can be found with the well sibling than with the ill or disabled child. In a study I did with families where a child was diagnosed as having cancer, the news was so shocking that, quite under-standably, everything became focused around the ill child and their treatment.[4] Nobody thought about the siblings. Nobody asked how they felt.'
– Tricia Sloper, Professor of Children's Healthcare

'One of my twin boys was worryingly little and had to be carefully monitored, so all of these things made me much more concerned for him. I was happy to wake for him through the night in a way I wasn't so happy to wake for his obviously healthy brother. The healthy boy was left to get on with it much more, and actually he was the one who in lots of ways was really needy of attention. I often wonder what affect that had.' – Amanda C.

Positives

'Well brothers and sisters may benefit from having a sibling with special needs. Siblings who have been actively involved in the management of their handicapped family member tend to be well adjusted . . . It may be that the critical variable is how the parents interact with their handicapped and non-handicapped offspring, for example, by providing ample time and by communicating their love and concern to all their children.'
– Milton Seligman, in 'Psychotherapy with Siblings of Disabled Children'[5]

Well siblings of people with special needs, chronic illness or learning difficulties are often very accepting of difference in others. They may seem unusually empathic and supportive of their brother or sister, irrespective of whether they are older or younger.[6] Some children recognise this as a strength in themselves and in the family as a whole.

'A lot of siblings said having a disabled or ill brother or sister made them more caring. They described themselves as becoming more mature, growing up, becoming more understanding of people and disability and illness, and seeing that as positive. Many children talked about closer family relation-ships in general. Clearly, that isn't the case for all families, it can go both ways, but many did talk about it drawing the family together.' – Tricia Sloper, Professor of Children's Healthcare

Regression and attention-seeking

Healthy siblings sometimes regress or imitate their brother or sister in an attempt to gain equal attention. This is particularly so among younger children and in times of particular stress, when concerned parental attention may be hard to come by. This can be maddening for parents who've more than enough to cope with already, but understanding the forces behind the behaviour may help us to be more understanding in our responses.

> *'One mother told me that when her two-year-old disabled child learned to crawl, his twin brother came down from his feet and started crawling, hoping for the same sort of acknowledgement and praise. Another mum told me how her healthy child positively welcomed it when she had an earache or whatever, because it meant she could have medicine "like her sister".'*
> – Dr Elizabeth Bryan, paediatrician

Family expectations

> *'If a child has a sibling who can't achieve as well, they may feel they must carry the success of the family. They may feel the focus of all their family aspirations, yet also feel guilty if they do succeed in ways their brother or sister can't. It can be quite complex for that child.'*
> – Corinne Abisgold, educational psychologist

Well children may feel they have to carry the burden of parental expectation, at school and beyond. If their ill or disabled sibling can't 'succeed', they may feel they must. If left unchecked, these feelings can inflict huge pressures and even a fear of failure that prevents the child from accepting new challenges.

We can help by ensuring each child knows they are loved for being themselves, not for what they may 'achieve', and by emphasising the many ways people can shine and bring pleasure to those around them (see Letting each child shine, page 175).

Expectations of behaviour can also take their toll. The behaviour of a 'good', quiet and withdrawn child may be positively welcomed by a family struggling against the odds, yet may be equally indicative of distress.

Bottling up feelings

'Well children felt they were not allowed to complain, be naughty, or get sick themselves because they didn't have a "proper" illness and should consider themselves lucky. In my discussions with well siblings, many felt they had an imposed identity. All the things that we in the rest of the population complain about, they didn't feel able to. Stress is always relative, and not being able to find your football socks can be as stressful for a child as having nebulised antibiotic, yet if mum's supervising the nebuliser with your brother or sister, you won't ask her about your socks. That definitely has the potential to influence the child's personal identity and affect their self-esteem.'
– Dr Mandy Bryon, consultant clinical psychologist,
Great Ormond Street Hospital for Children

A well child may resent limits to family activities imposed by their sibling's condition, and society's general lack of disability awareness. They may fear they are at risk of serious illness or disability themselves. They may feel angry or sad about the lack of concerned adult attention. They may feel guilty about feeling angry. They may feel guilty about being 'spared' the suffering of their brother or sister. And they may feel unable to express any of it.

Children often feel protective of their parents and try to hide their emotions and problems while parental time is focused on more urgent matters. They may become stereotyped as 'the child without a problem' (see Kids don't fit in pigeonholes, page 159) and, as they grow, may lose the ability to express, prioritise or even recognise their own feelings and needs[7] (see Expressing feelings, page 135).

'They tend not to express resentment. They felt guilty about it and they didn't want to upset their parents. These children were upset, anxious, sad about their brother or sister, angry and at the same time thinking, "I can't think this about them". That was hard for them to deal with.'
– Tricia Sloper, Professor of Children's Healthcare

The ill or disabled sibling

'I think from the point of view of the child who is ill or disabled, the sibling relationship is really important. It gives them the contact and activities with

non-disabled children, and can help them feel less isolated. It is a different relationship from the parent-child relationship and siblings can say things to each other they wouldn't necessarily say to parents and do different things together. It brings a great deal.' – Tricia Sloper, Professor of Children's Healthcare

The potential benefits of a sibling relationship for children with disability or special needs is often overlooked, as is the pain they may feel when the relationship changes.

The loss of companionship between siblings can be deeply felt by both when a child has to spend time in hospital or receives treatment that makes them feel tired or ill.[8] If new joint activities can be found, both children will benefit.

Parents also need to be alert to times when a child's anger, resentment or sadness at the differing life chances of themselves and their sibling may be particularly acute.

'Watching the difference happen can be painful for parents. Disabled adolescents' social lives may be much more restricted than their brother or sister's. The difference accentuates the older they become, and how to keep things going in the relationship can be a problem. We found that most siblings were very caring, very sensitive and would try to include their brother or sister in their lives. There were only a few who really separated themselves off. Yet the differences in the way they move through adolescence or, in the case of life-threatening illness, whether this is something the ill sibling will experience at all, can be very difficult to deal with. There aren't any easy answers.' – Tricia Sloper, Professor of Children's Healthcare

What may help them both

Time and attention

We've already seen how long-term differences in parental attention between siblings can crush the child who feels forgotten and fuel conflict between brothers and sisters[9] (see Facing up to favouritism, page 147). When a child is ill, disabled or has special needs, parents may be unable to give their children anything like equal time and care.

Yet if children are informed and reassured about why this is happening – that it is not because one child is loved more but because the ill child requires particular attention – the sibling relationship can thrive. If we give attention to all our children when we can, and fully explain when and why we can't, we will help all family members make the best of a hard situation.

'When there is very obvious differential attention from parents or carers, without a good explanation as to why, the well sibling may become quite attention-seeking, aggressive or argumentative. When parents are able to explain the differential attention, or manage the attention fairly, the sibling relationship isn't marked by high amounts of aggression and disagreement.'
– Dr Mandy Bryon, consultant clinical psychologist,
Great Ormond Street Hospital for Children

'Children need information about what's going on so they can make sense of all the changes in the family. It helps them put things into context and perspective, so they are able to say to themselves, "I know mum or dad is really irritable with me or isn't paying me much attention at the moment but I understand why. I know they are worried and I can deal with that, for the time being any way."' – Tricia Sloper,
Professor of Children's Healthcare

Ring-fencing time to spend one-to-one with the well child, and establishing this as part of the weekly routine, is invaluable if their needs aren't to be subsumed under the weight of other pressures. All children in the family will benefit as resentments diminish.

'If parents are quite clear – "I have to spend time with your brother today, but tomorrow at six o'clock we will spend some time together" – children are fairly flexible, especially when they have a good understanding of what is going on. Thinking about how you're going to protect time with your well child is really important. Of course you can't count for emergencies and I think children understand that, but it is possible to plan ahead and manage a time to go out together or just to talk. All children need to be able to look back and remember a special time with their mum or dad. It can really help.' – Clare Gibson, library and
information officer, Contact-a-Family

👤👤👤 *Emergency planning* 👤👤👤

Life with an ill or disabled child can be unpredictable. This can be unnerving for all children in the family, but some forward planning and discussion can help allay fears. 'I came across one case where a child was so worried about what would happen if his brother went to hospital that he wouldn't go to school in case he had to stand by the gates on his own and nobody collected him. He needed to know he was going to be collected and who would collect him,' says Clare Gibson of Contact-a-Family.

Her colleague Francine Bates agrees: 'Involving children in planning what happens in emergencies can help: "If your brother goes into hospital, would you rather stay with Aunty Susan or Mrs Bloggs?" Obviously the parent makes the final decision, but involving them in the process can bring back some sense of control in a situation which otherwise might seem every more scary.'

Discussion and information

'I had a child of eight tell me she was never going to get married because she had to look after her brother. She wasn't aware that someone else might do that job. She thought she had no choice. Being quite clear and giving information not only about the present but what the future may hold is really important.' – Clare Gibson, Contact-a-Family

'When the illness is not discussed, the message may be that everything is fine and dandy but children know very well that it isn't, so that breeds tension. We mustn't keep it a secret. We must give children information they can understand.' – Dr Mandy Bryon, consultant clinical psychologist, Great Ormond Street Hospital for Children

Open discussion and information helps children be more understanding of each other, of the family situation and of our limitations. All children need some basic facts about what is going on and what may happen in the future and some discussion about how family members feel about it (see Is it my turn next? page 227). If family outings have to be cancelled because of illness, for example, a healthy child is going to be much more understanding if their disappointment is acknowledged and they know the true reasons why, than if they are fobbed off with a lame excuse. If professionals and health workers are coming into the family home, it helps if all children know who they are and what they are doing.

No child should feel burdened with inappropriate responsibility for final decisions, yet involving them in concerned discussions – for example, having a family visit to a prospective respite care centre – can help the well child feel included and the ill or disabled child feel they have some control over their own destiny. Healthy siblings have been found to cope much better in adulthood when their curiosity about their brother or sister's illness was welcomed and open discussion encouraged.[10]

Is it my turn next?

'If as a small child you see your brother or sister being sick, being ill, going into hospital, coming back out, possibly even dying, and there's been no adequate explanation, a lot of children will think, "Is it my turn next? What did I do wrong? Have they been punished? Will the same thing happen to me?"' explains Dr Mandy Bryon, consultant clinical psychologist at Great Ormond Street Hospital for Children.

'Children will interpret according to their own sense and sensibilities what they see before them, and that may not actually be in the way we think. Parents often make the mistake of believing that if you don't tell a child they will be protected and innocent. Well, they won't. They'll make it up themselves, and will end up in a much more frightening world than if you had told them the truth.'

Accepting and respecting difference

Honest and open discussion involves an acceptance and respect of each child as they are, not as we might like them to be. Praising and emphasising individual achievements and helping each child in the family feel they can accomplish many things are extremely important (see Letting each child shine, page 175). So is facing up to the truth about ill or disabled children's difficulties. Refusal to acknowledge a child's problems is likely to fuel anger or make them feel they cannot express their feelings or anxieties for fear of upsetting others.

Expressing feelings

'Not being able to speak about fears or concerns breeds a tremendous amount of anxiety and disquiet that influences personality development and a child's sense of well-being.' – Dr Mandy Bryon, consultant clinical psychologist, Great Ormond Street Hospital for Children

All children need someone to listen to their feelings and fears (see Exploring emotions, page 125, and Message received? page 187). Children going through experiences as painful and confusing as chronic illness or disability, or who watch their brother or sister suffer, need that more than most.

Once alerted to the need of every child to be heard, most parents try their best to provide more opportunities. But restrictions on time and children's possible unwillingness to discuss their true feelings with their parents may make it especially important for them to have supportive relationships outside the immediate family. Whether it is a loved grandparent, family friend, teacher or someone who has been through similar experiences, what matters is that each child has someone to whom they can talk and who they trust will listen (see Someone who understands, page 229).

'When we were doing the research, just talking to families about siblings seemed to help. Some people said, "You've really made me think. Just having to sit down and talk about how our other child may be feeling has really made me realise, 'Gosh I don't know, and I should'." Families can get stuck in a cycle, whereby children don't talk about it because they don't want to upset the parent, so the parents don't know, so they therefore don't make the opportunities to talk. Somehow raising awareness did seem to make a difference. Where parents did start speaking to their children about these things and were more open, this seemed to help.' – Tricia Sloper, Professor of Children's Healthcare

Someone who understands

Someone who understands what you are going through can be an invaluable support for every family member. 'Children and parents need the opportunity to express feelings with someone who really understands, someone who is able to reassure them that it is quite normal and okay to feel that way,' says Tricia Sloper, Professor of Children's Healthcare at the Social Policy Research Unit, University of York.

Professor Peter Smith, Professor of Psychology at Goldsmiths College, University of London, agrees. 'A danger for someone with a disability, say, is that they are comparing themselves to others without a disability and that may be negative for them. In my work with deaf children it became clear that deaf children in a hearing family have lower self-esteem than deaf children in a deaf family. We have quite poignant interviews with children saying that their parents don't understand them and the difficulties they have with friendships – to a much greater degree than hearing children or even with deaf children in a deaf family.

'So what can you do if you have a child with a disability? I think you do all you can to communicate with them and respect them as fully as you can and to support their relationships with their siblings, and probably also try to facilitate friendships they may want with other children who have some form of disability, too. Talking openly in the family is important, but so is providing opportunities for children to mix with others who really understand their situation.'

Letting relationships grow

'Children with an illness may use a close sibling or their peers to discuss issues more often than they go to their parents. This can be a shock for parents, that their children are more likely to speak to peers and siblings, particularly in teenage years. If you have ensured that every member of the family has accurate information then you can feel more assured that they are giving good and appropriate support.' – Dr Mandy Bryon, consultant clinical psychologist, Great Ormond Street Hospital for Children

It is very understandable that parents may want to protect an ill or disabled child from the hurly-burly of normal sibling relationships. But if we do, we do them a disservice by denying them the chance to develop a powerful and potentially supportive bond.

'All siblings argue, yet parents can find it very hard when a well child says something against his or her brother or sister. We have to try to allow those situations and those feelings, and to allow normal family relationships to develop. It is really important to allow children, within reason, to find their own way.' – Clare Gibson, Contact-a-Family

Twins and more

'It's certainly not easy, but their ability to understand each other and make each other laugh can be a joy.' – Amanda C.

'Discipline's impossible at the moment. I'm the outsider and they're the team and sometimes they seem totally beyond being affected by anything I say or do.' – Louise R.

'I think being a twin is great, because you always have somebody to play with and somebody to argue with.' – Multiple Voices, Twins and Multiple Births Association[11]

Twins aren't a homogenous group and neither are their parents. There are too many variables for there to be one common experience,

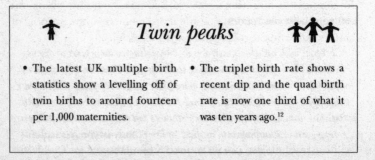

Twin peaks

- The latest UK multiple birth statistics show a levelling off of twin births to around fourteen per 1,000 maternities.

- The triplet birth rate shows a recent dip and the quad birth rate is now one third of what it was ten years ago.[12]

including the children's health and temperaments and the levels of support the parents receive. Yet there are issues common to most which will influence the children's view of themselves and of their sibling relationship. Many of these are also relevant to non-twin siblings close in age.

Managing time and attention

'The big problem for parents is how you give your undivided attention to both children, how you share yourself with each. It can be very difficult if one child is easier to relate to than the other or demands more attention. To give equal time and equal attention is not necessarily to be equally fair. You may have to give one child more attention at a particular moment, just as you would with children of different ages. My own feelings is that with the majority of children it will even out over time.' – Dr Elizabeth Bryan, paediatrician and founder of the Multiple Births Foundation.

'One of our girls is generally quiet and undemanding. Her sister is very loud and extreme with her emotions, I guess more obviously needy. I try to be with both the kids on their own sometimes, otherwise her sister's demands would swamp us.' – Judy F.

Most parents worry about their ability to respond to two, often competing sets of demands at any one time. There is no magic solution, and the only option is to do the best we can, and to realise that children do not need us to give them equal attention all the time but rather to respond to their individual needs as they arise (see You may want me, but your brother needs me right now, page 142). As long as the amount of attention each child receives roughly evens out over time, and the loudest doesn't always come first, the majority of families with twins negotiate this fairly successfully.

'I think we've just got to accept that we can't do it right for all of them all of the time. There were occasions when both needed a cuddle and they'd start fighting on my lap. In the end, I stuffed a pillow between them and sat them back-to-back on my knee so they didn't have to touch or look at each other. That helped. You find yourself jumping through hoops like that all the time.' – Emma S.

The impact on parents

'The families I support with Home Start reinforce the enormity of the responsibility of parenthood, particularly coping and managing with siblings. I gave one-night relief to a mother with an elder child and then triplets. It occurred to me after the twelfth feed, that in twenty-four hours we were only half way through and this mother had another twelve feeds to do. It can be so exhausting.' – Margaret Harrison, founder and life president of Home Start

For most parents, the early days of life with twins are a mix of joy, awe and very hard work under extreme circumstances. The demands made on parents of twin babies and young children are huge, physically, mentally, and economically. And these can take their toll on the parents, the children and their forming relationships.[13]

Three months after their twins' birth, seventy-six per cent of mothers in one study said they were exhausted, seventy-nine per cent said they had no time for them-selves and thirty per cent reported being depressed.[14] The mother of twins is five times more likely to have postnatal depression than the mother of singletons.[15] Tiredness and eating irregularly seems to make PND worse,[16] which may go some way towards explaining the disparity.

Parents of twins are particularly likely to be pushed to their limits and are far more likely to suffer drug and alcohol abuse, family violence and divorce, which is not the cheeriest news.

Ensuring each child has some one-to-one time alone with a parent will boost their language and social skills and help us give them the individual and relaxed attention they need.

'Most of us in life find one-to-one relationships more rewarding than trios, yet twins sometimes miss out on that. There is also a danger twins can have a strong one-to-one with each other but not with anyone else. I don't want for a moment to reduce the closeness of their friendship, but if it is a dependency, that's different. They need other one-to-one relationships.' – Dr Elizabeth Bryan, paediatrician and founder of the Multiple Births Foundation

But it is important. If we blind ourselves to the facts we may also blind ourselves to what may help and to the importance of looking after ourselves – for our own sakes and to enable us to properly care for our children. With so many other demands on our time and attention, we can slip to the bottom of the priorities list. Sometimes, that's a necessary part of parenthood, but if we remain at the bottom of the heap we're in trouble. Statistics aren't inevitabilities but rather a warning of what could be if we don't get the sleep, rest, food and support we need to keep going. So if you are the parent of young twins and haven't yet got the support you need, now's the time to start asking.

The good news is that life tends to become much easier as your twins grow and you experience the delight of a full night's sleep. Other issues arise as our children move through the stages of childhood and adolescence, but these can generally be negotiated successfully by supporting each child as an individual.

'You really feel, "Am I ever going to know these babies? Am I ever going to luxuriate in the look of a single individual because I am constantly juggling between the two?" In the early stages, it's just about surviving. But I remember a turning point, when they were about six weeks old. They were both sitting in these blue and white striped sleepsuits like a couple of very comfortable old men. They looked very established. I looked at them and laughed and from that moment on I felt "It's going to be okay".' – Sarah P.

'Twins need time to talk to their parents, not only about worries and fears but about practical day-to-day things. Ten minutes for each child will help.'
– Audrey Sandbank, honorary consultant family therapist for the Twins and Multiple Births Association (TAMBA)

Preferential treatment

'Unfairness is something that bothers them hugely. They watch me very closely.' – Amanda C.

Twins, who tend to compare every aspect of their lives almost constantly, may be particularly alert to preferential treatment by parents and extremely sensitive to its consequences. We cannot avoid having different feelings for two different children, and often those feelings will change over time as we and our children change and grow. We can ensure our feelings don't translate into entrenched, long-term disparity of treatment so a child ends up feeling less loved, or simply 'less than' their twin sibling (see Facing up to favouritism, page 147).

Conflict

Young twins can play together happily, then fight with a shocking lack of restraint. Biting is a speciality among twin toddlers. Yet so long as the conflict is managed firmly and consistently – and halted when it goes too far – they generally emerge unscathed.

Arguments and fights tend to decline in number and intensity as the children move away from toddlerhood. By school age many will have negotiated ways to either enjoy joint play more and fight less or, less commonly, to keep a safe distance.[17] But the very intimacy of the twin relationship means there is always the potential for volatility. As each knows precisely how to wind up the other, strategies to minimise and resolve conflict may be especially important (see He started it! page 83).

Parents of twins are so busy they tend to explain rules less and follow them through less consistently,[18] or attempt to educate their children in acceptable behaviour as a 'set'. Yet we might be rushed off our feet a little less, and certainly be less harassed, if we spent more time establishing the ground rules and gave each child clear guidance on their individual behaviour.

It helps to be alert to the continued dominance of one twin by another. In the early years, this seems linked to speech acquisition.[19] By school age, other factors come into play, including intellectual ability, physical prowess and interpersonal skills.[20] In boy-girl pairs, the girl tends to dominate, probably because of different developmental rates between the genders and girls' more advanced social skills. By adolescence, her greater physical maturity may still give her the upper hand. We can support both children by ensuring that neither one feels 'second best' or that their needs won't be recognised or opinions won't be heard (see Message received? page 187).

Identity

> *'The more closely coupled twins' lives have been, the more likely*
> *they are to become like two pieces of a jigsaw puzzle, each needing the*
> *other to become complete. Possibly the happiest twins are those who are*
> *able to allow each other freedom to develop independently while*
> *continuing a lifelong friendship.'* – Audrey Sandbank,
> family psychotherapist

> *'When Ben was little he came downstairs to see my aunt and uncle and said,*
> *"There's another one of me upstairs and it's called Rosie".'* – Multiple
> Voices, Twins and Multiple Births Association[21]

The influence twins have upon each other can be profound and life-long. They recognise and respond to each other within the first few months of life. Identical twins tend to be closer than fraternal (non-identical) twins, and same sex fraternal twins closer than boy-girl fraternal twins, yet all twins can display a bond that delights and tests themselves and their parents.

In the early years, twins may become each other's comforter or 'transitional object', like a teddy bear or blanket, providing security in an unfamiliar world. As they grow, they can cooperate and encourage each other in play and mischief-making, often working as a team to achieve together what they couldn't apart. In adulthood, it seems, most twins marry someone with a similar personality to their twin brother or sister.[22]

The dangers of treating twins as a 'matching pair' rather than two distinct individuals are generally acknowledged. At the extremes, twins may find such support and safety in their relationship that they withdraw from interaction with the world beyond. Some experience an intermingling of identity, with each child feeling part of a pair, one half of a whole, rather than a separate individual.[23]

What is less commonly acknowledged is the extent to which twins may emphasise their differences to establish their separate identities[24] – and the damage parents may do by exaggerating this natural process (see Exaggerating differences, page 161, and The danger of labels, page 168). Some studies have even suggested that identical twins separated at birth are *more alike* than those raised together, supporting the idea that close sibling pairs and those

Who's identical?

> *'If people take time to get to know us, they will see we may be the same on the surface but underneath we have our own beliefs and ideas.'* – Multiple Voices, Twins and Multiple Births Association[27]

Some twins are, of course, more similar than others. Identical twins result from the division of one fertilised egg. Fraternal twins are the result of two separate sperm fertilising two separate eggs. They are no more genetically similar than any other brothers and sisters, they just happen to be born at the same time.

While 'identical' twins sometimes show uncanny similarities they are not, of course, identical human beings. The differences between them begin in the womb, with ultrasound studies showing differences in foetal growth and activity patterns and in the way the intra-uterine environment may favour one twin above another.[28] Differences in birth order, birth weight, health and length of stay in hospital may all influence the mother-baby bond, and from their first moments, even identical twins may have very different experiences of life.

If twins are to grow up as fully rounded, bonded but healthily separate individuals, it's our job as parents to treat them as such. This isn't always easy – 'sets' of things have a neatness and cuteness that random 'separates' may not. It is a very human tendency to attempt to impose pattern and order on things. But perhaps that's a tendency best kept for the kids' sock drawer, not the kids themselves.

Dressing twins differently may help others distinguish between

around them may accentuate their differences to emphasise their individuality[25] (see Why are siblings so different? page 165).

These tendencies may be diluted if twins have older or younger siblings. Those who are treated as separate individuals and who are encouraged to have their own activities and friendships outside the family are also freer to be themselves and to develop all their skills.[26]

them. Dissimilar sounding names may help teachers and others confuse them less frequently. Separate classes at school, where possible, may help them progress at their own rate and avoid constant comparison.

Only you will know what feels right for your children, and there are certainly no rules. 'Yet I very much try to stress the importance of allowing twins to be the individuals they are,' says Dr Elizabeth Bryan, paediatrician and founder of the Multiple Births Foundation.

'The most important thing is that everyone can tell the children apart. If you want them to be dressed the same and they are easy to distinguish, that's fine. But it is important to remember that people are lazy and will confuse your twins unless it is very obvious who is who, so dressing them differently may help if they look similar. We know that twins often take longer to respond to their name because they so rarely hear it used. I don't know how you can treat someone as an individual if you don't know which twin they are, and therefore can't call them by their name.

'I am also very aware that many very loving, very sensible parents still find this a real difficulty. I remember a very nice mum who was all set to treat her twins as individuals. When they came to see me at three months they were indistinguishable in looks and dress! I asked her if she had changed her mind and she said, "I can hardly tell you, but I simply can't bring myself to dress them differently." I said, "This is really helpful and really interesting, will you keep me in touch with your feelings about this as time goes on?" At eighteen months she's decided now's the time to dress them differently but it was a real struggle for her. So I accept it is very easy for me to say this, but often much harder for parents to do.'

'Being compared is always painful, and being a twin you are compared a lot. It is a matter of being very careful not to take away people's uniqueness, by comparing or labelling them. My twin was always the one who was much more "athletic" than me. I was always "the bookworm". In fact, I now realise I actually enjoy some sports. My sister enjoys books and is taking a degree in later life.'
– Doro Marden, Parentline Plus facilitator

Language

'My twins are twelve so I really should know better, but I still sometimes find myself telling something to one of them and forgetting to repeat it to the other.' – Julia S.

Twins tend to experience far fewer verbal exchanges with their parents than singletons, and slight language delay is very common, partly because it is much harder to have a triangular conversation than it is to chat in couples.[29] Pairs who spend much time with each other may develop a private language. It is their 'Secret Garden', a place only they can enter.[30] Many twins have shared, made-up words for special items and people.

Differences in language acquisition for twins should be kept in perspective – most twins overcome any initial difficulties and speech therapy support (organised via your GP surgery or health centre) is very effective in turning around young children's language problems. But it helps to be alert to potential difficulties.

Children who cannot express how they feel tend to feel frustrated and may 'act out' their feelings through problematic behaviour. A child whose twin sibling's speech skills are far advanced of their own may become increasingly reticent to speak for themselves, preferring to use their brother or sister as mouthpiece and occasional translator. All can compound a child's feelings of inferiority.

Space

'We didn't all have a room of our own, so we swapped around. I shared with my younger brother and my younger sister at times, as well as with my twin. That helped.' – Doro Marden,
Parentline Plus facilitator

Each twin needs some territory they can call their own. It might be a bunk bed, a space behind the sofa, a corner of the bedroom. Wherever it is, ideally it should be somewhere they can sometimes be alone and keep belongings safe from siblings (see Caring and sharing, page 43).

Encouragement and Praise

Perhaps because of pressures on time and focused attention, twins tend to receive less parental praise and fewer overt expressions of affection than other children.[31] Descriptive praise (see page 72) can help redress the balance and make parental encouragement of siblings easier to accept.

When praise is a problem

'Encouraging and praising twins can be a real, real difficulty,' says Dr Elizabeth Bryan, paediatrician and founder of the Multiple Births Foundation. 'I have seen it in identical twin girls, when one always won the cup for diving and the other was always second. The second was a brilliant diver, but just happened to be second to her sister. That was devastating and spoilt it for both of them.

'I think it is less of a problem with non-identical twins because they are much more likely to have different interests and aptitudes, but identical twins tend to have the same skills and interests and it is unrealistic to say to one, "Stop diving, because that's your sister's great strength, too." It is also important to recognise that you cannot make life fair. One child is going to get more exams, score more goals, earn more money or whatever, so they and we have to be able to accept that.

'It's certainly not fair to hold back the more "successful" one, as I heard happen when only one child passed an exam so neither twin was allowed to go to a grammar school. That is when recognition of wider skills in life becomes so important. Every twin will have something we can make them feel good about.'

Other relationships

'He will butt in on his brother's friendships. It is almost as if he doesn't want his twin to have friends. I don't know how much to control the situation, how much to intervene. I think I'll have to try getting him out of the way

when his brother has friends round. I have tried having a friend round for each but that becomes gang warfare and we all run for cover.' – Amanda C.

Individual friendships through childhood and adolescence are essential if twins are to develop fully individual identities and the self-worth and social skills necessary to form happy and healthy adult relationships[32] (see When friends come to play, page 52).

Siblings of twins

'As well as my two beautiful new babies there was this little lost soul, our first child, who I so desperately wanted to take care of and be sensitive towards but who, in reality, barely got much of a look in during the first six weeks. I tried to keep some routines going, like our bedtime read together, but in truth it was absolute anarchy.' – Sarah P.

'He was seriously upstaged by their arrival and his behaviour did take a shocking nosedive.' – Jonathan T.

Older siblings are outnumbered by *two* new babies, who are often accorded celebrity status. They have to cope with all the adjustments that come with no longer being an 'only' child, and generally receive even less attention from exhausted parents. As the twins grow, their sibling may feel excluded from their close bond and isolated within the family.

From birth on, being the sibling of a twin affects a child's life just as much as being part of a twin pair. Yet if the relationship with the parent or another loved and trusted adult is sufficiently strong, this can be negotiated without too many problems.

'If there are two children before the twins arrive, there has already been a natural adjustment to life with siblings. If there has been the one precious child who's been the focus of attention for a long time, it can be very hard. Parents should be warned when twins are coming that their first child will inevitably find it difficult. Talking to other parents who've been through it seems to be very useful, and helps parents see that life does get easier.' – Dr Elizabeth Bryan paediatrician and founder of the Multiple Births Foundation

All the strategies to prepare and support older siblings of new babies will help (see Mum, you can send her back now, page 5). But with twins and more, it is even more important to get all the help and support you possibly can if you are to look after yourself and your children.

Time and attention

'The overwhelming problem is how does anybody get enough individual attention and airtime? In the mornings I have three children under five all pulling me and talking at once, often their big brother too, and all seemingly unaware that anyone else is speaking at the same time.' – Sarah P

Routines can be far more important in families with twins, as somewhere, somehow, you need to find time for each child to feel noticed, appreciated and heard.

Understanding behaviour

'One study on the siblings of twins found there were twice as many behaviour problems in the older child.[33] Some showed it by aggressive behaviour, some by regressive behaviour, some by negative attention-seeking, some by being "over good" to try to get attention, but maybe the most worrying ones were the children who just withdrew, obviously depressed. This can be overlooked because it is not disruptive. Parents may just be thankful their older child is so quiet and not demanding. That is very worrying.' – Dr Elizabeth Bryan, paediatrician and founder of the Multiple Births Foundation

We need to be alert to any signs of distress in siblings' behaviour. Each child will need our clear guidance, warm understanding, our praise and opportunities to express how they feel (see Exploring emotions, page 125).

'Twins are a hard act to precede and to follow. James, my youngest, responds by wanting to be a teenager at two-and-a-half. He is determined not to be left out and tries to keep up with great energy. George, my eldest, can be an absolutely wonderful big brother and is very protective towards them, but his sense of competition is less benign. His jealousy is very strong.' – Sarah P.

Other relationships

'In fairness, the parents can never give as much as they want to, so now's the time for a godparent, uncle or aunt to support in a big way. I think maybe not enough advantage is taken of people outside the family who could really become close to that child.' – Dr Elizabeth Bryan, paediatrician and founder of the Multiple Births Foundation

Opportunities to forge friendships with supportive adults and others outside the family are vital for siblings of twins. All children in the family will also benefit from having occasional one-to-one time with each other, so the twins are not always together and every child has a chance to get to know each sibling and play together in 'pairs'. This will help the twin bond seem less of an impenetrable charmed circle.

Divorce, step-families and family change

'I don't think we ever raised the subject with mum after he left. We'd talk about it between ourselves at night, imagining where he'd gone, but neither of us asked mum anything.' – Helen T.

'How parents get on after separation is as important as how parents get on when they are together. Separation does not mean that conflict between parents ceases automatically. Some children are harmed because their parents' relationship remains a battleground and they are the go-between. Other children benefit if their family relationships become more harmonious following parental divorce.'
– *Not In Front Of The Children*, One Plus One[37]

Parental conflict can affect children whether parents live together or apart, but separation, divorce and other times of family change bring particular stresses which may affect our children and their relationships with each other. We can ease or amplify these by our own behaviour as parents.

The children involved may feel angry, scared, sad, relieved,

♀ *Changing families* **♀♀♀**

- One in four children under five years old in England and Wales experiences their parents' divorce.[34]
- Many more have unmarried parents who separate.
- Half of these parents will repartner or remarry, forming new step-families.[35] Step-families comprise six per cent of all families in Britain where a parent is aged sixty or under.
- Almost nine in ten step-families consist of at least one child from a previous relationship of the female partner.[36]

resentful, safe, jealous, guilty, confused, or a mixture of all these and more at various times and in various measures. Brothers and sisters can be an important source of support,[38] but whether they are will depend on many factors, including the nature of their relationship prior to family change, the sensitivity of the parental support they receive and, crucially, how their parents manage their disagreements (see How do we deal with disagreements? page 114, and Parental conflict and children, page 245).

Whatever transition the family may be going through, our children need us to be honest and upfront, within reason. Concrete, age-appropriate information about how their lives may change, and reassurances that they are loved and are not in any way to blame, may help allay fears. We may also need to censor certain information, particularly our opinions of former partners and unnecessary details about the breakdown of the parental relationship.

If we are able, we should encourage each child to express their own mix of emotions in their own ways (see Exploring emotions, page 125). Of course, some of what they may need to say may be too painful for us to hear, so it helps if they each have someone else to talk to, perhaps a grandparent or a trusted friend.

We should also be aware of the gap between what we may think we have communicated to our children and what our children have actually taken on board. These are huge issues, with profound impact, and they are unlikely to understand all they need after one or two conversations. They will need time to 'process' information – to digest, consider, probe and question – and this generally requires repeated conversations over time.

> *'I think it helps to show that our feelings are sometimes ambivalent, that we don't always know the answers. As parents we can say, "I'm not sure about that right now, but I'll let you know as soon as I can". And we can demonstrate that ambivalence is something we all have to struggle with. We can let our children see, for example, that it's okay and understandable in difficult times to love and hate someone at the same time.'* – Cheryl Walters, psychotherapist and Head of Research at Parentline Plus

> *'This may sound strange, but now I'm a mother I admire how my parents managed their divorce. We were never left in any doubt that they loved us all and we talked most things through. I'm grateful for that.'* – Emma H.

Divorce and separation

Managing conflict

> *'I know when I am a bit wound up I say or do things, or have telephone conversations which I think the children can't hear, but they do. They pick up on little things when you think they're out of earshot. I've had to become more aware of that.'* – Karen S.

> *'We had some huge rows, but we tried to keep them away from the house so the kids didn't feel like they were in a war zone. You can't fool kids. They know what's going on. But I think you can at least protect them from the worst excesses.'* – Deborah O.

> *' Children can experience problems if exposed to embittered and angry conflict, but they are not deceived by closed doors. Supposedly "hidden" conflict can also be troubling, for conflict between parents pervades family life.'* – Not In Front Of The Children, One Plus One[39]

Children seem to cope with life as well as those from non-separated families two to three years following their parents' divorce, provided they do not experience continued or additional conflict or stress.[40] During the first two years, however, children may display an increase in problematic, argumentative or aggressive behaviour, which is often directed towards brothers and sisters.

Understanding the feelings underlying such behaviour may help us be more constructive in our responses. The conclusions of recent research are unambiguous. The most important factor in influencing children's resilience to the impact of divorce and separation is our own behaviour as parents. Children experiencing the upheavals of family change need us to be loving, warm and responsive, to encourage good family communication and also to provide firm, clear and fair guidance on behaviour.[41]

'A health visitor described it to me as "testing" behaviour. That he was seeing if I would still be there for him no matter how horrible he was to me or to his brothers. He was testing us to see if we'd stand by him or leave, like his dad. That made a lot of sense, and it helped me see how much he needed our support.' – Jill N.

Parental conflict and children

'Parents argue in different ways. Three types of parental conflict have been identified as having an effect on children:

1. **Destructive Conflict** is particularly detrimental to children's well-being. Children are at risk when:

- Conflict is frequent and intense
- Disputes are full of aggression
- Partners treat one another with quiet contempt
- One partner withdraws during an argument

- The child is the subject of disagreements

2. In contrast, children may learn from observing **constructive conflict**, whereby parents manage and resolve disputes effectively, whether they are together or apart.

3. Similarly, children may learn from **productive conflict**, where problems are openly discussed but not necessarily resolved.'

Source: Not In Front Of The Children, *One Plus One*[42]

Divided loyalties hurt

'Parental conflict is often reflected on the younger generation in that sometimes one parent has an "ally" in one of the children and the other parent has an "ally" in another child. These alliances and conflicts inevitably have a bearing on the sibling bond.'
– Desa Markovic, family therapist

Children need to be allowed to love both their parents. This can be hard, especially if we feel great bitterness or anger towards our ex-partner. But if children are encouraged to love or care more about one parent than the other, or to take one's side against the other, they can become distressed and confused. Parent-child allegiances can result in marked differential treatment of siblings, which in turn sparks conflict and distrust between brothers and sisters[43] (see Facing up to favouritism, page 147).

Allowing each child to express their feelings, and making it clear that a family is made up of separate individuals with different and valid viewpoints and emotions, will also help children see the split as a problem between parents. They are not 'to blame'.

'Adults need to take responsibility here. We need to be able to say to the children that we understand how they may be feeling. That we know they love daddy or whatever, and that's okay.' – Cheryl Walters, psychotherapist and Head of Research at Parentline Plus

Different children feel differently

Each child's perspective and responses may be very different, and each will need expression. Someone each child can talk to outside the immediate family may help – and this needn't be the same person for all. Talking to other children, especially those who've lived through similar experiences, may help a child feel less isolated and lonely (see Exploring emotions, page 125, and Message received? page 187).

Step-families

'The foundations are so important and have to be put in place first. Good relationships are about hard work every day. They don't just happen and we need to break the myth that they do.' – Cheryl Walters, psychotherapist and Head of Research at Parentline Plus

'He's my brother, not by birth but by all that matters. And I love him.' – Michael W.

'One of the strongest messages in these stories [of growing up in step-families] was the power of these memories in shaping people's lives and self-understanding. They conveyed vividly how the past can hang as a shadow over a life or provide recurrent strength, and how crucial reflection can be in turning the experiences of the past into an enabling force for the future.' – Growing Up In Stepfamilies, Gill Gorell Barnes et al[44]

Adjusting to life with a new step-parent or step-family will inevitably impact on sibling relationships. Equally, how children get on with their brothers, sisters, half-siblings or step-siblings is central to their experiences of step-family life.[45]

Their circumstances will vary widely, not least because of the wide-ranging roots and components of step-families. Some children may be full or part-time members of new households; many will be sharing their lives with new children as well as new adults; some may come to step-family life after divorce, others after single-parenthood, separation of co-habiting parents or the death of their mother or father.

There are, however, issues common to most siblings' experiences of step-family life.

Time and patience

'You can't make instant families and you can't make instant brothers and sisters.' – Jude, aged fourteen

'I want time with my husband to build our relationship, but the kids take up so much of it. It's hard not to resent that.' – Cathryn D.

Relationships with new step-brothers and sisters or with a new adult in the family can work well. However, most children find the transition hard, and may reflect this in increased conflict with their siblings. In time, however, as relationships grow and new family routines and customs develop, aggression between brothers and sisters tends to decrease to levels found in families generally.

Realistic expectations of our children's behaviour and a recognition of their complex and often conflicting emotions as they adjust to their new lives may help us maintain the mix of firm, clear parental guidance and warmth, responsiveness and understanding that they need.

> 'We get on fine now, and I think the kids genuinely like each other and enjoy each other's company, but I was too tough to begin with. I'd get so upset when they'd argue. I remember sobbing to my husband one night that I wanted to live in a house full of love, not a house full of rage and resentment. But I think it was all wrapped up in me wanting everything to be okay this time round. I'd had my fill of arguments and wanted some familial bliss. But that wasn't really fair on them.' – Karen O.

Tolerance of difference

> 'The boys are so different, and sometimes the only way to negotiate that is to highlight it and ask them to respect it. "So Tom does it this way and you do it another way, but actually you both manage to do it. So where's the problem?" It's something that all parents with more than one child have to deal with, but in a merged family like ours it's definitely higher up the agenda.' – Sarah P.

Imagine. You are spending most of your time in one house with one set of rules but some of your time in another house with another set of rules. In one house you are the eldest child. In the other you are number three. Your brothers and sisters don't feel the same as you do. The two homes and the people in them sound different, feel different, act different, even smell different. Each contains at least one person, your parent, whom you love.

If different is taken to mean 'better' or 'worse', your life will be even

Adjusting to step-family life

Some groups of children tend to find step-family life harder than others. Children aged between nine and fifteen may have particular difficulty accepting a step-parent. Those coping with the birth of a baby to a parent and step-parent can, understandably, take time to come to terms with the living proof of their new family order.

Girls who become very close to their mothers following divorce tend to have more long-term difficulties adjusting to a step-family and often remain more disengaged from siblings, spending less time interacting with full and step-brothers and sisters. Boys, who tend to have more problems inside and outside the home following divorce, seem to gradually adapt and benefit from contact with a supportive step-father.[46]

Interestingly, the 'emotional pitch' seems higher among full siblings than among half- or step-siblings in step-families. Research indicates that while full siblings are more often loved by children than are half- or step-brothers and sisters, they are also more often disliked. Intense hostility, relatively common among full siblings, seems relatively rare among other sibling types once step-families become established.[47]

more confusing and strained. If you and everyone around you is encouraged to see 'different' as simply that – another valid way of behaving, being, feeling – you are likely to feel more accepting and accepted. Tolerance involves an acknowledgement of feelings and an understanding that differences can coexist. It is something we parents can encourage by what we do and say, and how we encourage tolerance and understanding among all children in the family (see Building tolerance, page 176). It is an essential of step-family survival.

'We can foster the idea that difference is okay, that difference means that we expand ourselves, that we don't all have to be the same and that there are different ways to be a family. At its simplest, if your stepchild tells you, "Mummy always does the roast chicken like this", you perhaps could accept

that and say, "Yes, there are lots of different ways to cook chicken." This is how you can begin to help children accept difference and it is such an important life skill. We shouldn't be afraid of difference, threatened by it or diminished by it.' – Cheryl Walters, psychotherapist and
Head of Research at Parentline Plus

The risks of preferential treatment

In all families, preferential treatment fuels sibling conflict. In step-families, the impact of parental favouritism can be particularly marked, perhaps because the temptations to show preference are so much greater and the competition between step-siblings to find their place in the family system is so keenly felt (see Facing up to favouritism, page 147).

Some adults simply don't get on with their step-children. Some children within step-families simply don't get on with each other. But we can try to avoid marked and long-term differences in the affection or irritability displayed to each child and to ease the transition to step-family life for all the children involved (see What must it feel like? page 251).

Building a sense of belonging

'There were two happy homes with children – one my dad's and one my mum's – and I wasn't really a part of either. I was welcome, I suppose, but I wasn't sought after. I wasn't missed if I wasn't there. There was nowhere I really belonged.' – Andrew S.

'I used to love staying with my half-sister. We'd do things I'd never do at home – make camps in the bedroom, talk to each other through walkie-talkies in the garden, eat Jaffa Cakes in front of the telly.' – Mike T.

Many children spend time in both parental homes, or at least visit regularly. They may not only face picking up the threads of their relationship with mum or dad, but also sharing time with other children. This can work wonderfully well or be excruciatingly hard, depending on the circumstances.

What must it feel like?

It is important for all parents to occasionally put themselves in children's shoes and look at life from their perspective. It helps us have a far better grasp of their feelings and anxieties, and enables us to respond with far greater sensitivity and effect. 'But it is even more vital for step-parents,' says Cheryl Walters, a psychotherapist and Head of Research at Parentline Plus.

'The moment they do so they get a far better understanding of the child, whether they like the child or not. The moment they can imagine themselves in that situation and are able to think "Oh God, I would probably hate this as well!" is the moment that there is a space to develop in the relationship.

'Separate time is so important. Of course, go off and have a particular time with your own child, but if you also spend time alone with your step-child the chances increase of something developing between you that maybe you weren't expecting. It won't be the same, but it may actually be okay and even become valuable to you both.'

As well as allowing all relationships the potential to develop, it also helps to accept the differences between them. 'It is important not to knock our relationships with step-children because they aren't the same as with our own,' says Cheryl Walters. 'Again, it's about accepting difference, about recognising that you might be able to have something with this child that you don't get with yours, or saying "Okay, it's not ideal, there are problems, but this relationship is actually worth having".'

We can ease children's sense of belonging by trying to ensure they have somewhere of their own to keep clothes and possessions. Family chores, projects and activities may help unite children in a joint goal, even temporarily (see Caring and sharing, page 43). Children with a wide age gap between themselves and children in the family they are visiting sometimes feel more comfortable if they bring a friend along, at least to begin with. Planning activities around a favourite hobby may help them feel recognised and welcomed.

♀ *Children calling . . .* ♀♀♀

The following 'snapshots' of recent calls to ChildLine show just some of the issues children face when living in a step-family – and the number of problems that might be eased by better family communication and understanding.

- A fourteen-year-old girl whose mother had died has always lived with her dad and gran. After her dad remarried, two step-sisters moved in. She finds it 'hard to cope'. Apart from finding her step-mum 'bossy', she is feeling 'pushed out' by her step-sisters and feels she has rivals for her dad's affections.

- An eleven-year-old does not get on with her step-sister aged four-teen. She thinks she killed her hamster.

- A twelve-year-old girl rang because she had been 'kicked out' by dad's girlfriend who 'doesn't want me, doesn't care about me'. 'My step-brother is two, and I feel completely left out, I don't want to go home. I'm very cold and hungry and I'm scared to sleep in the dark outside.'

- A boy aged twelve whose father had remarried now felt he was 'number two', compared with his father's new partner. He was 'very sad' and felt his dad did not love him any more.

Reproduced with the kind permission of ChildLine[48]

Reviewing boundaries

Children, particularly in their early teens, may feel uncomfortable when confronted with the idea of their parents as sexual beings. Keeping overt shows of sexual attraction between parent and step-parent to a minimum can help avoid embarrassment and set an important example about appropriate behaviour in the family. This is particularly important when adolescent children who haven't grown up together suddenly find themselves sharing a home.

'While it is important that children see their parents affectionate, I think that anything that is overtly sexual is not fair, it can set up uncomfortable images in a child's mind. Adults should remember that how they want to be isn't

necessarily what the children want or need to see.' – Cheryl Walters,
psychotherapist and Head of Research at Parentline Plus

Knowing our role

'Why should we take any notice? He's their dad, not ours.'
– Simon, aged twelve

As a step-parent, we can be loving, supportive and caring but
we cannot be an instant replacement mother or father. Studies indicate that even those step-parents who display warmth and
responsive concern for their step-children risk rejection by them
if they attempt to exert control or impose discipline too soon. Those
who show warmth, who support their partner's parenting and only
later attempt involvement in the children's discipline and behaviour
management stand a much better chance of acceptance by their
step-children.[49]

*'My step-sons live with me, my partner and our other children for just
under half the time. They have a devoted father and a mother who is very
responsible and committed, who loves them completely and who they love
completely. So they have a full parenting quota. I am enormously fond of
them both but I am not their parent. I feel absolutely clear about that and
I think that's probably why we do all get on as a family. They have
been pleasantly surprised that moving in with us does not entail
me trying to control or rejig their lives.'* – Sarah P.

Getting together

*'Every fortnight we get together to discuss what's going on and how
everyone's feeling. Last night's big discussion was about who messes up the
videos and who should clear them up.'* – Lisa B.

*'With a big family there's never a time when you are not worried about some-
body. It is very rare to have a complete bill of health. With three it's rare
enough; when all the children are here and we're six, it's pretty well never.
There's always going to be at least one you are fretting about or who needs*

Family meetings

'Not interrupting is the first idea to take on board. If it seems this is going to be difficult, give whoever wants a notebook to jot down points they want to bring back later, but ask them not to interrupt. If one person tends to dominate family conversations, it could be useful to give them a time limit, say five minutes, after which others are allowed to talk. That way everyone can have their say.' – Cheryl Walters, psychotherapist and Head of Research at Parentline Plus

The basic idea is to provide a forum for every step-family member's opinion to be heard and to encourage children to suggest solutions to family problems. Topics up for discussion can include everything from feelings in the family to house rules, to who keeps leaving the towel on the bathroom floor.

Some children find it easier to write down questions or worries, or may need a parent to raise a particular matter for them: 'Some of you feel there's nowhere to be quiet in this house at the moment. Can any of you think why having a quiet place is important, and what we can do about it?'

Encouraging all children to make constructive suggestions and to listen to other people's contributions can help foster mutual respect and a sense of 'all being in this together'. Once they have suggested possible solutions, each child can choose their favoured alternative.

Our job is to help the discussions happen, not to dominate proceedings or get our own way. If solutions aren't agreed, however, we may have to outline the pros and cons of each suggestion and add a few of our own (see When they can't sort it out themselves, page 112).

Time limits to discussions and the number of items discussed can stop meetings dragging on. 'Bribes' such as snacks may help keep all participants in one place for a while. Discussing fun items, such as family outings and treats, can help lighten the mood.

'We have to let children have their own opinions and encourage them to express them. This is so important in step-families but it's great training for all kids. It's a skill for life.' – Cheryl Walters, psychotherapist and Head of Research at Parentline

attention. The ideal is to be super-observant but it's hard to keep up. Sometimes I just need to get lost in a book or a flowerbed.' – Sarah P.

With all the competing demands of step-family life, some voices may not be heard and some relationships may go relatively unsupported. It helps to remember that each child needs to get to know every other family member, not just those of their birth family or those they gravitate towards initially. Arranging activities for each 'pair' – anything from trips out to reading to little ones – can help forge bonds.

'Family meetings' can also help step-families open up communication and sort out issues children seem to find hard (see page 254). This may sound rather formal, but many families find that a structure for discussions helps ensure every family member has their say.

Extra pressures:
key approaches

Illness, disability and special needs	**Remember the well child**: lack of attention can lead to long-term problems. **Allow feelings**: every child needs someone to listen to their feelings and fears. **Provide information**: understanding the illness or disability and the family situation reduces aggression and disagreements between siblings. **Let the relationship grow**: each child can benefit.
Twins and more	**Manage time and attention**: each child needs individual attention and one-to-one time. **Manage conflict**: avoid treating twins as 'a set'. Each will need clear guidance on their behaviour. **Encourage individuality**: acknowledge and appreciate each child as an individual, allowing them their own space, their own friends and individual recognition for their unique special qualities. **Siblings of twins**: need attention, understanding and opportunities to forge relationships outside the family, too.
Divorce and family change	**Allow feelings**: children need to know their feelings are understood and respected, even when they are

	different to their parents', brother's and sister's. **Give appropriate information**: so each child can better understand what's happening in their lives. **Lessen the impact of conflict**: by letting children see their parents deal with it as calmly and constructively as they can.
Step-families	**Allow time and patience**: for children to adjust and relationships to grow. **Encourage tolerance**: help children understand that differences can coexist. **Avoid marked preferential treatment**: it will only fuel conflict between children. **Build a sense of belonging**: with shared activities and family meetings to discuss issues and problems. **Know our role**: Step-parents are not instant or replacement parents, and children's relationships will benefit if we respect that.

Key message:

Watch for moments to respond to each child's needs. We can, and it counts.

9

Growing pains:

adolescence and beyond

'Establishing identity becomes a huge issue as kids become teenagers. The jump-cuts you face as a parent can be so dramatic. All of a sudden this person you thought you knew suddenly becomes someone very different, and you think to yourself, "But yesterday you were this! And today you're that! Who is this?" It can be baffling for brothers and sisters, too.' – Mary MacLeod, chief executive, National Family and Parenting Institute

'There are so many new things to tease and hurt each other about once they hit adolescence – friends, dates, bodies, clothes. Their emotions are so heightened they can be in agony over the smallest slight, ignore each other for weeks then get closer again and have a good laugh.' – Linda G.

To parents, a child's journey through adolescence to young adulthood can be poetic as well as turbulent. To a brother or sister, it can seem plain weird. Sibling relationships change in adolescence, often dramatically.

The middle childhood years (from about six to nine) and even pre-adolescence (from roughly ten to the beginnings of puberty) tend to be the least eventful in sibling relationships.[1] The bonds between our children may develop, sometimes stronger, sometimes looser but, short of dramatic upheaval in their lives, the nature of their relationship tends to be relatively familiar and stable.

Then come sex hormones. New friends. New freedoms. New emotions. New vulnerabilities. New attitude. New spots. Our children will change shape and increase in sexual maturity, thinking capacity and emotional sophistication. Overall, the developmental changes they experience will be as numerous and as life-shaping as those of infancy and toddlerhood. Hardly surprising then, that siblings' influences on each other in adolescence may be profound and dramatic, for good, bad and both.

The challenge is to connect with and support each of our children and their relationships with each other in new and age-appropriate ways. This isn't always easy, and we need to inject a note of realism. Parents cannot wave magic wands. As with any stage of our children's development, we can nurture and encourage sibling relationships, but we can't force them. If we try during the volatile years of adolescence, our efforts are very likely to backfire.

Yet by continuing to love, respect, support and respond to our children as individuals, and by helping them communicate with and understand each other, we can help them still connect as they change and grow. And the rewards can be great, with richer and more sophisticated family relationships as the next generation matures.

'It helps if parents cast back and remember what their own needs were at that stage of their lives, and how far they were met and not met. Adolescents are finding out who they are, what they like and what they are good at, how to be liked and respected by their peers and to form relationships. This is their time to learn, to find these things out, to not be too constrained but to still have boundaries, to be able to be a child one day and an adult the next.'
– John Bristow, chartered psychologist and psychotherapist

Changing relationships

Growing up requires children to develop and establish adult identities, different and separate from their parents and from brothers and sisters. In the process, some children may become cool and distant, others may become volatile and angry and many move between the two as they seek to wean themselves and others off childhood dependencies. Their siblings may experience a profound sense of loss of the relationship that once existed between them. All family members may benefit from better awareness of the key factors in these shifting family bonds.

Change is unsettling

'One of the natural transitions is when the older one goes off to senior school and the younger one is left at primary school. Suddenly the horizons are different and the older child is expected to be much more grown up. That, coupled with the changes through puberty, can make a chasm open up between them. Some siblings won't want strong sibling relationships for any number of reasons, and we have to allow that. But if they had a strong bond before, they'll usually reconverge later on.' – Dr Sarah Newton, specialist in children's psychological health

'I can't say I was particularly affected when my brother left home because we were never that close, but my sister mooched about for weeks like a jilted girlfriend. The difference was quite pronounced. I hardly noticed, and she grieved.' – Charlotte V.

Some siblings stay close through their teenage years, but many adolescents pull away from brothers and sisters as they begin to establish their adult identities. This can be painful for the sibling 'left behind' in the developmental journey, who may yearn for the former relationship and not know how to relate to their new-style brother or sister. Children who watch older siblings leave home may feel a particularly sharp jolt.

As there is fear in the unknown, it may help to talk to our children about the nature of adolescence, the common feelings it may stir in families and the shifts in sibling relationships that may occur as they grow. Explaining that relations with a brother or sister can go through tough or fallow times then blossom again, may reassure a child that the bond hasn't broken beyond repair. Talking about issues as they arise is generally more constructive than formal 'sit-down-and-let-me-explain-why-your-sister-is-acting-strangely' conversations (see Message received? page 187).

> *'Puberty and adolescence are so volatile, the feelings so intense, that I think brothers and sisters often run for cover.'* – Ros T.

🏃🏃🏃 *What do we expect?* 🏃🏃

Family ties often weaken around adolescence. Whether they re-establish may be influenced by societal and cultural expectations, as well as direct family relationships.

'Attachment to parents and siblings may weaken at this stage of life as children have new experiences, make new friends and try to establish an identity apart from the family,' says Professor Victor G. Cicirelli, one of the world's leading researchers into sibling relationships throughout life. 'Siblings at this stage tend to fight, disagree and annoy each other. Typically, siblings feel closer again in young adulthood, although they may become preoccupied with getting an education, finding a mate, developing a career, and so on.

'In industrialised society, there is little formal support for sibling relationships compared to non-industrialised societies. In addition, sibling relations in today's families are more complex, with step-siblings, half-siblings and adoptive siblings often competing with biological siblings. This may make it still more difficult to maintain supportive sibling relationships.'

The pace of puberty

There is a wide age range for the onset of puberty among children, and even children in the same family may mature physically at different times in their lives and at different rates. This can be most marked between genders, as girls sometimes shoot ahead of slightly older brothers. Obvious differences in maturity can be painful.

> *I was a year younger than my brother but started going out with boys who were at least one year above him at school. They treated him like the squirty*

kid brother. That must have been hard. Also, I had boyfriends when he didn't have a girlfriend for years. That must have been torture.' – Susan K.

'Growing up with someone of similar age but different gender teaches you a lot, I think. I've a twin sister, so adolescence was very different for both of us, but that maybe helped me understand more about women. Certainly more about her. How can you ever know what you'd have been without your sibling? You can't. But that's what I sense.' – Malcolm D.

The impact of sibling behaviour

Siblings can have a life-transforming impact on each other in the teen years. A teasing, undermining brother or sister can crush self-esteem at this vulnerable time, while a more supportive one can help a child negotiate the changes in themselves and their life with greater ease and understanding.

Research worldwide also emphasises the link between siblings and delinquent behaviour in adolescence – if one goes off the rails, their brother or sister often follows (see Siblings and delinquency, page 264).

Comparing 'success'

'Some adults don't want things to be good for their friends. It's a very grown-up position to take, and it's often easier to be jealous and competitive. So maybe it's too much to expect our children to be generous about each other just yet.' – Lisa S.

Adolescents tend to measure their achievements against the yardstick of sibling accomplishments – who is the more 'successful', rich, attractive, popular, loved?

One sibling may idolise another for a while. One child may feel irritated beyond belief by their brother or sister. It happens. By accepting feelings (see Exploring emotions, page 125), talking about family members' feelings and needs (in a way that doesn't make them vulnerable to derision), supporting each child individually and discussing

Siblings and delinquency

'If the first child becomes delinquent, it is very likely the second child becomes delinquent, too. Siblings in general are very different, but one thing they are surprisingly likely to share is antisocial behaviour.'
– Dr Gavin Nobes, senior lecturer in
developmental psychology

The fact that adolescent siblings often display similar problematic or antisocial behaviour is clear. A growing body of research shows the link between siblings and alcohol and drug misuse, and violent and delinquent behaviour.[2]

But why is the link so strong? 'It seems partly a question of kids in a family getting drawn into the antisocial activities of a sibling,' explains child psychiatrist, Professor Michael Rutter. 'It may also be in part a shared genetic vulnerability,

though that cannot explain it fully. The genetic influence on antisocial behaviour and ordinary depression are about the same, yet depression usually affects just one child in the family while antisocial behaviour affects several children.'

While acknowledging that children in the same family have very different experiences of childhood (see Why are siblings so different? page 165), Professor Rutter stresses that some problems a family may face are likely to affect all the children

Keeping track

Adolescents need us to keep track of what's happening in their lives and in their relationships with friends, brothers and sisters. We need to be generally aware of where they are, what they are doing and with whom (see Siblings and delinquency, page 264).

As they grow our children will

require less direct supervision, but still need us to observe and communicate with them, their friends and other adults who know them. Heavy-handed interrogation or attempts to track their every move will usually lead to open revolt. However, most adolescents consider appropriate 'monitoring' of their welfare

within it. 'It is really important not to assume that because children grow up in the same family their experiences are the same. It is also very necessary that we take on board that there are some sorts of problems that usually affect several children in the same family.

'The implication is that shared environmental effects – shared experiences – are likely to be more important for antisocial behaviour in children than they are for other outcomes, such as depression. Such shared experiences with effects on delinquency include unresolved family conflict and discord, a lack of social problem-solving, and poor supervision of the children's activities.'

'It's one of those enormous questions, isn't it, why some children become self-destructive and delinquent? My boys can see each other as unique individuals. We all celebrate each other's talents and strengths, but I think it still doesn't wipe out the enormous messages that we get about who we are. I certainly couldn't control it. My elder boy said, in effect, "The most important thing in life for me is to be a macho street boy" and then the one who came just eighteen months behind him said, "I'm going to be an even bigger, macho, drug-taking street boy". They could have chosen many other messages to receive but those were the two they chose. I don't know why.' – Barbara Dale, counsellor, mother and long-term foster parent

as a sign that their parents care.[3]

We can aim to be alert to their needs but not overly intrusive. We can attempt that delicate balance if we:

- **Observe, listen and communicate** with each of our children (see Making connections, page 270).
- **Monitor their progress** with teachers and others.
- **Get to know their friends**, or at least know who they are.
- **Talk to other adults** they come into contact with.
- **Be aware of changes** in their behaviour and their relationship with each other.
- **Let each child know they can tell us anything.**
- **Let each child know we're available when they need us.**

different ways of being, we may encourage our children to accept each other more generously.

> 'Things that helped them gain insight into each other's differences seem to help. Kids can be on top of each other, yet still not really see or understand each other. Our son imagined we thought everything of his sister and nothing of him. We certainly weren't that impressed with a lot of his behaviour at the time. Then my husband took him to visit his sister who was working in Rwanda. He saw her as an adult, working in a job, and he got a totally different perspective on her. Their relationship has changed for the good ever since.' – Barbara Dale, counsellor

Establishing and maintaining family 'traditions'

> 'We all complained about having to be home for Sunday lunch, but I would have been horrified if they'd stopped happening.'
> – Lisa S.

Children who feel disappointed or rejected by changes in their sibling relationship may be particularly appreciative of one-to-one time with a parent. We can also provide a framework for family relations by maintaining old and establishing new ways of getting together, from meals together to family days out. This is far from an assurance of improved communication between our children, but at least the opportunity is there if they are in the same place at the same time. Even if it is not taken up, the children are having shared experiences which may make it easier for them to reconnect in adulthood.

Children who have the advantage of shared interests – from football to fishing, cooking to rock climbing – may still take pleasure in each other's company and common pursuits, but may need our help to make it happen. Billing them as 'family' activities rather than 'children's' pursuits may mean older children are less dismissive of a younger siblings' companionship and efforts.

> For me, divorced and then remarried, it has been very important to build rituals of constancy, permanency. I think these can help in all families as they change and the children grow. It was important that at

certain times in the week, for example, the children and I would have meals
together, and that we did certain things at weekends. Now the children are
grown, we have new rituals, like meeting for lunch. The rituals we
have established over the years have become amended but not broken,
so there is quite a strong sense of continuance.'
– Jim Wilson, systemic psychotherapist

Stuck in the past?

Some sibling relationships become 'stuck', anchored in past perceptions and prejudices and unable to move on. We can help liberate
each child by refusing to label individuals or their relationships and
by being alert to the dangers of one child feeling less favoured than
another (see Kids don't fit in pigeonholes, page 159 and Facing up to
favouritism, page 147).

It is especially important during the teen years that children's sense
of their own potential is not limited by parents or siblings still applying
old 'labels' – the 'good' sister or 'wayward' brother, the 'naughty' or
'responsible' one – introducing new ones, or treating them as the
young children they once were rather than the adolescents they have
become.

Searching for adult identity is hard enough without also having to
negotiate inappropriate parental assumptions and aspirations[4] (see
A fragile confidence, page 268). Are we aware of each child's new
interests, skills, achievements, passions, ideas, fears? Are we treating
them each as different people at different developmental stages and
with different abilities and needs, or as some sort of homogenous 'job
lot'? Are we alert to labels other family members may be sticking to
our kids?

'Because they were close, twenty-one months between them, I often
expected my children to be the same. You can then have expectations
and anxieties that are totally unrealistic, about the youngest child
especially. Actually she was absolutely fine, just younger.'
– Mary MacLeod, National Family and Parenting Institute

'My mum always asked my daughter about her GCSE course work and
my son about his cricket. Always. In the end I had to have a word. I tried

✦✦✦ *A fragile confidence* ✦✦✦

Comparisons between children can have serious consequences at any age, but the potential for damage can be greater as they move through adolescence and form new views of themselves and their world.

'I remember a client, a woman in her twenties, who suffered depression and lack of motivation,' says family therapist Desa Markovic. 'She felt a failure in whatever work she attempted and finally gave up doing anything.

During our therapeutic conversations she discussed her past family experiences and particularly her relationship with her brother with whom she once had been close. Their relationship began to change as he became more academically successful. While concentrating on his studies he was showing less interest in spending time with her and she felt rejected, uninteresting and not clever. She found his behaviour intimi-

dating and it undermined her self-confidence.

'It became like a vicious circle; the more she was hearing that she was not good enough, the "less good" she became. By withdrawing into her room and avoiding the world, she was trying to protect herself from further hurt.

'This is an extreme example of how things can go wrong, and there are probably many factors involved, including cultural and gender beliefs. Yet the parents had not been aware of the sibling influence on their daughter's sense of worth. Our family sessions helped them learn about this connection.

'I think there is much that parents can do to avoid such situations. Their encouragement of each child as an individual throughout their lives is a crucial component in the development and strengthening of their self esteem.'

to put it positively, asking her if she'd help me boost my son's confidence about college by taking an interest and ease my daughter's anxieties about exams by talking to her about other things. The effect was quite marked. They've started having real conversations together. I hope they can keep it up.'
– Susan W.

The importance of friends

'When there is a difference in emotional or physical development between siblings, friends become very important. Children want contact with others who are at the same stage as themselves and interested in the same things.'
– Dr Elizabeth Bryan, paediatrician and founder
of the Multiple Births Foundation

'Through adolescence, the influence of peers increases. It is quite rare that even a couple of siblings who are eighteen months apart will spend much time with the same group of friends. More often, because they are usually in different classes at school, they will hang out with different groups. If they are different genders, they are even more likely to have different friendship groups.' – Dr Gavin Nobes, senior
lecturer in developmental psychology

Friendships take on new importance and meaning in adolescence, as most parents can testify on examining telephone bills or watching their children declare individuality by dressing the same as their peers.

The potency of peer pressure in delinquency and drug misuse is clear, and we can help our children resist pressures to follow the crowd by encouraging them from early childhood to value themselves, their feelings and their own decisions.[5] Yet we should not allow the negative associations of peer pressure blind us to the benefits that close teen friendships can bring. They can be intense, intimate, and rooted in great trust and mutual understanding, and they seem central to adolescents' experiences of independence outside the family and to their understanding of acceptable social behaviour and adult relationships.

They can also be hugely consuming of an adolescent's time and attention, and devastating for a sibling excluded from the group. Yet the excluded child's friendships and outside interests can also be an invaluable source of fun and understanding when relationships with a brother or sister seem to falter.

'If one child considers themselves to be too grown up to be bothered with a sibling, we can look to the rejected child's resources. What do they get satisfaction from? What do they enjoy? What makes them feel good? These are things to build on.' – Jim Wilson, systemic psychotherapist

Making connections

'As the need for independence gets stronger, so does the need to be valued and heard. Adolescents don't need us any the less. Their need for our love, approval, boundaries, affection, attention and listening ear doesn't stop just because they become spotty teenagers.' – Sarah Darton, health visitor

Communicating with our adolescent children will help them express their feelings, better manage their behaviour and reduce levels of sibling conflict. That much we know (see Message received? page 187).

What may take us by surprise is the degree to which our children need to communicate and the lengths they will go to avoid it. As their need for privacy increases, so their sharing of personal information may become more selective. A child who shouts their opinions out loud in the morning may be the child who communicates by grunt in the afternoon. Maintaining links with teenagers isn't easy, but essential. Parents, professionals and adolescents themselves have suggested the following approaches:

1. **Listen first, speak later.** If we want to find out what is on an adolescent's mind, we should be prepared to listen and to wait.

2. **Keep direct questions to a minimum.** Interrogating teens about thoughts, feelings and deeds invites communication clampdown. If the issue's important, expressing our own thoughts and concerns, then inviting our children to talk about them, may work better: 'It worries me that you two seem so angry with each other. If you want to talk about it, I'll listen and try to understand.'

'You know, really understanding parents can be a pain in the butt, just as much as parents who don't understand at all. We need to remember that, we need to be able to scroll back, keep our nose out sometimes and remember what adolescence felt like for us.'
– Cheryl Walters, psychotherapist and Head of Research at Parentline Plus

3. **Respect views.** Adolescents often try out new views and opinions for size before deciding whether they fit, so it helps not to over-react or assume that what is being voiced today will necessarily be an opinion they will hold in adulthood or even tomorrow. This does not mean that their opinion doesn't count.

Listening to, respecting and exchanging ideas in a non-judgemental way is key to maintaining communication links, to understanding how they are feeling and what they are doing, and to them extending the same courtesy to brothers and sisters.

'Some teenagers are almost trying on different outfits and deciding what fits. They are beginning to launch away from the family and finding out who they are and what they think. They've got to suck it and see before they find what they're comfortable with. And we should let them.' – Sarah Darton, health visitor

'Parents' respect for their children's opinions and wishes needs to be even more visible once they reach adolescence. It doesn't mean we have to agree with our children, but we need to show them we respect what they're saying. Hopefully sometimes we will be able to say, "Actually I haven't thought of it like that, you have a point". At others we may say, "Well, I understand what you are saying and I can remember where you are coming from, but actually that is a bit dangerous." Sometimes we can look for a middle road, sometimes it's going to be a straight "No", but even that doesn't mean we have to rubbish their opinions.' – Cheryl Walters, psychotherapist and Head of Research at Parentline Plus

4. **Consider complex emotions.** Adolescents develop an increasing ability to identify and communicate complex emotions and to understand the emotions of others in more sophisticated ways.[6] By talking about emotions we can help our children better understand their own feelings and those of other family members (see Exploring emotions, page 125). This may help them be gentler on themselves and on their irritating parents, brothers and sisters.

5. **Be alert to anxieties.** Expressing

hurt or need can be hard for a teenager desperate to appear 'cool' in front of friends and 'grown up' in front of parents and siblings.

Much adolescent anxiety can be hidden by stroppy or surly behaviour. It is our task to be clear what behaviour we find unacceptable and, crucially, to consider the feelings that may lay beneath their actions.

'She's been vile to her brothers for weeks. Calling them horrible names, refusing to reply when they speak to her, tutting and rolling her eyes when they said anything, even walking out of the room if they came in. As far as I can make out, it's because she's fallen out with a friend. Whatever's happened, it doesn't seem to have much to do with the people she's taking it out on.' – Sally P.

6. **Seize the moment.** Some teens still appreciate hugs and physical expressions of affection. Many don't, especially boys, and especially in public. It's our job to show physical affection when appropriate and appreciated, to find new, more mutually acceptable ways of expressing our love and regard, and to grasp opportunities when they arise.

Children who feel unable to express their affections or who feel deprived of affection in adolescence can feel increasingly isolated, angry and sad. Acknowledging the positives of our children's developing personalities, interests and achievements will help them feel better understood and appreciated.

'I think mum or dad could go to the teenager and say, "You're still not too big for me to give you a hug". We can teach them that it's okay to still be physically affectionate. Or if they would find that hard, we can do it the other way round, say, "I'm feeling a bit low, could you do me a favour and give me a hug.' – Cheryl Walters, psychotherapist and Head of Research at Parentline Plus

'Parental recognition is important at any age, whether you're five or fifty, isn't it?' – Ian B.

7. Look beyond immediate family.

*'All my sisters are important people in my children's lives and we
support each other's children at difficult times. That really
helped, especially when my children were teenagers.'*
– Barbara Dale, counsellor

Adolescents may sometimes talk to a trusted adult outside the family – perhaps a teacher or a friend's mum – more easily than they talk to their parents. What matters is that they are able to talk to someone.

*'This is a time when children are a storm of feelings, when they are
pulling away from family and when schools are often less equipped to
support them emotionally. These children need someone to talk to about
their feelings. It may be the most dominant aspect of their lives, yet
through the secondary years we risk acknowledging them the least.'*
– Corinne Abisgold, educational psychologist

8. Letting them know they are loved. We should tell them and we should show them, by taking an interest in what each of our children is doing and feeling and by making ourselves available when they need us.

Arguments and fights

*'The "he's got", "but she's got" rivalry seems to last forever. My twenty-year-
old, would you believe, was upset when my husband brought home sweets for
the younger ones and he didn't get any. Crazily, it still carries on.'* – Eileen
Hayes, writer and parenting adviser to the NSPCC

*'Siblings can't argue in isolation. With every disagreement comes a
lifetime's worth of resentments, misunderstandings and shared
childhood moments. For the most part, I believe we simply
learn to dance around the eggshells.'*
–Brian C.

Adolescent children will argue with us and with their brothers and sisters. And that's as it should be. It is one of the ways they work out who they are and what they think, and it helps alert us to their changing needs and increasing maturity.[7] The good news is that they probably won't argue as much as sitcoms suggest, and their more sophisticated understanding of other people's emotions means they are now better equipped to resolve disagreements constructively. When they feel like it.

When they don't, conflict between siblings can still be ear-splitting, abrasive or aggressive. Our role is to be sufficiently alert and emotionally available to support, step in and guide behaviour when necessary (see He started it!, page 83 and Conflict in perspective, page 275).

Forewarned is forearmed

'My sister was like a snake – deadly, and you wouldn't see it coming. One false move, and she'd get you by the throat with a vicious comment. She was awful to us for years.' – Lisa S.

Children tend to physically fight less often as they get older, although adolescents may still attack each other verbally or punch, hit and slap each other when tempers erupt. Gone may be the days when we can forcibly separate them, but they should be left in no doubt as to our low opinion of such behaviour and our expectation that they behave otherwise in future (see He started it! page 83).

Play fighting, or rough and tumble, becomes less common and should be watched closely as it can slide further away from 'play' and closer towards 'fighting' as they grow.

'In rough and tumble play, younger children are learning how far they can go while keeping it playful. But it seems things start to change as you get into adolescence because some children then take advantage of rough and tumble play to actually hurt their opponent or impress others with being dominant. There's quite a bit of evidence for that.'
– Professor Peter Smith, Professor of Psychology at
Goldsmiths College, University of London, and
Head of the Unit for School and Family Studies

Conflict in perspective

'They don't argue often, but when they do they turn from teenagers into toddlers. They're slamming doors and sending rude text messages to each other's phones rather than throwing Lego, but essentially I've seen it all before.' – Christine P.

'Adolescence is a time when we rework the experiences of infancy, particularly those of separation.' – Audrey Sandbank, family psychotherapist

What we expect and how we support the relationships between our children may now be influenced by two basic misunderstandings.

The first is that extreme conflict is almost inevitable in families with teenagers. While studies show that arguments often increase, most families negotiate their way through these to calmer times. Fewer than ten per cent of families report worrying relationship difficulties through the teenage years and many of these are a continuation of childhood tensions rather than problems that erupted as a result of adolescence.[8]

The second is that when adolescents say 'No', something is going 'wrong'. Remember toddlerhood? Adolescence is a much bigger version of the same sorts of transition. Sometimes our adolescents will behave like children and sometimes they'll behave like young adults and nobody, least of all them, will know in advance which it's going to be.

Teenagers who suddenly become more antagonistic or challenging to siblings and other family members are often testing the boundaries of behaviour and moving towards greater independence. In other words, growing up. And just as in toddlerhood, many psychologists believe a marked increased in negativity often precedes a developmental leap.

It is our job as parents to hold firm the important, non-negotiable boundaries of behaviour while allowing some rules to bend and accommodate our maturing children.[9]

Flexible and firm, as necessary

> *'Adolescence is usually talked about in terms of children drawing apart from their parents, but that is a half truth. Yes, they have increased activities away from their parents and they follow the peer group in such things as music and dress but, in the majority of families, children still defer to their parents quite a lot on the things that really matter. They may not say so very often, but it is a fact that parents continue to have a lot of influence and if that is handled in a way that recognises children's rights to increasingly make their own decisions, they will go on having influence. So it may help to give way on the little things. Children suddenly appearing with green hair may not seem like a little thing at the time, but in the bigger scheme of things, it is.'*
> – Professor Michael Rutter, child psychiatrist

Our children don't need us any less, they just need us differently. Teenagers tell researchers that they neither need nor want their relationships with their parents to become distant, but rather to respect and adapt to the changes they are experiencing.[10]

Despite the increasing importance of friends in their lives, adolescents still tend to turn to parents for advice on major life decisions.[11] They still need us to maintain and explain important family rules and routines, but now more than ever they also need us to acknowledge their views when setting limits to their behaviour with siblings and others. The precise balance we choose between firmness and flexibility will depend on many factors, from cultural traditions to the safety of the home neighbourhood, yet most adolescents and their siblings will benefit when

- **Discipline is used to educate** rather than to exact revenge or express parental frustrations (See He started it!, page 83).
- **Adolescents feel their opinions and beliefs are listened to**, acknowledged and considered when limits to behaviour are set or adjusted.
- **Rules are explained and fairly administered** (no favouritism because of age, gender, etc).
- **We show through example** that it's okay to admit mistakes, to consider other viewpoints, to reconsider opinions in the light of

new information, and to reach compromises rather than collapse under another person's anger or battle to the death on every point.

- **We don't take it personally**. When our adolescent child oversteps the mark, it may help not to take it as a personal slight but rather as a signal to renegotiate or reinforce agreed boundaries to behaviour.

The court of last resort

Children's thinking skills typically improve dramatically through the teenage years, enabling them to think through and predict situations in ways they could not have done in earlier childhood.[12]

They are more able to be empathic – putting themselves in other people's shoes – consider other people's perspectives more consistently[13] and use more sophisticated strategies for decision making, problem solving and conflict resolution.[14] This means that we can more often leave them to it, encouraging them sort out their problems between themselves.

But not all the time. Teaching our children how to resolve conflict is a subtle and on-going process of example, explanation, discussion and decision-making. With a little prompting and guidance from their parents, most children in their teens can tackle disputes in ways which respect their opponents' views as well as their own. But if one child seems dominated by another, or if they show no sign of surfacing from squabbles, they may still need our more direct intervention (see When they can't sort it out themselves, page 112).

We should, however, increasingly consider ourselves as the court of last resort and, as far as possible, allow our growing children opportunities to find their own way out of their own disputes.

'My personal style is to prefer to leave certain decisions about behaviour to the child, where possible. My children, adult now, certainly saw that as a very striking feature of their upbringing. They were well aware of my views so they needed to think about those, but the choice was often with them. They view that as a mixed blessing. It wasn't an easy option because it implied a responsibility of having to decide matters for themselves.' – Professor Michael Rutter, child psychiatrist

Sexual curiosity and sexual abuse

Recent reports highlighting the sexual abuse of children by other children, including siblings, left many parents in shock.[16] The tabloids had a field day, accusing researchers of scaremongering, yet providing families with little constructive information or advice. So, for the sake of ourselves and our children, it may help to look at this most difficult of subjects with calm and perspective.

Fleeting moments of childhood sexual curiosity and experimentation of the 'you show me yours and I'll show you mine' type are perfectly normal. Not all siblings do it, but very many do. Siblings of different genders do it; same sex siblings do it. It is a common part of growing up.

Sexual abuse is not 'normal' sibling behaviour and is not a common part of growing up. It may involve deliberate physical or mental abuse. Sometimes it is consensual, with children seeking some connection among the wreckage of confused and despairing family relationships. Its victims may display compulsive and persistent sexualised behaviour. It may have lifelong damaging consequences, but this is not inevitable. It is vital to get help for children affected by sexual abuse. Child protection advisors stress the importance of giving children a say in deciding the form and timing of counselling or other help they receive.

Often, as they journey through adolescence, siblings may catch a glimpse of a brother or sister's body and feel embarrassment tinged with sexual excitement. This

Sexuality and boundaries

Privacy is an important part of separateness. Children need to learn to respect each other's physical and psychological space.'
– Audrey Sandbank, family psychotherapist

'I'm having to take the lead from them at the moment, because some of the things they feel comfortable with and uncomfortable with surprise me.

may leave the child feeling confused, and emphasises the importance of appropriate guidance and respect of privacy and boundaries.

Our role as parents is to understand how our children develop and what is perfectly normal behaviour as they grow, while also being calm and very clear to our children about boundaries of acceptable conduct. If we support our children emotionally, encourage good communication and provide them with the information and support they need to make sense of their sexuality and development, we can help to assuage their anxieties and confusions, and provide them with a clearer sense of appropriate behaviour.

'There is incredible amnesia around this issue, some of it actual, some of it rooted in what some people find best forgotten. Adults of my generation remember a total silence around these issues, but of course children sometimes touch each other and of course many adults will think back to some episodes with a little embarrassment. One has to be very careful around issues of sexuality because they are handled and managed in very different ways in different cultures. There are, for example, differing opinions about access to materials that may help young people make sense of what is happening to them and what they are feeling. But personally, I think it helps to recognise that this sexual curiosity exists and to deal with it in a way that neither denies or condones it, but which rather guides children about appropriate behaviour without shaming or being punitive or punishing.' – Mary MacLeod,
National Family and Parenting Institute

My eleven-year-old daughter will shut the door when bathing or changing, and then march through the house with nothing on but a towel on her head. Her thirteen-year-old brother slams the door shut when changing or even brushing his hair but he doesn't bat an eyelid when he's in the shower and people walk into the bathroom.' – Helen D.

'Inevitably, all those things about who's attractive and who has a girlfriend or boyfriend come into play and can make another area of rivalry and

conflict. For the parents, it can be tricky. For the children, it can feel terrible.'
– Eileen Hayes, writer and parenting adviser to the NSPCC

Children's bodies can as much as double in size through adolescence.[15] They develop sexual characteristics, they begin to learn how to manage their sexual feelings and start establishing a sexual identity. They may engage in sexual behaviours. They need privacy, respect and information. They do not need a sibling always tagging along or bursting into the bathroom or bedroom uninvited.

We can support their new boundaries of privacy by talking about issues openly and honestly. 'I think you're all growing up and grown ups like their privacy, so maybe we need some new family rules. Like always knocking on closed doors, and not opening them until your brother or sister says it's okay.'

We can set examples by respecting the rules ourselves; the fact that they apply to all family members is a point some parents fail to grasp. Children generally indicate when they'd like more privacy – they shut doors, they spend more time in their rooms alone – and by respecting the boundaries they set, we show our respect and acknowledgement of the changes they are experiencing. If children share bedrooms, it may help to find some space or time they can spend by themselves, should they wish.

Older children can be encouraged to recognise and respect younger siblings' needs not to be exposed to explicit or inappropriate material, information or behaviour. The simplest and most effective way may be to explain the younger child's vulnerability and level of understanding and to ask for their older brother or sister's supportive sensitivity.

Sexual development can have a huge impact on sibling relationships. The more sexually developed child may no longer be interested in spending time with their brother or sister. The less developed (not necessarily the youngest) may be left feeling confused and inadequate. All will need our support, along with clear and straightforward guidance about themselves, their bodies and their feelings.

'Children will reach an age when they'll want to close the door and have their own privacy, and I think parents have to be respectful of that. Children may need to be guided as to what is appropriate and inappropriate,

*but if family members are generally respectful of each other's privacy, they
will accept when a sibling is approaching adolescence and needs time
and space of their own.'* – Christine Puckering, clinical psychologist
and co-developer of the Mellow Parenting Programme

*'By talking to the child and explaining, we can help them feel good about
being the eldest while also helping them understand that their younger
siblings will need to be protected in a different way.'* – Cheryl Walters,
psychotherapist and Head of Research at Parentline Plus

Roles and Responsibilities

Providing adolescents with meaningful new roles and family responsibilities can give a great boost to their sense of worth and capability. Offering opportunities to contribute to family well-being may help them feel more adult, and stimulate their interests in helping siblings and others more often. Or it may backfire.

Family tasks sometimes make an adolescent feel put upon and taken for granted. So it helps to think through what is fair to ask of our children and why, and what may minimise the risks of rebellion.

- **It's those labels again.** Any imposition of rigid roles may limit people's view of the child and the child's view of themselves. Whether it's help with the cooking, shopping, cleaning, mowing the lawn or reading to younger children at bedtime, tasks are best assigned to all children capable of them, not just those deemed most 'responsible' or 'compliant'. It also helps to swap roles around (see Children as childminders, page 282).

- **Balance responsibilities with free time.** Adolescents who have plenty of time to spend with their own friends and on their own activities are generally less resentful when contributing time to the family good.

- **Notice and praise.** Adolescents who feel they contribute something of value feel valued in themselves.

- **Make it do-able.** Tasks should match children's capabilities. Too

Children as childminders?

'Burgeoning adolescents are not always going to want to have responsibility for younger siblings while parents go to work or out for the evening. It is not fair to impose on them and sometimes they are simply not responsible enough. It can build up resentment. What goes on between siblings can also be abusive if there is not enough adult supervision.' – Dr Sarah Newton, specialist in children's psychological health

'I was one of five and the eldest. As the eldest I did feel a lot of responsibility, in fact at times I felt like a small mother. It was chaotic and very child-centred but a lot of fun.' – Belinda Phipps, National Childbirth Trust

In some societies and cultures, where children are expected to care for their siblings and are valued for doing so, older children are educated for the job, often first sharing the tasks with their parents.[17] In modern western societies, where sibling relationships tend to be less valued, adolescent children may receive little training or information about the needs and care of younger children but may still be expected to 'babysit' their siblings for periods of time.

This can be a positive experience for both. 'For the carer it offers an opportunity to do something positive, to demonstrate maturity and a responsibility for another human being and that's to be valued,' says Peter Wilson, director of Young Minds.

'The downside is that this may be at a cost to their own development and wider opportunities. One can't turn a blind eye to the resentment that must reside somewhere in a child assumed to carry this responsibility. So yes, it is an opportunity to care, to be of use and to be socially responsible – as we all should be by not taking kids for granted.'

The degree to which adolescent children are 'trained' in the care of younger siblings can vary greatly between families and cultures. Studies in the United States, for example, indicate greater support and information for older children in Italian-American families than in traditionally protestant communities.[18] Where little training was given, 'babysitting' and looking after siblings was found to consist of basic 'custodial' duties – preventing younger children doing things – rather than anything more caring or constructive.[19]

This concerns Victor Cicirelli, Professor of Developmental and Ageing Psychology at Purdue University, USA: 'There are potential dangers in sibling caretaking, and we should recognise the importance of preparing siblings for the role, especially given the increasing participation of mothers in the full-time work force. Society needs to consider these issues as a matter or urgency, so siblings are not simply left adrift with each other.

'For one thing, siblings in our culture are not generally expected to be caretakers or have any special societal roles regarding brothers and sisters. Due to the value placed on individualism, older children tend to want to follow their own interests. This may lead to caretaking that is careless and without real concern.'

Sibling 'caretaking' can lead to a set hierarchy among the children, with older children tyrannising younger ones or even younger ones tyrannising older ones as the 'caretaker' tries to appease the younger child and keep parents happy, Professor Cicirelli warns. 'Parents should certainly be alert to the potential tyranny of sibling caregivers, as well as to the potential for a dark side to sibling relationships involving sibling violence or even sexual abuse of younger siblings under circumstances where there is absolutely no adult supervision.

'When sibling caregivers are used, making the caregiving an activity shared with the parent, increasing parental supervision and emphasising constructive activities in which the siblings can share can all help.'

Contrary to popular belief, there is no legal minimum age under which children are not allowed to babysit in the UK. However, parents can be prosecuted if a child is thought to be at risk because he or she is inadequately supervised.[20]

demanding, and we deny them the opportunity to feel good about what they have achieved.

- **An opt-out clause may help.** Whether this is possible will depend on family circumstances. If you are a single parent or a tired working mum, it may not be realistic to let a child know they don't have to do the dishes if they really don't want to. But, where possible, options often help. Children tend to be happier about helping if they know they're appreciated for what they do willingly rather than if they're forced into it.

Siblings as adults

'My own personal view, being an only child, is that I envy people who have brothers and sisters. I think I have a slightly romantic view that not having a sibling, not having another person to have a shared history with, is a kind of deprivation. I know full well from people who have siblings that it's not as hunky dory as all that, but at a very fundamental level, I know that there's not anyone around in my life who has shared the same mother and father and the same moments of fun, excitement, difficulty and tragedy – the same memories.' – Peter Wilson, director of Young Minds

'The real significance of my relationship with my brothers became clear to me after my mother died. I hadn't realised we were as close as we were before then. They are the only two people left now who know my whole personal history and two of the few I know who have travelled a similar journey through race and class. They walked me up the aisle.' – Gary Younge, newspaper columnist and author

In early adulthood, siblings may have relatively little to do with each other as they follow their individual interests, careers and relationships, and they continue to explore their autonomous and separate identities. The nature of their relationship will depend on many interacting factors – the distance between their homes, their choice of partner, socio-economic differences, family and cultural expectations – but it is not uncommon for young adult brothers and sisters to maintain contact only through infrequent visits, telephone calls and family gatherings. So it may still be down to parents to support connections between children, letting each know of the progress of the other and organising get-togethers.

Yet all this tends to change as siblings grow older and the urge to reconnect with brothers and sisters, to support each other and to share memories, becomes increasingly powerful.

> *'I wouldn't want to be without him. If I didn't have a brother I could trust absolutely I could write all men off at times, but having my brother, who's such a good man and such a good dad, stops me.'* – Linda G.

> *'As we've got older we've become less prickly. We're more willing to see the good in each other whereas before we were always on the lookout for the bad. And she does matter to me in a way that surprises.'* – Helen D.

More of the same?

> *Sometimes, as adults, things come out which have been buried and resented for a very long time, even between siblings who looked like they got on fine during childhood. I've seen that in my own family.'* – Eileen Hayes, writer and parenting adviser to the NSPCC

> *'We're behaving like bickering children. I'm the youngest and I'm forty-three. I had hoped we'd have grown beyond this.'* – Rob N.

Any brother or sister of any age can revert to how they behaved and felt with their siblings as a child. Memories can be stirred decades later, and sequences and hierarchies replayed. Depending on the circumstances, this can be comforting or maddening, enriching or crushing. Whether we want to maintain the patterns and rituals or not, it may help us and our adult relationships with our brothers and sisters, if we reassess our behaviour and responses towards each other through adult, not child, eyes.

> *Family patterns are very important and patterns that persist through life and over generations can be refreshed and triggered. At Christmas, say, you*

Rediscovering a relationship

'As the firstborn son to a Sikh family, one is the centre of attention, love and adoration,' explains Dilraj S. 'My sister was born when I was six and I was always told that it was my duty to look after and protect her. The reason given was that I would always be part of my family, yet one day she was destined to leave and live with another.

'Growing up as a teenager in Nottingham I was given a certain amount of freedom – clothes, music, the ability to work part-time. My sister was encouraged to play a more domestic role and this often led to cries of "Unfair! If he can go out with his friends why can't I?" And we had the usual sibling hostilities about the size of bedroom, etc.

'But our relationship was almost non-existent, due to the age gap and the family perception that my "behaviour" would have a direct impact on family prestige. So I distanced myself from not only my sister but also from my parents. I didn't want to take that particular guilt trip.

'By the time my sister was married, I was not. I was always introduced as "This is my son, such as he is . . ." While I showed my sister dutiful respect at formal events there was no real love of the person. Our relationship at this point was probably at an all-time low.

'Upon my marriage and the birth of my son the family kicked off its shoes and claimed the liberal highground – integrated marriages, modern times, boys will be boys . . . ! This upset me, as they had always denied my sister the same. So when her marriage failed, I felt drawn to comfort and protect her.

'A relationship as adults, equal members of an increasingly aged family, started to grow. She and her new partner live in the same city as us and we're family to each other now. We talk fondly of times spent as children and the characters we lived around. Perhaps we had to drift apart because we were still developing our sense of the world, I don't know. But now those middle years seem never to have happened.'

might recreate the sibling hierarchy by seating people in a certain way or by who interrupts whom, so you end up with the same patterns re-emerging or you feel the same emotions coming back. Just because patterns have been established early on doesn't make them bad, it just means that you may need to reappraise them in adulthood.' – Jim Wilson, systemic psychotherapist

'Stereotypes and roles can be comfortable. Sometimes we might stay within them because we know that within that frame, the relationship functions. But there comes a time to step outside them. For me, it was having my own children. I needed to call a halt to my brother's jibes at my son, so I stopped being 'little sister' and responded like a mum.' – Hilary N.

Maintaining bonds

'My mum is still in the middle of my sister and me. She still likes to be the arbitrator, the giver of messages, and she's seventy-four. Actually, I'd like us to have a relationship with each other, without filtering everything through mum first.' – Jenny T.

'In some situations, there may be little communication between siblings because both think the other doesn't want it. The feeling of being less favoured can also create mutual resentment. So many times, when adults decide to talk at last to their siblings, the reactions are, "I thought you were the favoured child?" / "But I thought you were!"'
– Desa Markovic, family therapist

'Sibling relationships are the longest relationships that one will have in life, and are worth nurturing.' – Victor Cicirelli,
Professor of Developmental and Ageing Psychology,
Purdue University

Brothers and sisters often find comfort in the thought of siblings as 'safety nets' – people who will always be there for them in times of need. In reality, however, many young adult siblings make little effort to maintain regular or significant contact.

Yet the importance of siblings to our view of our lives and of ourselves continues. Rivalries can carry on through young adulthood into middle age and beyond, with brothers especially often measuring

🚶🚶🚶 *Grown-ups can still hurt* 🚶🚶🚶
like children

'One of the things I remember so strongly from my childhood are my feelings around my siblings. I have a photograph of me crying in a corner, with my back to the other four children. I remember that precisely, how it felt to be the littlest. If I'm honest I can still return today to being weak and powerless, or frightened in my siblings' presence, and they don't provoke that consciously. They can do it with a glance, a gesture, something so intimate that you associate only with your family.' – Barbara Dale, counsellor

'I'm going to have one child. I was one of six, so I know what it's like having brothers and sisters. I don't want that for my kid.'
– Chris W.

Unresolved arguments and perceptions of parental favour can fuel damaging conflicts throughout adulthood. 'This is a big problem, even in adult life, and I think people just don't acknowledge it,' says Eileen Hayes, writer and parenting adviser to the NSPCC. 'It spoils a lot of adult family relationships if there are underlying, unresolved sibling conflicts and rivalries that have been there forever, hidden but absolutely huge in significance. They can mean some siblings just don't see each other or keep in touch,

their achievements against sibling success.[21] Parental behaviour towards siblings can still hurt or lift the spirits, with parental approval boosting an adult's sense of worth and perceived favouritism lying at the root of much adult sibling conflict (see Grown-ups can still hurt like children, this page).

The frequency and nature of adult sibling contact will obviously depend on the closeness of the relationship generally, but other factors also come into play. Family and cultural expectations of gender behaviour, for example, can also have a powerful influence[22]

perhaps because a brother was the preferred child when they were small.

'Just as you would allow a child to air their feelings, I think it is really helpful to air and listen to these feelings and have open discussions about them instead of keeping a lid on things, because they won't just go away and their impact can be life-long.'

Family therapist Desa Markovic agrees, but stresses that the timing and circumstances for such con-versations has to feel right. 'Sometimes meeting with your siblings in adult life brings you right back to times you don't particularly wish to remember; or you feel you've moved away so much but your siblings keep treating you as a little brother or a little sister, for example, and you respond in the same "old" way, you become a helpless little child again. In order to avoid that pattern, you may avoid meeting them.

'It is important to make a distinc-tion between whether the siblings want to communicate and don't know how, whether they feel the other one doesn't want to, or they simply don't want to themselves – the time has passed by and they feel very distant from their brothers and sisters.

'There are many sibling relation-ships where people communicate simply because of the fact that they are siblings and feel that it is contrary to their choice; in this situ-ation pressure to communicate is not likely to make the relationship successful. In others, the pressure to communicate may help maintain the relationship, keep it alive. For some people, this can mean a significant connection and feeling of belonging, loyalty to the family history and keeping the family bond.'

(see Who makes the connections? page 290).

But, as ever, these are statistical trends and not inevitabilities. If, as parents, we want to encourage communication and supportive relationships between all our children, we should support direct communication and shared events and activities throughout their lives, regardless of gender. As siblings ourselves, it may be worth looking at the 'roles' assigned to us and asking whether our relationships might be happier and more fulfilling if we broke free.

Who makes the connections?

In a review of research worldwide into the bonds between brothers and sisters, Professor Victor Cicirelli found that sister-sister adult relationships seemed closest in industrialised societies.[23] Brother-sister pairs were 'intermediate' in closeness and brother-brother pairs least close.

'Pairs of sisters may have their arguments, conflicts, and jealousies, but in the long run they maintain closer and more affectionate relationships than do brothers. This close relationship is important to their morale and general well-being even into old age,' he writes. 'Sisters tend to work together as a team to maintain relationships within the family. Sisters seem to be very important for the emotional security of their brothers in later life.'

By contrast, in non-industrialised societies, the relationship between brothers tends to be closest and of central social and economic importance.

So what are we to make of these differences? Key messages, says Professor Cicirelli, are the power of social and familial expectations and the role parents can play in preventing set gender roles limiting adult relationships between their children.

'Recent research suggests that some gender differences in temperament and behaviours are real. But these things interact with cultural and family expectations to shape sibling relationships according to gender roles,' he explains. 'Whether sister-sister relationships or relationships with brothers are more important generally may depend on social norms. But I think parents can strive to keep sibling roles from becoming rigid.

'Parents can promote sibling relationships across gender lines by encouraging all their adult children in "kin-keeping" duties – that is, keeping track of the members of the extended family by telephone and/or correspondence, arranging family get-togethers, and so on. Typically, the family matriarch assumes this role, and when she becomes more frail the oldest daughter often takes it on. What I suggest is that the male members of the family also take on some responsibility for the nurturance of family relationships, and not just appear on special occasions.'

♟♟♟ *Siblings in the future* ♟♟♟

Social change may make sibling relationships even more significant in shaping and defining adult identity, believes Professor Victor Cicirelli, of Purdue University.

'I think our industrialised societies tend to emphasise children's relationships with same-age-peers such as schoolmates more than relationships with siblings. Yet, the geographic mobility of many families and the instability of marriages make the relationship with siblings more important as a nucleus of family identification. Mates may come and go, but sibling relationships are permanent. If nurtured, these relationships can add richness and stability to adult lives.

'What's the best way for parents to deal with this? I think to encourage good sibling relationships in childhood and adolescence. The better siblings can build their relationships in childhood and adolescence, the greater the probability that siblings will try to maintain these relationships despite the obstacles of later life.'

The urge to reconnect

'She still infuriates me. I moved down to be near her after my husband died but I sometimes wonder why.' – Eleanor T., aged eighty-six

'What happens between brothers and sisters in their childhood years seems to be of real significance to people in their seventies and eighties.'
– Professor Judy Dunn, developmental psychologist

As we grow older, we reflect on our memories and our lives, our successes and our struggles. Siblings are often the only people in the world able to share some of those memories or fill in the missing pieces. Even sibling relationships marred by jealousies and misunderstandings in earlier life tend to grow in significance and mutual support as brothers and sisters journey into old age (see Older and wiser? page 292).

♦♦♦   *Older and wiser?*   **♦♦♦**

'There are eight years between my younger sister and I, so we were always out of step growing up. I was going to school when she was born; when she started school I was off to secondary school; when she started university I was getting married; we never quite linked up. Also she deliberately chose to take a different path to me. I liked art school so she deliberately chose science courses, and so on. It was very much about being different, very different. Now it's all changed. Through our shared experiences of careers and families and sustaining our marriages over the years we have become so linked. In fact she has moved in with us for four nights a week because she's started a new job. It's the first time we have lived together since being children.'
– Margaret Harrison, founder and life president of Home-Start

As people get older, a supportive sibling relationship can increase in significance, says Professor Victor Cicirelli. 'It can represent a core of stability for the individual, in a society increasingly characterised by single-hood, divorce, loss of friendships through mobility, and so on. Such a supportive relationship may involve listening to each other's problems and helping to solve them, providing emotional understanding, giving financial help on occasion, exchanging services, and partici-

The processes of reflection are not always comfortable and another's very different interpretation of events or circumstances can cause some sibling relationships to crack under the strain. In adulthood, just as in childhood, a recognition that siblings have very different experiences within the same family may bring about greater understanding, tolerance of difference, and a more gentle, accepting and less conflictual relationship (see Why are siblings so different? page 165).

Even those siblings who do not or cannot go as far as to reconcile their various recollections and feelings tend to become increasingly aware that continued rivalry is fairly fruitless and that an accepting relationship with their brother or sister can provide important emotional security as they enter the later stages of their lives.

pating together in social and recreational activities.'

In non-industrialised societies, continued sibling solidarity throughout life is common, sometimes obligatory. In industrialised societies, the renewed significance of siblings in adult lives tends to develop over time.[24] In a study by Professor Cicirelli of siblings at all stages of life only five per cent of siblings didn't feel at all close to their siblings by middle age, while sixty-eight per cent felt close or extremely close. By old age this had increased to eighty-three per cent.[25]

'Even when there is sibling conflict in adulthood, the relationship can be improved if both siblings attempt to talk things out and change things for the better,' comments Professor Cicirelli. 'Like any other relationship, siblings have to work at it, initiating getting together, overlooking each other's faults, and building on things they have in common.

'Research shows that most adults desire to have better sibling relationships in adulthood and most older adults remain in contact with siblings until the end of their life. Siblings can then offer emotional support, and in many cases can assist with caregiving when their brother or sister's health declines. They can offer advice, set examples as to how to deal with the problems of aging and, because they are the only ones remaining who shared early experiences in life, they can aid in the life review and reminiscences of our final years by validating one another's recollections.'

As the journey to old age begins many of us will find that the urge to reconnect with brothers and sisters proves irresistible. Once again, even at the end of our lives, our sibling relationships affect who and how we are.

'My uncle knows how to hold a grudge and still won't speak to my father. Dad wrote to him again recently, but there's been no response. It's very sad.'
– Hannah C.

'My mother and her sister were crossing the road in front of me last week and, just for a moment, they held hands. It struck me how lucky they are. Here they are, facing the uncertain journey of aging, and they've still got a hand to hold.' – Helen D.

Adolescence and beyond: key approaches

Allow adolescents freedom to grow	Adolescents are establishing their adult identities. They need to become distinct and separate from their parents, their siblings, and their past.
Support any child 'left behind'	They may feel alienated or rejected. They need their friends and they need us.
Support new boundaries	Every family member needs to respect adolescents' desire for privacy.
Monitor and observe	Adolescent siblings influence each other's behaviour. For the sake of every child in the family, we need to keep track of adolescents' whereabouts, activities and friends.
Be firm, be flexible	Maintain key family rules and values, but be willing to renegotiate the rest.
Provide meaningful roles	Adolescents respond well to new responsibilities. But avoid using siblings as reluctant, untrained and unsupported childminders.
Maintain connections	Communicate with adolescents respectfully and constructively. Continue old family 'traditions' and establish new ones. Times together help maintain links and shared memories.

Reassess adult relationships	Can grown siblings enjoy shared childhood memories and yet respond to each other as adults, not children?
Reconnect	Sibling relationships gain in significance as people grow older.

Key message:

Sibling ties may change, but their significance remains.

References

1. Life support: why sibling relations matter

1. 1999 figures. National Statistics (2001). Households and families. In, *Social Trends*, No. 31, 2001. (The Stationery Office, London). Sibling percentages relevant to UK, US and Europe.

2. Mum, you can send her back now: a new baby arrives

1. Cicirelli, V.G., Sibling relationships in cross-cultural perspective. *Journal of Marriage & the Family*, Vol. 56 Issue 1, 1994
2. Dunn, J., *From One Child to Two*, Ballantine Books, New York 1995
3. Dunn, J. and Kendrick, C., *Siblings: Love, Envy and Understanding*, Grant McIntyre, London, 1982.
4. Based on a search of Childline data 1999–2000
5. Legg C., Sherrick I., Wadland W., 'Reactions of preschool children to the birth of a sibling', *Child Psychiatry Human Development*, 5; 1974, 3–39
    Thomas A, Chess S., *Temperament and Development*, Brunner-Mazel, New York, 1977
6. Lamb, M.E., 'The Development of Sibling Relationships in Infancy: A Short-Term Longitudinal Study', *Child Development 49* (1978), 1189–96
7. Dunn, J. and Kendrick, C., *Siblings: Love, Envy and Understanding*, op cit
8. Ibid
9. Including Brody, G.H., Stoneman, Z., MacKinnon, C.E., MacKinnon, R., 'Role relationships and behaviour among preschool-aged and school-aged sibling pairs', *Dev. Psychol.* 21, 1985, 124–9
    Buhrmester, D., 'The development courses of sibling and peer relationships', in *Children's Sibling Relationships: Developmental and Clinical Issues*, eds Boer, F., Dunn, J., Erlbaum, Hillsdale, N.J., 1992
    Dunn, J., 'Connections between relationships: implications of research on mothers and siblings', in *Relationships within Families: Mutual*

Influences, eds Hind, R.A., Stevenson-Hinde, J., Clarendon, Oxford, 1988

10. Dunn, J. 'State of the Art: Siblings', *The Psychologist*, Vol. 13, No. 5, 2000

11. Dunn, J., Kendrick, C., MacNamee, R., 'The reaction of first born children to the birth of a sibling: mothers' reports', *J. Child Psychol. Psychiatry*, 22: 1981, 1–18

12. Dunn, J., *Sisters and Brothers: The Developing Child*, Harvard University Press, Cambridge, Mass., 1985

13. Including those detailed in Dunn, J. and Kendrick, C., *Siblings: Love, Envy and Understanding*, op cit.

14. Including Dunn, J., *Young children's close relationships: Beyond attachment* (vol 4), Sage, Newbury Park, CA, 1993
    Stewart, R., Mobley, L., Van Tuyl, S., and Salvador, M., 'The firstborn's adjustment to the birth of a sibling', *Child Development*, 58, 1987, 341–55

15. Dunn, J. and Kendrick, C., *Siblings: Love, Envy and Understanding*, op cit

16. Houston, D.M. and Marks, G., *Employment Choices for Mothers of Pre-school children: A psychological perspective*. End of Award Report to ESRC, 2001

3. Caring and sharing: building positive relationships

1. Dunn, J., 'Children as psychologists: The later correlates of individual differences in understanding of emotions and other minds', *Cognition and Emotion*, 9, 1995, 187–201, and Dunn, J., 'Making sense of the social world: Mindreading, emotion and relationships', in Zelazo, P.D., Astington, J.W. and Olson, D.R., (eds) *Developing theories of intention: Social understanding and self control*, Lawrence Erlbaum, Mahwah, NJ, 1999, 229–42

2. Dunn, J., Slomkowski, C., Beardsall, L. 'Sibling relationships from the preschool period through middle childhood and early adolescence', *Development Psychology*, 30, 1994, 315–24

3. Reprinted, with kind permission, from *Multiple Voices, Listening to Twins, Triplets and More*, by Mary Lowe and Pat Preedy, Twins and Multiple Births Association, Wine Press, Feb 1998

4. Dunn, J., *From One Child to Two*, Ballantine Books, New York, 1995

5. Ram, A. and Ross, H., 'Problem-solving, contention, and struggle: How

siblings resolve conflicts of interest', *Child Development* (in press)

6. Ross, H.S., Negotiating principles of entitlement in sibling property disputes. *Developmental Psychology*, 32, 1996, 990–101

7. Dunn, J., and Kendrick, C., *Siblings: Love, Envy and Understanding*, op cit.

8. Including Dunn, J., Brown, J. and Beardsall, L., 'Family talk about feeling states and children's later understanding of others' emotions', *Dev. Psychol.*, 27, 1991, 448–55

9. Dunn, J., Brown, J., Slomkowski, C., Tesla, C. and Youngblade, L., 'Young children's understanding of other people's feelings and beliefs: individual differences and their antecedents', *Child Dev.* 62, 1991, 1352–66

10. Including Brody, G.H., Stoneman, Z., Burke, M., 'Family system and individual child correlates of sibling behaviour', *American Journal of Orthopsychiatry*, 57, 1987, 561–9

    Brody, G.H., Stoneman, Z., McCoy, J.K., 'Contributions of family relationships and child temperaments to longitudinal variations in sibling relationship quality and sibling relationship styles', *Journal of Family Psychology*, 8, 1994, 274–86

    Hetherington, E.M., 'Parents, children and siblings six years after divorce', in *Relationships Within Families: Mutual Influences*, eds Hinde, R.A., Stevenson-Hinde, J., Clarendon, Oxford, 1988

    Dunn, J., and Kendrick, C., *Siblings: Love, Envy and Understanding*, op cit

11. Baumrind, D., 'Current patterns of parental authority', *Developmental Psychology Monographs*, 4 (No. 1, Pt. 2), 1971, 1-1-0

4. He started it! tackling sibling conflict

1. Katz, A., Buchanan, A., and Bream, V., *Bullying in Britain: Testimonies from Teenagers*, Young Voice, 2001

2. Brown, J.R., Dunn, J., 'Talk with your mother or your sibling? Development changes in early family conversations about feelings', *Child Dev.* 63, 1992, 336–49

    Dunn, J., Brown, J., Beardsall, L., 'Family talk about feeling states and children's later understanding of others' emotions', *Dev. Psychol.* 27, 1991, 448–55

    Dunn, J., Brown, J., Slomkowski, C., Tesla, C., Youngblade, L., 'Young children's understanding of other people's feelings and beliefs: individual differences and their antecedents', *Child Dev.* 62, 1991, 1352–66

3. For example, Kelly, F.D., Main, F.O., 'Sibling Conflict in a single-parent family: an empirical case study', *American Journal of Family Therapy* 7, 1979, 39–47

4. Newson, J., and Newson, E., *Seven Years Old in the Home Environment*, Penguin, Harmondsworth, 1970

5. Raffaelli, M., 'Sibling Conflict in early adolescence', *Journal of Marriage and the Family*, 54, 1992, 652–63

6. The full version of Marina Fraser's story, 'A Thief in the Family', appeared in *The Guardian*, 29 December 1999

7. Including Brody, G.H. and Stoneman, X., 'A risk-amelioration model of sibling relationships: conceptual underpinnings and preliminary findings', in Brody, G.H. (ed), *Sibling Relationships: Their Causes and Consequences*, Ablex, Norwood, NJ, 1996, 231–47
   Hetherington, E.M., Reiss, D., and Plomin, R., *Separate social worlds of siblings: The impact of nonshared environment on development*, Lawrence Erlbaum, Hillsdale, NJ, 1994

8. Katz, A., Buchanan, A., and Bream, V., *Bullying in Britain: Testimonies from Teenagers*, op cit

9. See *The development of an individual's potential for violence: understanding and preventing violence*, Reiss, A.J. and Roth, J.A. (eds), National Academy Press, Washington DC, 1993; and *Children and Violence*, Report of the Commission on Children and Violence convened by the Gulbenkian Foundation, Calouste Gulbenkian Foundation, London, 1995

10. Bank, L., Patterson, G.R., Reid, J.B., 'Negative sibling interaction patterns as predictors of later adjustment problems in adolescent and young adult males', in *Sibling Relationships: Their Causes and Consequences*, op cit

11. Including Loeber, R., 'The analysis of coercive chains between children, mothers and siblings', *Journal of Family Violence*, 1, 1986, 51–70. Patterson, G.R., *Coercive Family Process*, Castalia, Eugene, OR, 1982

12. Including Conger, R.D. and Rutter, M.A., 'Siblings, parents and peers: A longitudinal study of social influences in adolescent risk for alcohol use and abuse', in Brody, G.H. (ed.), *Sibling Relationships: Their Causes and Consequences*, op cit 1–30

Lauritsen, J.J., 'Sibling resemblance in juvenile delinquency: findings from the National Youth Survey', *Criminology*, 31, 1993, 387–409

13. Ross, H.G., Milgram, J., 'Important variables in adult sibling relationships: a qualitative study', in *Sibling Relationships: Their Nature and Significance Over the Lifespan*, ed Lamb, M.E., Suton-Smith, B., Erlbaum, Hillsdale, NJ, 1982, 225–47

14. Dunn, J., Slomkowski, C., Beardsall, L. and Rende, R., 'Adjustment in middle childhood and early adolescence: Links with earlier and contemporary sibling relationships', *Journal of Child Psychology and Psychiatry*, 35, 1994, 491–504

15. Bank, L., Patterson, G.R., Reid, J.B., 'Negative sibling interaction patterns as predictors of later adjustment problems in adolescent and young adult males', in *Sibling Relationships: Their Causes and Consequences*, op cit
Dunn, J., Slomkowski, C., Beardsall, L. and Rende, R., 'Adjustment in middle childhood and early adolescence: Links with earlier and contemporary sibling relationships', *Journal of Child Psychology and Psychiatry*, 35, 1994, 491–504

16. *Sibling Relationships: Their Causes and Consequences*, op cit

17. Perlman, M. and Ross, H.S., 'The benefits of parent intervention in their children's disputes: An examination of concurrent changes in children's fighting styles', *Child Development*, 1997, 690–700

18. Dunn, J., and Munn, P., 'Becoming a family member: Family conflict and the development of social understanding in the second year', *Child Development*, 56, 1985, 480–92

19. Ross, H.G. and Milgram, J., 'Important variables in adult sibling relationships: a qualitative study', in *Sibling Relationships: Their Nature and Significance Over the Lifespan*, ed Lamb, M.E., Suton-Smith, B., op cit

20. Brody, G.H., Stoneman, Z., McCoy, J.K., Forehand, R., 'Contemporaneous and longitudinal associations of sibling conflict with family relationship assessments and family discussions about sibling problems', *Child Development*, 63, 1992, 391–400

21. 'Changing Our School: promoting positive behaviour', Highfield Primary School, Plymouth and the Institute of Education, University of London, 1997

22. Including Bryant, B.K., 'Conflict resolution strategies in relation to children's peer relations', *Journal of Applied Developmental Psychology*, 13, 1992, 35–50 and Chung, T.-Y., and Asher, M., 'Children's goals and

strategies in peer conflict situations', *Merrill-Palmer Quarterly*, 42, 1996, 125–47

23. *Not in Front of the Children: How conflict between parents affects children*, ed Jenny Reynolds, One Plus One, Marriage and Partnership Research, London, 2001

24. Dubow, E., Tisak, J., 'The relation between stressful life events and adjustment in elementary school children: the role of social support and problem-solving skills', *Child Development*, 60, 1989, 1412–20; Fabes, R.A., Eisenberg, N., 'Young children's coping with interpersonal anger', Child Development, 63, 1992, 116–28

25. Brody, G.H., 'Sibling Relationship Quality: Its Causes and Consequences', *Annu.Rev. Psychol.* 49, 1998, 1–24

26. *Not in Front of the Children: How conflict between parents affects children*, op cit

27. Tesla, C. and Dunn, J., 'Getting along or getting your way: The development of young children's use of arguments in conflicts with mother and sibling', *Social Development* 1, (2), 1992, 107–21. See also Dunn, J., *Young children's close relationships*, Sage Publications, Newbury, CA, 1993

5. Exploring emotions: understanding feelings in families

1. Pernier, J., Ruffman, T. and Leekham, S.R., 'Theory of mind is contagious: You catch it from your sibs', *Child Development*, 65, 1994, 1228–38

2. Based on a search of ChildLine data, 1999–2000

3. Including Dunn, J., Brown, J. and Beardsall, L., 'Family talk about feeling states and children's later understanding of others' emotions', *Dev. Psychol.* 27, 1999, 448–55

4. Feinstein, L. 'The relative economic importance of academic, psychological and behavioural attributes developed in childhood', Discussion Paper 443, Centre for Economic Performance, London School of Economics, 2000

5. Including Brody, G.H., Stoneman, X., 'A risk-amelioration model of sibling relationships: conceptual underpinnings and preliminary findings', *Sibling Relationships: Their Causes and Consequences* op cit, 231–47 Hetherington, E.M., Reiss, D. and Plomin, R., *Separate social worlds of siblings: The impact of nonshared environment on development*, op cit

6. Brody, G.H. 'Sibling Relationship quality: Its causes and consequences', *Annual Review Psychology*, 49, 1998, 1–24

7. Katz, A., Buchanan, A. and Bream, V., *Bullying in Britain: Testimonies from Teenagers*, op cit

8. Fraiberg, S., Adelson, E. and Shapiro, V., 'Ghosts in the nursery: A psychoanalytic approach to the problems of impaired infant mother relationships', in *Clinical Studies in Infant Mental Health, The First Year of Life*, ed. Selma Fraiberg, Tavistock Publications, London, 1980

6. Kids don't fit in pigeonholes: identity and individuality

1. Pinker, S., *How the Mind Works*, Allen Lane, The Penguin Press, London, 1997

2. Schachter, Frances Fuchs, et al, 'Sibling Deidentification', *Developmental Psychology*, 12, 1976, 418–27

3. Plomin, R., *Development, Genetics and Psychology*, Erlbaum, Hillsdale, NJ, 1986
   Rowe, D.C., Plomin, R., 'The importance of nonshared environmental influences in behaviour development', *Development Psychology*, 17, 1981, 517–31

4. Based on a search of ChildLine data 1999–2000

5. Prof Jerome Kagan, Harvard University. Issues discussed in *Three Seductive Ideas*, Jerome Kagan, Harvard University Press, 2000

6. Reprinted with kind permission, from *Multiple Voices, Listening to Twins, Triplets and More*, by Mary Lowe and Pat Preedy, Twins and Multiple Births Association, Wine Press, Feb 1998

7. Brody, G.H., 'Sibling Relationship quality: Its causes and consequences', op cit

7. Message received? family communication

1. Katz, A., Buchanan, A. and Bream, V., *Bullying in Britain: Testimonies from Teenagers*, op cit

2. McGurk, H. and Hurry, J., *Project Charlie: An Evaluation of A Life Skills Drug Education Programme for Primary Schools*, Home Office Drugs Prevention Initiative, 1995

Hurry, J. and Lloyd, C., *A Follow-Up Evaluation of Project Charlie*. Home Office Drugs Prevention Initiative, 1997

8. Extra pressures: illness, disability and special needs; twins and more; divorce and family change

1. Bryon, M. 'The Impact of Cystic Fibrosis and the Influence of Mothers on Childhood Sibling Relationships', PHD thesis, 1998, held at the University of Wales
2. Ibid
3   Bank, S.P. and Kahn, M.D., *The Sibling Bond*, HarperCollins, 1982
4. Sloper, P., 'Experiences and support needs of siblings of children with cancer', *Health and Social Care in the Community*, 8, 2000, 298–306. Sloper, P. and While, D., 'Risk Factors in the Adjustment of Siblings of children with Cancer', *Journal of Child Psychology and Psychiatry*, 37, 1997, 597–607
5. Seligman, M., 'Psychotherapy with Siblings of Disabled Children', in *Siblings in Therapy: Life Span and Clinical Issues*, eds Kahn, M.D., Lewis, K.G., W.W. Norton, New York, 1998
6. Bryon, M., The Impact of Cystics Fibrosis and the Influence of Mothers on Childhood Sibling Relationships, op cit
7. Winnicott, D.W., *The Maturational Processes and the Facilitating Environment*, International Universities Press, Madison, CT, 1965
8. Sloper, P., 'Experiences and support needs of siblings of children with cancer', op cit;
    Sloper, P. and While, D. 'Risk Factors in the Adjustment of Siblings of children with Cancer', op cit
9. Including Brody, G.H. and Stoneman, X., A risk-amelioration model of sibling relationships: conceptual underpinnings and preliminary findings, in Brody, G.H. (ed), *Sibling relationships: Their causes and consequences*, op cit
    Hetherington, E.M., Reiss, D. and Plomin, R., *Separate social worlds of siblings: The impact of nonshared environment on development*, op cit
10. Including Hannam, C., *Parents and Mentally Handicapped Children*, Penguin, Harmondsworth, 1975
11. Reprinted with kind permission from *Multiple Voices, Listening to Twins, Triplets and More*, by Mary Lowe and Pat Preedy, op cit
12. 1999 figures. National Statistics (2001). Households and families, in

Social Trends, 31, The Stationery Office, London, 2001

13. Lytton, H., *Parent–child interaction: the socialization process observed in twin and singleton families*, Plenum, New York, 1980

14. Hay, D.A. and O'Brien, P.J., 'The role of parental attitudes in the development of temperament in twins at home, school and in test situations', *Acta Geneticae Medicae et Gemellologiae* 33, 1984, 191–204

15. Twins and Multiple Births Association, 2001

16. The Association for Post Natal Illness, 1999

17. 'Parenting Twins', Lytton, H. et al, University of Calgary, in *Handbook of Parenting*, ed., Bornstein, Marc H., Lawrence Erlbaum, 1995

18. Lytton, H. *Parent–child interaction: the socialization process observed in twin and singleton families*, op cit

19. Lytton, H., Watts, D. and Dunn, B.E., 'Twin-singleton differences in verbal ability: Where do they stem from?' *Intelligence* 11, 1987, 359–69

20. Koch, H., *Twins and twin relations*, Chicago University Press, Chicago, 1966

21. Reprinted with kind permission from *Multiple Voices, Listening to Twins, Triplets and More*, op cit

22. Byng-Hall, J., *Rewriting Family Scripts*, The Guildford Press, New York and London, 1995

23. Shopper, M., Twinning reactions in non-twin siblings, *Journal of the American Academy of Child and Adolescent Psychiatry*, 13, 1974, 300–18

24. Sandbank, A.C., 'The importance of understanding the psychology of twin and triplet relationships', in *Twin and Triplet Psychology*, ed Sandbank, A.C., Brunner-Routledge, London, June 1999

25. Ibid

26. Bryan, E., *Twins, Triplets and More: Their nature, development and care*, Penguin Books, London, 1992

27. Reprinted with kind permission from *Multiple Voices, Listening to Twins, Triplets and More*, op cit

28. Alessandra Piontelli, 'Twins in utero: Temperament development and intertwin behaviour before and after birth', in *Twin and Triplet Psychology*, Brunner-Routledge, June 1999

29. Tomasello, M., Mannie, S. and Kruger, A.C., Linguistic environment of 1 to 2-year-old twins, *Developmental Psychology* 22, 1986, 169–76

30. Zazzo, R. *Les Jumeaux – Le Couple et la Personne*, Presses Universitaires de France, Paris, 1960, Zazzo, R. 'The Twin Condition and the Couple

Effect on Personality Development', *Acta Geneticae Medicae et Gemellologiae* 25, 1976, 343–52

31. Lytton, H., *Parent–child interaction: the socialization process observed in twin and singleton families*, op cit

32. Lytton, H., Watts, D., and Dunn, B.E. 'Twin-singleton differences in verbal ability: Where do they stem from?' op cit

33. Hay, D., *Australian Journal of Early Childhood*, 13, 1987, 25–8

34. 1999 figures. National Statistics (2001). Households and families, in *Social Trends* 31, op cit

35. Parentline Plus, 2001

36. National Statistics (2001). Households and families, in *Social Trends* 31, op cit

37. *Not in Front of the Children: How conflict between parents affects children*, op cit

38. Dunn, J., 'State of the Art: Siblings' *The Psychologist*, vol 13, No 5, 2000

39. *Not in Front of the Children: How conflict between parents affects children*, op cit

40. Hetherington, E.M., 'Parents, children and siblings six years after divorce', op cit
    Gorrell Barnes, G., Thompson, P., Daniel, G. and Burchardt, N., *Growing Up In Stepfamilies*, Clarendon, Oxford, 1998

41. Hetherington, E.M., 'Parents, children and siblings six years after divorce', op cit;
    Stepfamilies: Challenges, myths and rewards, Parentline Plus, 2000;
    Golombok, S., Parenting: *What Really Counts*, Routledge: London 2001

42. *Not in Front of the Children: How conflict between parents affects children*, op cit

43. Hetherington, E.M., 'Parents, children and siblings six years after divorce', op cit

44. Gorrell Barnes, G., Thompson, P., Daniel, G. and Burchardt, N., *Growing Up In Stepfamilies*, op cit

45. Ibid

46. Hetherington, E.M., 'Parents, children and siblings six years after divorce', op cit

47. Gorrell Barnes, G., Thompson, P., Daniel, G. and Burchardt, N., *Growing Up In Stepfamilies*, op cit

48. Based on a search of ChildLine date 1999–2000
49. Hetherington, E.M., 'Parents, children and siblings six years after divorce', op cit

9. Growing pains: adolescence and beyond

1. Simpson, A. Rae, *Raising Teens: A Synthesis of Research and a Foundation for Action*, Centre for Health Communication, Harvard School of Public Health, Boston, 2001
2. Including, Conger, R.D. and Rutter, M.A., 'Siblings, parents and peers: A longitudinal study of social influences in adolescent risk for alcohol use and abuse', op cit;
   Lauritsen, J.L., 'Sibling resemblance in juvenile delinquency: findings from the National Youth Survey', *Criminology*, 31, 1993, 387–409
3. Gray, M.R. and Steinberg, L., 'Unpacking Authoritative Parenting: Reassessing a Multidimensional Construct', *Journal of Marriage and the Family* 67(3), 1999, 574–87
4. Demo, D.H., Allen, K.R. and Fine, M.A., *Handbook of Family Diversity*, Oxford University Press, New York, 2000
   Grotevenat, H.D., Dunbar, N., Kohler, J.K. and Esau, A.M.L., 'Adoptive Identity: how contexts within and beyond the family shape development pathways', *Family Relations*, 49(4), 2000, 379–87
5. *Project Charlie: An Evaluation of A Life Skills Drug Education Programme for Primary Schools*, op cit;
   Follow-Up Evaluation of Project Charlie, op cit
6. Larson, R. and Richards, M.H., *Divergent Realities: The Emotional Lives of Mothers, Fathers and Adolescents*, Basic Books, New York, 1994;
   Brown, D., Affect Development, Psychopathology, and Adaptation, in Ablon, S.L., Brown, D., Khantzian, E.J. and Mack, J. (eds), *Human Feelings: Explorations in Affect Development and Meaning*, Analytic Press, Hillsdale, NJ, 1993, 5–66
7. Holmbeck, G.N. and Hill, J.P., 'Conflictive engagement, positive affect, and menarche in families with seventh-grade girls', *Child Development* 62, 1991, 1030–48
8. Collins, W.A. and Laursen, B., 'Conflict and relationships during adolescence', in Shantz, C.U. and Hartup, W.W. (eds), *Conflict in Child and Adolescent Development*, Cambridge University Press, New York, 1992

9. Lamborn, S.D., Mounts, N.S., Steinberg, L. and Dornbusch, S.M. 'Patterns of competence and adjustment among adolescents from authoritative, authoritarian, indulgent and neglectful families', *Child Development* 62, 1991, 1049–65

10. Simpson, A. Rae, *Raising Teens: A Synthesis of Research and a Foundation for Action*, Center for Health Communication, Harvard School of Public Health, Boston, 2001

11. Ibid

12. Fischoff, B., Crowell, N.A. and Kipke, M., *Adolescent Decision Making: Implications for Prevention Programs*, National Academy Press, Washington, DC, 1999;
    Fischer, K.W. and Rose, S.P., 'Dynamic Development of Coordination of Components in Brain and Behaviour: A framework for Theory and Research', in Dawson, G. and Fischer, K.W. (eds), *Human Behavior and the Developing Brain*, Guildford, New York, 1994

13. Damon, W. and Hart, D., 'The Development of Self-Understanding from Infancy through Adolescence', *Child Development*, 53(4), 1982, 841–64;
    Eisenberg, N., Murphy, B.C. and Shepard, S., 'The Development of Empathic Accuracy', in Ickes, W. (ed), *Empathic Accuracy*, Guildford, New York, 1997, 73–116

14. Fischoff, B., Crowell, N.A. and Kipke, M., *Adolescent Decision Making: Implications for Prevention Programs*, op cit

15. Simpson, A. Rae, *Raising Teens: A Synthesis of Research and a Foundation for Action*, op cit

16. *Child Maltreatment in the United Kingdom: A study of the prevalence of child abuse and neglect*, NSPCC, 2000

17. Cicirelli, Victor G., Sibling relationships in cross-cultural perspective, *Journal of Marriage and the Family*, op cit

18. Ervin-Tripp, S., 'Sisters and brothers', in Zukow, P.G. (ed), *Sibling interaction across cultures: Theoretical and methodological issues*, Springer-Verlag, New York, 1989

19. Bryant, B.K., 'The child's perspective of sibling caretaking and its relevance to understanding social-emotional functioning and development', in Zukow, P.G. (ed), *Sibling interaction across cultures: Theoretical and methodological issues*, op cit

20. Citizen's Advice Bureau, UK

21. Cicirelli, Victor G., Sibling relationships in cross-cultural perspective, *Journal of Marriage and the Family*, op cit

22. Ibid
23. Ibid
24. Ibid
25 Cicirelli, V.G., 'Siblings Helping Siblings', in Allen, V.L. (ed), *Inter-Age Interaction in Children*, Academic, New York, 1976

Contributors

Corinne Abisgold is an educational psychologist.

Francine Bates is Chief Executive of Contact-a-Family, a charity helping families who care for children with any disability, special need or rare disorder.

Clare Beswick is an early years and childcare consultant.

Christine Bidmead is a qualified health visitor, RGN and midwife, trained psychodynamic counsellor and training facilitator at the Centre for Parent and Child Support, South London and Maudesly NHS Trust. In 1998, she founded the CPHVA (Community Practitioners and Health Visitors Association) Interest and Development Group for Parenting and Family Support.

John Bristow is a chartered psychologist and psychotherapist in independent practice. His clients include individuals, families and organisations.

Gene H. Brody is Distinguished Research Professor of Child and Family Development, The University of Georgia, USA.

Dr Elizabeth Bryan is Consultant Paediatrician at Queen Charlotte's and Chelsea hospital, London, founder of the Multiple Births Foundation and president of the International Society for Twin Studies.

Dr Mandy Bryon is Consultant Clinical Psychologist at the Department of Psychological Medicine, Great Ormond Street Hospital for Children NHS Trust, London.

Professor Victor G. Cicirelli is Professor of Development and Ageing Psychology in the Department of Psychological Studies at Purdue University in West Lafayette, Indiana, USA. He is a Fellow of the American Psychological Association, the American Psychological Society, and the Gerontological Society of America. He has written extensively on sibling relationships.

Barbara Dale is a counsellor and psychotherapist.

Sarah Darton is a health visitor. She also trained as a group facilitator with Parent Network (now Parentline Plus).

Professor Judy Dunn, MRC Research

Professor at the Institute of Psychiatry, King's College, London, has led some of the world's foremost research into sibling relationships. She has written many books on sibling relationships, including *From One Child to Two* (Ballatine), *Sisters and Brothers, Young Children's Close Relationships* (Sage) and, with Carol Kendrick, the book that prompted systematic research on siblings, *Siblings: Love, envy and understanding* (Harvard University Press).

Pat Elliot is a psychotherapist in private practice specialising in parenting and bereavement issues. She also works as tutor at the Psychosynthesis and Education Trust with trainee therapists, and as a consultant to schools in bereavement issues. She is the author of *Coping With Loss* (Piccadilly Press).

Dr Leon Feinstein is Research Director at the Wider Benefits of Learning Research Centre, a centre funded by the Department for Education and Skills, at the Institute of Education in London, to investigate the social and non-pecuniary effects of learning. He is also an associate of the Centre for Economic Performance and the Centre for the Economics of Education, both at the London School of Economics.

Professor Robert Fisher is a teacher trainer and directs the Centre for Research in Teaching Thinking at Brunel University. He has published more than 20 books on education, including the highly acclaimed *Stories for Thinking* series (see www.teachingthinking.net). He is involved in research and training with schools and LEAs, and is an adviser to the QCA and DES on literacy and thinking skills.

Hugh Foot is Professor of Psychology and Vice-Dean (Research) in the Faculty of Arts and Social Sciences at the University of Strathclyde and the course director for the Masters degree in Research Methods in Psychology.

Clare Gibson is Library and Information Officer for Contact-a-Family.

Kitty Hagenbach is a Transpersonal Psychotherapist and Child Psychotherapist, working at Viveka, 27A Queens Terrace, London NW8 6EA. She specialises in working with parents regarding the emotional and psychological aspects of parenting.

Carol Ann Hally is a health visitor and community practice teacher.

Margaret Harrison is Founder and Life President of Home-Start, the voluntary family support organisation, which now offers support, friendship and practical help to around 50,000 children, together with their parents, each year in the UK. Home-Start has also developed in 12 other countries. She is a founder member and trustee of the National Family and Parenting Institute.

Eileen Hayes is Parenting Adviser to the NSPCC and Vice-chair of the Parenting Education and Support Forum, for which she chairs a Media and Parenting Working Group. She is also an author and magazine columnist on child behaviour and a frequent broadcaster on radio and TV.

Adrienne Katz is Founder and Executive Director of Young Voice, a charity 'working to make young people's views count'. An author and journalist on issues of concern to families and children for 20 years, she has worked on social research projects in association with Dr Ann Buchanan of Oxford University since 1996.

Mary Macleod is Chief Executive of the National Family and Parenting Institute. Prior to this she was Director of Policy and Research at ChildLine.

Doro Marden is a parent educator.

Desa Markovic is Assistant Director at the Institute of Family Therapy, London. She has been working as a family therapist, supervisor and tutor for 11 years in the UK and has written extensively on the subjects of couple and family therapy, and clinical supervision.

Brenda Meldrum is Head of Training at The Place to Be, a charity offering emotional support to children in mainstream primary schools. She trained as a psychologist at the London School of Economics and is a Registered Dramatherapist, Supervisor and Play Therapist.

Andrew Mellor is Manager of the Anti-Bullying Network. A teacher with 25 years' experience, he conducted the first substantial research on bullying in Scotland. As the Scottish Anti-Bullying Development Officer from 1993 to 1995 he played a major role in highlighting the seriousness of bullying in schools and contributed to a large number of workshops and conferences.

Dr Sarah Newton is Consultant Clinical Psychologist and Head of Clinical Psychology Services, Plymouth Primary Care Trust, and Associate Fellow of the British Psychological Society. She is a specialist in the psychological health of children, young people and their families, with particular interest in development disabilities, physical health and the impact of traumas.

Dr Gavin Nobes lectures in developmental and forensic psychology. His research interests include children's social development – especially the development of morality and antisocial behaviour – families, physical punishment and abuse, and children's understanding of science.

Belinda Phipps is Chief Executive Officer of the National Childbirth Trust.

Christine Puckering is Consultant Clinical Psychologist at the Royal Hospital for Sick Children, Glasgow and Senior Research Fellow in Child and Adolescent Psychiatry, University of Glasgow.

Professor Michael Rutter is Professor of Developmental Psychopathology at the Institute of Psychiatry, Kings College, London and consultant physician at the Maudesly Hospital. He has been involved in family research for over 40 years and has a particular interest in integrating clinical and developmental perspectives in both his research and clinical practice. He established the Medical Research Council Child Psychiatry Research Unit in 1984 and the Social, Genetic and Developmental Psychiatry Research Centre a decade later, retiring from his post as Director in 1998.

Professor Hildy Ross is Professor of Developmental Psychology at the University of Waterloo, Canada where she has studied young children's social relationships over the past 30 years. Her current work is focused on children's conflicts with family members, with emphasis on the contributions of children and parents to the resolution of young children's disputes. She is also collaborating on a major project at the University of Chicago into relations between parents' and children's understanding and negotiation of family conflict.

Audrey Sandbank is a family therapist, now in private practice. She is honourary Consultant Family Therapist to the Twins and Multiple Births Association (TAMBA) and author of *Twins in the Family*. She also edited *Twin and Triplet Psychology*, a professional guide to working with multiples. She is a professional adviser to the Young Mind's Information Service helpline for parents and professionals, and is a regular writer and broadcaster on multiple and family issues.

Professor Tricia Sloper is Professor of Children's Healthcare at the Social Policy Research Unit, University of York. She has many years' experience in research on the experiences of disabled or chronically ill children and their siblings.

Professor Peter K Smith is Professor of Psychology at Goldsmiths College, University of London and Head of the Unit for School and Family Studies there. He is leading a research group examining school bullying, the causes of bullying and ways of preventing it in school. He has also carried out research on children's play, especially rough-and-tumble and physical activity play. He is author (with H. Cowie and M. Blades) of *Understanding Children's Development* (Blackwell); and co-edited *The Nature of School Bullying: A Cross-National Perspective* (Routledge) and *The Family Systems Test (FAST): Theory and applications* (Brunner/Routledge).

Cheryl Walters is Head of Research at Parentline Plus, and an individual, psychosexual and marital psychoanalytical psychotherapist in private practice.

Jim Wilson is a UKCP systemic therapist, author of *Child-Focused Practice: A Collaborative Systemic Approach* (Karnac Books), and director of the Centre for Child-Focused Practice at the Institute of Family Therapy, London. The Centre offers a therapy and counselling service for children and their families.

Peter Wilson is Director at the children's mental health charity, Young Minds, where he has developed a parents' information service, a consultancy and training service and a range of publications designed to inform the public of child and adolescent mental health issues and to influence policy at national and local level.

Gary Younge is a columnist and feature writer for the *Guardian* and author of *No Place Like Home: A Black Briton's Journey Through The American South* (Picador).

Contacts

Advisory Centre for Education (ACE)
1c Aberdeen Studios
22 Highbury Grove
London N5 2DQ
Tel: 020 7354 8318
General advice line: 0808 800 5793
Exclusion line: 020 7704 9822
www.ace-ed.org.uk
An independent advice centre for parents, offering information about state education in England and Wales for 5–16-year-olds. Offers free advice on many topics, including exclusion from school, bullying, special educational needs and school admission appeals.

Anti-Bullying Network
Moray House School of Education
The University of Edinburgh
Edinburgh EH8 8AQ
Info Line: 0131 651 6100
www.antibullying.net
Established by the Scottish Executive, for teachers, parents and young people to share ideas about tackling bullying.

The Association for Post-natal Illness
145 Dawes Road
Fulham
London SW6 1BE
Tel: 020 7386 0868
Helpline: 020 7386 0868
www.apni.org
Provides information, advice and support for sufferers of post-natal depression and their relatives/friends.

Barnardos
Tanners Lane
Barkinside, Ilford
Essex 1G6 1QG
Tel: 020 8550 8822
Helpline: 0845 7697967
www.barnardos.org.uk
The country's largest children's charity, offering a wide range of supportive projects in the following areas: disability, education, children needing families, disadvantaged communities, disadvantaged young people and families with young children.

Benefits Agency
Child Benefit – Central Helpline: 0845 3021444
Family Tax Credit – Central Helpline: 08456 095000
Your local benefits agency is listed in the telephone directory under B.

Bliss
68 South Lambeth Road
London SW8 1RL
Tel: 0870 7700337
Freephone helpline: 0500 618140
www.bliss.org.uk
The premature baby charity providing information and support for families of premature and sick newborn babies.

The Brazelton Centre
For training and information contact:
Dr Joanna Hawthorne
Box 226, NICU
Addenbrooks NHS Trust,
Hills Road
Cambridge CB2 2QQ
Tel: 01223 245791
www.brazelton.co.uk
The centre aims to provide an understanding of infant development and foster strong infant–parent eelationships. Training programmes for healthcare professionals are available.

British Association for Counselling and Psychotherapy
1 Regent Place
Rugby
Warwickshire CV21 2PJ
Tel: 0870 443 5252
www.counselling.co.uk
Can provide a list of qualified counsellors in your area.

The British Psychological Society
St Andrews House
48 Princes Road East
Leicester LE1 7DR
Tel: 0116 254 9568
www.bps.org.uk
Can provide directory of qualified chartered psychologists and child psychologists by area.

Centre for Counselling and Psychotherapy Education
Beauchamp Lodge
2 Warwick Crescent
London W2 6NE
Tel: 020 7266 3006
www.ccpe.org.uk
Offers individual, couple and child/adolescent psychotherapy on a sliding-scale rate.

Child Growth Foundation
2 Mayfield Avenue
London W4 1PW
Tel: 020 8994 7625
www.heightmatters. org.uk
For parents who are concerned about the growth of their children. Information and support groups.

Child Psychotherapy Trust
Star House
104–108 Grafton Road
London NW5 4BD
Tel: 020 7284 1355
www.childpsychotherapytrust.org.uk
Provides publications on request on a wide range of subjects concerned with the emotional development of children.

ChildLine
Freepost 1111
London N1 0BR
Helpline (24 hr): 0800 1111
www.childline.org.uk
The 24-hour national helpline for children and young people in trouble or danger. All calls are free and confidential and children may call about any problem.

Children 1st
83 Whitehouse Loan
Edinburgh EH9 1AT
Tel: 0131 446 2300
www.children1st.org.uk
Scotland's own childcare agency for prevention of cruelty to children.

Children's Legal Centre
University of Essex
Wivenhoe Park
Colchester CO4 3SQ
Tel: 01206 872466 (office)
Adviceline: 01206 873820
www.childrenslegalcentre.com
Free advice by telephone or letter regarding legal issues involving children and children's interests.

The Children's Society
Edward Rudolph House
69–85 Margery Street
London WC1X 0JL
Tel: 020 7841 4400
www.childrenssociety.org.uk
Independent charity working with children, young people and their families throughout England and Wales.

Contact-a-Family
209–211 City Road
London EC1V 1JN
Helpline: 0808 808 3555
www.cafamily.org.uk
Provides advice and information on all issues affecting families of children with disabilities, special needs, or rare disorders.

Cruse Bereavement Care
Cruse House
126 Sheen Road
Richmond
Surrey TW9 1UR
Tel: 020 8940 4818 (office)
Helpline: 0870 167 1677
www.crusebereavementcare.org.uk
Offers free help to those affected by bereavement with opportunities for social support and practical advice.

CRY-SIS Helpline
BM CRY-SIS
London WC1N 3XX
Tel: 020 7404 5011
www.cry-sis.com
Self-help and support for families with excessively crying, sleepless and demanding babies from birth to 18 months.

Daycare Trust
21 St George's Road
London SE1 6ES
Tel: 020 7840 3350
www.daycaretrust.org.uk
A charity promoting high quality affordable child-care for all.

DFEE
www.parents.dfee.gov.uk
Provides information and ideas on how parents can help at school. See the 'discover' section for help with homework.

Disables Parents Network
Unit F9
89–93 Fonthill Road
London N4 3JH
Tel: 0870 2410450
Information line: 0800 0184730
www.disabledparents network.org.uk
Offering peer support for disabled parents, disabled people looking to become parents, and family, friends and allies of disabled people.

Disability Pregnancy and Parenthood International
Unit F9
89–93 Fonthill Road
London N4 3JH
Freephone: 0800 0184730
www.dppi.org.uk
Information for disabled parents, disabled people looking to become parents, and family, friends and allies of disabled people.

Drugscope
Waterbridge House
32–36 Loman Street
London SE1 0EE
Information: 0870 774 3682
www.drugscope.org.uk
The drugs information charity providing straightforward informa-

tion on drugs, the common terms, their effects and associated risks. Clicking on the 'Find a Drug Service' button links to a database of local drug treatment and help services.

Family Caring Trust
8 Ashtree Enterprise Park
Newry
Co. Down BT34 1BY
Tel: 028 3026 4174
Fax: 028 3026 9077
www.familycaring.co.uk
A Northern Ireland-based charity concerned with the care of the family. Resources for parents and parenting groups available via website.

Family Links
New Marston Centre
Jack Straws Lane
Oxford OX3 0DL
Tel: 01865 454004
Fax: 01865 452145
www.familylinks.org.uk
An Oxford-based charity promoting emotional literacy, nurturing and relationship skills in families, schools and communities. It runs the Nurturing Programme parenting course, with a parallel PSHCE course for primary schools, and offers training courses for professionals working in education and in health.

Family Welfare Association
501–505 Kingsland Road
London E8 4AU

Tel: 020 7254 6251
www.fwa.org.uk
Offers financial advice to families
and individuals.

Fathers Direct
Herald House
15 Lamb's Passage
Bunhill Row
London EC1Y 8TQ
Tel: 020 7920 9491
www.fathersdirect.com
Provides a range of resources,
research and training for working
fathers.

**FSID (Foundation for the Study of
Infant Deaths)**
Artillery House
11–19 Artillery Row
London SW1P 1RT
Tel: 0870 787 0885
Helpline: 0870 787 0554
www.sids.org.uk/fsid
Provides support to bereaved fami-
lies, advice to anyone concerned
about cot death and promotes infant
health.

General Osteopathic Council
Osteopathy House
176 Tower Bridge Road
London SE1 3LU
Tel: 020 7357 6655
www.osteopathy.org.uk
Provides information and list of
registered osteopaths.

Gingerbread
7 Sovereign Close
Sovereign Court
London E1W 3HW
Tel: 020 7488 9300
Adviceline: 0800 018 4318
www.gingerbread.org.uk
Runs a network of self-help groups
for single parents.

Gingerbread Wales
Tel: 0292 047 1900
Gingerbread Scotland
Tel: 0141 576 5085

Homoepathic Medical Association
6 Livingstone Road
Gravesend
Kent DA12 5DZ
Tel: 01474 560336
Supplies a list of qualified home-
opaths and an information leaflet.

Home-Start
Central Office
2 Salisbury Road
Leicester LE1 7QR
Tel: 0116 233 9955
Helpline: 0800 068 6368
www.home-start.org.uk
Support, friendship and practical
advice to families with children
under five in their homes, provided
through local schemes.

**Hyperactive Children's Support
Group** (HACSG)
28 Worple Road
London SW19 4EE

Tel: 020 8946 4444
www.hacsg.org.uk
Monthly workshops and clinics for parents of children with behavioural problems or learning difficulties.

Information Service of the Early Years Diagnostic Centre
272 Longdale Lane
Ravenshead
Notts NG15 9AH
Tel: 01623 490 879
For parents of children with communication disorders.

Institute of Family Therapy
24–32 Stephenson Way
London NW1 2HX
Tel: 020 7391 9150
www.instituteoffamilytherapy.org.uk
Couple and family counselling and mediation.

The International Society for Twin Studies (ISTS)
www.ists.qimi.edu.au
The society aims to further research and public education in all fields related to twins and twin studies, for the mutual benefit of twins and their families and for scientific research.

Kids Company
Arch 259
Grosvenor Court
Grosvenor Terrace
London SE5 0NP
Tel: 020 7703 1808
www.kidsco.org.uk

Provides caring adults to whom children can talk about their concerns and who can visit them in their schools or homes. It also has a children's centre where children refer themselves for support.

Kidscape
2 Grosvenor Garden
London SW1W 0DH
Helpline: 0845 104590
www.kidscape.org.uk
For parents of children being bullied.

Meet-a-Mum (MAMA)
77 Westbury View
Peasdown St. John
Bath BA2 8TZ
Tel: 01525 217064
Helpline: 0208 768 0123
www.mama.org.uk
Provides friendship and support to all mothers and mothers-to-be, and those suffering from post-natal depression.

Multiple Births Foundation
Hammersmith House Level 4
Queen Charlotte's Hospital
Du Cane Road
London W12 0HS
Tel: 020 8383 3519/20
www.multiplebirths.org.uk
Provides specialist professional advice and information to parents of twins and more, and to health professionals in the field.

**National Association of Citizens
Advice Bureaux** (NACAB)
115–123 Pentonville Road
London N1 9LZ
Tel: 020 7833 2181
www.citizensadvice.org.uk
The national association of 1,400
Citizens Advice Bureaux, which
provide information and advice on
subjects such as housing benefits,
immigration, finance, consumer
complaints and family matters.

National Autistic Society
393 City Road
London EC1V 1NG
Tel: 020 7833 2299
Helpline: 0870 600 8585
www.nas.org.uk
A parent-led charity providing
support and information for people
with autism and their parents and
carers.

National Childbirth Trust
Alexandra House
Oldham Terrace
Acton
London W3 6NH
Tel: 0870 444 8707
Breastfeeding Helpline: 0870
4448708
www.nctpregnancyandbabycare.com
The NCT offers information and
support in pregnancy, childbirth
and early parenthood and aims
to enable every parent to make
informed choices. It campaigns
on behalf of parents for improve-

ments in maternity and post-natal
care.

National Childminding Association
8 Masons Hill
Bromley
Kent
BR2 9EY
Tel: 020 8464 6164
Advice Line: 0800 169 4486
www.ncma.org.uk
Help and advice to those looking
after other people's children.

National Children's Bureau
8 Wakley Street
London EC1V 7QE
Tel: 020 7843 6000
www.ncb.org.uk
A charity concerned with making the
voice of children heard.

NCH
Central Office
85 Highbury Park
London N5 1UD
Tel: 020 7704 7000
www.nch.org.uk
A leading children's charity
running projects in the UK and
abroad and campaigning on behalf
of children and their families.

**National Council for One-Parent
Families**
255 Kentish Town Road
London NW5 2LX
Tel: 020 7428 5400
Helpline: 0800 018 5026

www.oneparentfamilies.org.uk
Information service for single
parents.

National Family Mediation (NFM)
9 Tavistock Place
London WC1H 9SN
Tel: 020 7485 8809
www.nfm.u-net.com
Fostering the provision of independent family mediation services to
couples experiencing separation or
divorce whilst focusing on the
children involved.

**National Family and Parenting
Institute**
430 Highgate Studios
53–79 Highgate Road
London NW5 1TL
Tel: 020 7424 3460
www.nfpi.org
Set up by the government in 1999 to
support families in raising children.
The institute wants to make it easy for
parents to find out what help is available and to ensure that parenting
services provided by small and large
organisations are more widely publi-
cised.

National Health Service Direct
Tel: 0845 4647
www.nhsdirect.nhs.uk
24-hour health information by
phone or on the Internet.

National Newpin
Sutherland House
35 Sutherland Square

London SE17 3EE
Tel: 020 7358 5900
www.nationalnewpin.freeserve.co.uk
Peer support, training, individual
counselling, group therapy and
family play therapy for parents and
children.

**National Society for the Prevention
of Cruelty to Children** (NSPCC)
National Centre
42 Curtain Road
London EC2A 3NH
Helpline (24 hr): 0808 800 5000
www.nspcc.org.uk
The NSPCC is the UK's leading
charity specialising in child protection and the prevention of cruelty to
children. Their helpline provides
counselling, information and advice
to anyone concerned about a child at
risk of abuse.

One-Parent Families Scotland
13 Gayfield Square
Edinburgh EH1 3NX
Tel: 0131 556 3899
www.opfs.org.uk
Scottish organisation for single
parents.

One Plus One
The Wells
7–15 Rosebury Avenue
London EC1R 4SP
Tel: 020 7841 3660
www.oneplusone.org.uk
An independent research organisa-
tion whose role is to generate

knowledge about marriage and relationships and uses the findings in a practical way, setting up working projects to support families and couples.

Osteopathic Centre For Children
109 Harley Street
London W1G 6AN
Helpline: 020 7628 2128
A charity providing fully qualified osteopaths for children (a donation is requested for each treatment).

Parenting Education and Support Forum
Unit 431 Highgate Studios
53–79 Highgate Road
London NW5 1TL
Tel: 020 7284 8370
www.parenting-forum.org.uk
An umbrella organisation for all groups and agencies involved in parenting education and support.

Parentline Plus
Head Office
Unit 520 Highgate Studios
53–79 Highgate Road
London NW5 1TL
Tel: 020 7284 5500
Adviceline: 0808 800 2222
Free textphone helpline: 0800 783 6783 (for hearing and speech impaired people)
www.parentlineplus.org.uk
Parentline Plus is a national charity dedicated to providing help and information to parents and carers via

a free helpline, parenting courses, interactive website and information service. Parentline Plus also provides training to professionals working with families.

Parents at Work
1–3 Berry Street
London EC1V 0AA
Tel: 020 7253 7243
Helpline: 020 7253 4664
www.parentsatwork.org.uk
A charity which supports parents and help employers in developing family-friendly policies

Parents Information Network (PIN)
www.pin.org.uk
An independent service providing guidance for parents about computers and education, including advice on software and website evaluation, home learning and safety on the Internet.

PIPPIN (Parents in Partnership – Parent Infant Network)
Derwood
Todds Green
Stevenage
Herts SG1 2JE
Tel: 01438 748478
www.pippin.org.uk
A national charity providing structured parenting courses for expectant and new parents.

The Place to Be
Royal Mint Street
London E1 8LG

Tel: 020 7780 6189
www.theplace2be.org.uk
This charity offers emotional support to children in mainstream primary schools.

Refuge
2/8 Maltravers Street
London WC2 R3EE
Domestic violence helpline:
0870 599 5443
24-hour helpline for domestic violence.

Relate
Herbert Grey College
Little Church Street
Rugby
Warwickshire CV21 3AP
Tel: 01788 573241
www.relate.org.uk
This office will provide information regarding your local Relate centre, offering counselling help for marriage and family relationship needs.

The Royal College of Speech and Language Therapists (RCSLT)
2 White Hart Yard
London SE1 1NX
Tel: 020 7378 1200
www.rcslt.org
Information on speech and language therapy and speech and language therapists.

Royal London Homeopathic Hospital NHS Trust
Greenwell Street
London W1W 5BP
Tel: 020 7391 8833
Provides information on services including a children's clinic. All services are free.

Samaritans
The Upper Mill
Kingston Road
Ewell
Surrey KT17 2AS
Tel: 020 8394 8300
www.samaritans.org
National Helpline: 08457 909090
A charity available 24 hours a day to provide confidential emotional support for anyone experiencing feelings of distress or despair, including those which may lead to suicide.

Society of Homeopaths
2 Artizan Road
Northampton NN1 4HU
Tel: 01604 621 400
www.homeopathy-soh.org
Provides information leaflet plus a register of professional homeopaths throughout the UK.

The Speech Language and Hearing Centre
Christopher Place
Charlton Street
London NW1 1JF
Tel: 020 7383 3834

www.speech-lang.org.uk
A new centre for pre-school children with hearing impairment and delay in speech or language.

TalkToFrank
(Formerly the National Drugs Helpline)
Confidential 24-hour helpline: 0800 776600
www.talktofrank.com

Trust for the Study of Adolescence
23 New Road
Brighton BN11W2
Tel: 01273 679907
www.tsa.uk.com
Registered charity and independent research and training organisation, promoting knowledge and understanding or young people. It stocks a range of publications for parents and professionals.

Twins and Multiple Birth Association (TAMBA)
2 The Willows
Gardener Road
Guildford
Surrey GU1 4PG
Helpline: 0800 1380509
www.tamba.org.uk
Information and support for families with twins, triplets or more.

Women's Aid Federation (England)
PO Box 391
Bristol BS99 7WS
Tel: 0117 944 4411

www.womensaid.org.uk
National Helpline: 08457 023468
Offers advice and refuge to women and children threatened by violence.

Working Group Against Racism in Children's Resources
Unit 63A Eurolink Business PArk
49 Effre Road
London SW2 1BZ
Tel: 020 7501 9992
Information on books, toys and resources which provide positive representation of all children and communities.

Young Minds
102–108 Clerkenwell Road
London EC1M 5SA
Tel: 020 7336 8445 (office)
Helpline: 0800 018 2138
www.youngminds.org.uk
National charity committed to improving the mental health of all children. Parents' adviceline and information line for those concerned with the mental heath of a child.

Young Voice
12 Bridge Gardens
East Molesey
Surrey KT8 9HU
Tel: 020 8379 4991
www.young-voice.org
A charity working to make young people's views count.

Youth Access
1/2 Taylors Yard
67 Alderbrook Road
London SW12 8AD
Tel: 020 8772 9900
Information on local contacts for
counselling, advice and information
for young people.

Republic of Ireland Contacts

Association for Children and Adults with Learning Difficulties (incorporating the Dyslexia Association)
Suffolk Chambers
1 Suffolk Street
Dublin 2
Tel: 01 679 0276
Fax: 01 679 0273
Email: acld@iol.ie
Website: www.iol.ie/~acld/
Promoting awareness of dyslexia and supporting adults and children with Specific Learning Difficulties.

Barnardos
Christchurch Square
Dublin 8
Tel: 01-453 0355
Email: info@barnardos.ie
Website: www.barnardos.ie
Offers a wide range of services to children and their families including family support services, a national children's resource centre, a bereavement counselling service and adoption advice service.

Caint
Tel: 01 840 4349
Email: caint@indigo.ie
Website:
http://indigo.ie/~caint/Default.htm
Parent to parent support and information for mothers and fathers of languages impaired children.

ChildLine
Tel: 1800 666 666
Free-to-use national helpline for children.

Childminding Ireland
The Enterprise Park
The Murrough
Wicklow Town
Tel: 0404 64007
Email: childm@indigo.ie
Website: www.childminding-irl.com
National organisation promoting high standards in family-based day care. Childcare vacancy service for parents wanting to find a registered childminder in their area.

Children's Rights Alliance
13 Harcourt Street
Dublin 2
Ireland
Tel: 01 4054823
Email: info@cra.iol.ie
Website: www.childrensrights.ie
Protecting, promoting and advancing children's rights. Providing information, including an

online Children's Rights Information Centre detailing children's rights and services in Ireland.

Cuidiú Irish Childbirth Trust
Carmichael Centre
North Brunswick Street
Dublin 7
Tel: 01 8724501
Website: www.cuidiu-ict.ie
Parent to parent community based voluntary support group providing support for families throughout all stages of parenthood – from pregnancy to adolescence. Branches and groups nationwide.

Family Mediation Service
A free, state-run service, staffed by professionally trained mediators, helping couples experiencing separation or divorce address the needs of all family members. Free information packs on issues such as How Children React To Separation, Managing The Stress Of Separation And Divorce, Managing The Financial Issues.
Regional Offices:
Dublin: 1st Floor
St. Stephen's Green
Earlsfort Terrace, D2
Tel: 01 6344320
Galway: 1st Floor
Ross House
Merchants Road
Galway
Tel: 091 509730
Cork: Hibernian House

80A South Mall
Cork
Tel: 021 252200
Limerick: 1st Floor
Mill House
Henry Street
Limerick
Tel: 061 214310
Part-time offices:
Athlone: c/o CIC
St Mary's Square
Athlone
Co. Westmeath
Tel: 0902 20970
Castlebar: Family Centre
Chapel Street
Castlebar
Co. Mayo
Tel: 094 25900
Dundalk: 3 Seatown Place
Dundalk
Co Louth
Tel: 042 93594210
Tallagh: The Rere
Tallaght Social Services Centre
The Square
Dublin 24
Tel: 01 4145180
Tralee: c/o Kerry Family Resource & Counselling Centre
Balloonagh
Tralee
Co. Kerry
Tel: 066 7186100
Wexford: Distillery Road
Wexford
Tel: 053 63050

Gingerbread Ireland
Carmichael House
North Brunswick Street
Dublin 7
Tel: 01 814 6618
Website: www.gingerbread.ie
Email: info@gingerbread.ie
Voluntary body providing practical, friendly advice and support for single parents and their families.

Irish Association of Speech and Language Therapists
29 Gardiner Place
Dublin 1
Tel: 01 878 0215
Website: www.clubi.ie/iaslt
Helping parents locate and contact speech and language therapists working privately in their area.

Irish Multiple Births Association (IMBA)
Carmichael Centre
North Brunswick Street
Dublin 7
Tel: 01 874 9056
Email: twinsplusimba@eircom.net
Website:
www.carmichaelcentre.ie/imba
Supporting families with twins, triplets and more.

Irish Pre-school Playgroups Association (IPPA)
Unit 4
Broomhill Business Complex
Broomhill Road
Tallaght
Dublin 24
Tel: 01 463 0010
Fax: 01 463 0045
Email: info@ippa.ie
Website: www.ippa.ie
Promoting quality play-based early childhood care and education.

Irish Society for the Prevention of Cruelty to Children (ISPCC)
20 Molesworth Street
Dublin 2
Tel: 01 679 4944
Fax: 01 679 1746
Email: ispcc@ispcc.ie
Website: www. ispcc.ie
Ireland's leading children's charity specialising in the prevention of cruelty to children. Every year the Society works with thousands or children and parents to foster better relationships between parents and children while promoting better understanding of children's needs.

Mental Health Ireland
Mensana House
6 Adelaide Street
Dun Laoghaire
Co. Dublin
Tel: 01 284 1166
Email: info@mentalhealthireland.ie
Website: www.mensana.org
Information on maintaining mental health and coping with mental health problems including stress, anxiety and post natal depression.

Website carries support group listings.

National Children's Nurseries Association
12C Bluebell Business Park
Old Naas Road
Bluebell
Dublin 12
Tel: 01 460 1138
Email: info@ncna.ie
Website: www.ncna.net
Advice on how to choose a quality nursery. Lists of registered nurseries by area.

Parentline Republic of Ireland
Carmichael House
North Brunswick Street
Dublin 7
Helpline: 1890 927277
Email: parentline@eircom.net
Website: www.parentline.ie
Parentline offers a confidential service to parents, grandparents, guardians, health care professionals, teachers and all concerned with parenting and family life, via a helpline, face-to-face support and parenting groups.

Republic of Ireland Department of Health and Children
Hawkins House
Hawkins Street
Dublin 2
Tel: 01 635 4000
Website: www.doh.ie

RollerCoaster
Website: www.RollerCoaster.ie
Website for parents in Ireland

Treoir
National Information Centre for Unmarried Parents
14 Gandon House
Custom House Square
IFSC
Dublin 1
Tel: 01 670 0120
Fax: 01 670 0199
Email: info@treoir.ie
Website: www.treoir.ie
The national co-ordinating body for both statutory and voluntary agencies providing services for unmarried parents and their children in Ireland. It is a voluntary organisation supported by Government, health boards and other agencies. It provides a free, confidential, accessible and up-to-date information service.

Index

Jan Parker and Jan Stimpson

Raising Happy Children

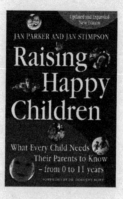

'This book tackles the complex and contentious issues facing all
parents bringing up young children today, offering insight, support
and real solutions. I couldn't recommend it more highly.'
Mary MacLeod, ChildLine

'Finally, a sensible, balanced and really useful handbook that tells
you how to deal with children as they are, rather than as people
would like them to be.'
Kate Figes, author of *Life After Birth*

'The mixture of personal experience, professional expertise and large
helpings of humour make this a much needed and very accessible book.'
Vivienne Gross, The Institute of Family Therapy

'*Raising Happy Children* is not about spoiling children, but about how
to help children grow up feeling comfortable with themselves and
with other people, and having the courage to face the
inherent difficulties of life.'
Dr Dorothy Rowe, psychologist and writer

'Parker and Stimpson have succeeded in providing a readable, highly
informative book which tackles some of the toughest issues facing
parents and children today.'
Amazon.co.uk